ORGANIZE YOURSELF!

NEW AND REVISED EDITION

Ronni Eisenberg
with Kate Kelly

Macmillan • USA

To Alan and George

MACMILLAN
A Simon & Schuster Macmillan Company
1633 Broadway
New York, NY 10019-6785

Library of Congress Cataloging-in-Publication Data

Eisenberg, Ronni.

    Organize yourself! / Ronni Eisenberg with Kate Kelly. — New and rev. ed.
      p.   cm.
    Includes index.
    ISBN: 0-02-861507-7
    1. Home economics. 2. Time management. I. Kelly, Kate.
II. Title.

TX147.E47   1997   96-44615
640—dc21   CIP

10 9 8 7

Printed in the United States of America

CONTENTS

Introduction   *vii*

Part I: **Getting Control of Your Time**   *1*

  1 Procrastination   1
  2 Managing Interruptions   10
  3 The Telephone   13
  4 Getting Out of the House on Time   23
  5 Preserving Personal Time   25
  6 Twenty-Two Time Wasters to Avoid   27
  7 How to Use a Kitchen Timer to
     Manage Time   30

Part II: **Paperwork**   *31*

  8 Books   33
  9 Calendars   36
 10 The Family Computer   42
 11 Desk Organization   49
 12 Filing Systems   56
 13 Health Records   65
 14 Mail, E-Mail, and Faxes   67
 15 Resource File   76

Part III: **Financial Records**   *81*

 16 Banking   83
 17 Bill-Paying   89
 18 Budgeting   96
 19 Financial Master List   103

20 Investments 106
21 Medical Payments and Insurance
    Reimbursements 111
22 Personal Property Inventory 113
23 Safe-Deposit Box and Strongbox 116
24 Income Taxes 119

Part IV: *Household Matters* 123

25 In Case of Emergency 125
26 General Household 129
27 Closets 133
28 The Kitchen 138
29 The Refrigerator 145
30 Supermarket Shopping and
    Inventory Control 147
31 The Laundry 152
32 The Medicine Chest 154
33 Hiring Household Help 158

Part V: *Main Events* 165

34 Tag Sales 167
35 Preparing for the Painters 174
36 Moving 178
37 Job Search 191
38 Party Planning 198
39 Travel Planning 204
40 Travel Packing 210

Part VI: *Personal Agenda* 219

41 Beauty Routine 221
42 Dates to Remember 224
43 Doctors: Organizing a Selective Search 227
44 Errands 231
45 Gift Shopping 236

46 Handbag   239
47 Briefcase   242
48 How to Stop Losing Things   245
49 Organizing Your Spouse   247
50 Wardrobe Shopping for Women   250
51 Wardrobe Shopping for Men   255

Part VII: *Children*   **261**

52 Pregnancy Checklist   263
53 Post-Pregnancy: Organization
    After the Baby Is Born   269
54 Children's Rooms   276
55 Teaching Children About Organization   281
56 Traveling with Children   287
57 When Travel Means Leaving the Kids
    Behind   293

    About the Authors   ***303***

    Index   ***305***

INTRODUCTION

In the eleven years since I wrote *Organize Yourself!*, our world has changed a great deal. Today we are overwhelmed by voluminous amounts of e-mail as well as regular mail; we have fax machines spewing out paper so fast that the pages seem to be begging to be read instantly; and electronic organizers or calendars on laptop computers have often replaced date books.

The world also offers more options for making life convenient. Today we can have our paycheck deposited directly into our bank account, and we can leave a standing order for payment on some of the regular bills, or if we prefer, we can pay our debts electronically from the comfort of our own computer screen. The latest phone systems offer terrific features that make life easier, and computers and those paper-spewing faxes are actually real time-savers when used properly.

When I thought about all the changes that needed to be incorporated to bring the book into the twenty-first century, I also thought about another thing: *The basic advice for getting organized still stands the test of time.* I'm going to be showing you how to take the principles I wrote about eleven years ago and apply them to our world today.

People's concern about getting more control over their lives has also remained constant. I still get the same response when I tell people that I make my living teaching others how to become better organized. "Boy, could I use you!" is what I hear. Often that comment is followed by a sigh and a true confession: "Organizing takes too much time. I just can't be bothered." Other familiar statements I hear are:

- "I don't know how."
- "It's easier to let things go."
- "I have children." (!)
- "If I get organized, I won't be creative anymore."

- "My problems are different from those of everyone else (I get more mail, I have more appointments, responsibilities, etc.), so I can't get organized."

While people may believe these excuses are true, the fact remains that people who are successful share a common secret. They know that to get ahead, they must plan, set priorities, and always follow through. In the process, they develop systems that work for them.

Their reward? Peace of mind and a gift of extra time—no more looking for the missing file folder, the other sock, or a friend's telephone number. (It's frightening to imagine the hours *wasted* on disorganization!)

Organization is being able to find what you're looking for—getting things done—being in control of your life. Why spend time looking for your keys when you could be locking the door and heading out to have a good time?

With most people, I find that there comes a time when they simply have to face the fact that because of disorganization, their lives aren't working for them: For one client things got so bad she had to move out of her apartment; another came to me because she couldn't stand having her checks bounce anymore; a third telephoned saying her desk "looked like an archaeological dig, there were so many levels of civilization to uncover . . ."; a fourth called after she bought a new evening dress and shoes and had her hair done for a black tie event—only to go on the wrong night. One called immediately after he had seen my name in the newspaper. I was impressed with his efficiency until he said, "I was afraid that if I didn't call you now, I would lose the little scrap of paper I've written your number on." The list goes on and on.

I recently met a woman who said, "I'm so disorganized that I go to the supermarket and I forget why I'm there. I get to a meeting, and I've left the papers I needed behind; I'm always late . . . . My life would be so simple if only I were organized."

"Why do you avoid getting organized?" I asked her.

"I guess I just don't know how," was her reply.

You've bought this book, so you must have decided that—for you—*now* is the time to learn how to get organized. And I've got good news for you: Anybody can get organized if they want to badly enough.

Organization is a skill that can be learned. The most difficult part is breaking those lifelong bad habits (like letting your paperwork pile up). The key to getting better organized is to start with one small step and then take others, one at a time. You may find that what you've put off for years takes only an hour to do! And once you see the benefits in one part of your life, you'll be motivated to go on.

If you implement the ideas given here, you'll be free from chaos and feel in charge of your life. Just do me one favor. Once you've started, stick with it. Getting organized is the first step; persistence and follow-through will keep you that way.

You may want to read the book straight through or go directly to the chapter that interests you most. Just keep working away, and keep *Organize Yourself!* around for easy reference. You'll find it handy to refer to time and again. Now let's get started.

PART I

Getting Control of Your Time

1 Procrastination

2 Managing Interruptions

3 The Telephone

4 Getting Out of the House on Time

5 Preserving Personal Time

6 Twenty-Two Time Wasters to Avoid

7 How to Use a Kitchen Timer to Manage Time

Procrastination

Are you a procrastinator? Here are some warning signs:

- Do you often wait until the last minute to start a project?
- Do you frequently send belated birthday cards?
- Do you usually finish filling out your tax form on April 15 or later?
- Do you do all of your holiday shopping on Christmas Eve?
- Do you regularly put off going to the doctor or dentist?
- How long have you been waiting to clean out your closet/ drawers/kitchen/medicine cabinet?
- Do you often put off making a decision about something?
- Are you waiting for the "right" time to make that dreaded phone call, confront your boss about a well-deserved raise, or start an exercise program?
- Did you leave this chapter for last?

Most of us procrastinate in one area or another. Some people procrastinate about everything. It's only natural. As children, we learned that procrastination brought a certain element of satisfaction. If we delayed something (like Mom's request that we clean our room), we at least gained some control over the task; we had to do it, but at least *we* said when. That's important to a child who has so little say over many things. What's more, if we procrastinated long enough, we learned that someone (good old Mom) might sometimes do it for us—and that was worth waiting for!

As adults, procrastination generally signals some type of internal conflict. While we've made the decision to do something, there is still a part of us that holds back. Some of the reasons people procrastinate are the following:

- *They feel overwhelmed.* This usually happens when there is an overload of information or too many details.

- *They overestimate time needed.* They think the task is too time-consuming, that it will take *forever.* A variation of this is thinking that they have forever to finish something.

- *They'd rather be doing something else.* Anything seems better than what awaits them.

- *They think that if they wait long enough, it will go away.* The project will be canceled or the appointment postponed, and so forth.

- *They want to do it perfectly.* People often fear turning in a report or finishing a project because they worry about failing on "judgment day." They delay until the last minute, and then if it doesn't measure up, they say, "Oh, I would have done better if I'd had more time."

- *They don't want to assume responsibility.* After all, if they never complete the project, no one will hold them responsible.

- *They fear success.* If they complete something and succeed, will they be able to continue to live up to that standard? How will others relate to them once they are successful?

- *They say they enjoy the last-minute adrenaline rush.* Often people feel that they do their best work "under pressure." What they fail to remember are the times when they had a terrible cold or there was a family emergency during the time they had intended to devote to the project.

Identifying Your Reasons for Procrastinating

- First you must determine which situations generally cause you to procrastinate. Consider the following questions:
  - In what types of situations do you usually procrastinate?
  - How has it worked against you?
  - What price did you pay for the delay?

- • When you procrastinated for a long time and then finally
  did it, what finally got you going? (Imminent deadline?
  Reward? Some outside pressure?)

- ▪ When you find yourself procrastinating about something
  specific, consider the following:
  - • What about this situation causes conflict for you? What are
    you avoiding?
  - • If you delay, what is likely to be the result?
  - • If the question really is when to do it (and there is really no
    possibility that you won't do it), ask yourself if you truly
    want to pay the price of a delay.

Twenty-Seven Ways to Stop Procrastinating

- ▪ The hardest part is getting started. Once you're in motion, it will
  be easier to keep going. You may well find that it isn't as bad as
  you expected, and once you're *involved,* you've overcome the
  highest hurdle.

- ▪ A more realistic sense of time will aid in getting things done.
  Procrastinators often have an unrealistic sense of time; you may
  have the feeling that a project will take *forever* or that you have
  "plenty of time." The more realistic you become, the less likely
  you'll be to procrastinate. To get a better sense of time, start
  keeping a log of how long various projects take. (Use your desk
  calendar or your computer calendar to keep track. You can do a
  tally at the end of each month.) How long did you *really* spend
  making those sales calls? Only one hour? That wasn't so bad.
  How long did it take to pack for a family vacation? How much
  time did you spend doing your family budget?

- ▪ Work with the time available to you. Sometimes people estimate
  that a project will take ten or twelve hours, so they keep waiting
  for a day when they can devote that amount of time to it. Of
  course, that day never comes. Break the project down into small,
  manageable parts. List each step you need to take in order to

complete the task. For example, if you're planning a household move, begin by researching which moving company to use. Ask friends for referrals, and price some of the companies that have advertised. Keep a record of what you learn, and you'll soon be prepared to make a decision. (And note that selecting a mover is just one part of the very large task of moving.)

- Consider your To Do list inviolate. Once a task from the project gets written down on that list, then it *shall* be done.

- Remember that even five minutes is enough time to get something done. Two phone calls or more can be completed in that time.

- If it seems like there really is no time, carve out a half hour or so from your existing schedule. If you *really* want to take up jogging, try getting up a half hour earlier each day (or on weekends). If you want to do it, you'll find the time.

- Consider your workspace—perhaps it's simply not convenient. One client constantly complained that she never had time to write, though she enjoyed it. When I visited her I saw why. Her computer was in one part of the house; her notes and files were in a closet, and her books were scattered on the floor—she then had to carry everything to a fourth location where she liked to work. Simply setting-up was such a big project, small wonder she never wrote!

- Clear your work area of all else so you don't let your eyes wander.

- You don't always have to start at the beginning. If that first step seems the hardest, start with another part of the project instead.

- Some people like to do the worst first. If they accomplish what they dislike most, the rest of the project seems to proceed more smoothly.

- Set small deadlines for yourself. For example, a major desk organization schedule might include:
  - Purchase desktop organizers by April 20.
  - Establish a Desk Workbook by April 30.
  - Finish sorting through papers by May 8.

For more information, see Chapter 11.

- Tell someone else what your deadline is. Often you will be motivated by not wanting to disclose to them that you did not meet the deadline.

- Try tricking yourself: "If I don't finish writing this proposal by 5 P.M., then I will have to cancel my plans for tonight." Working against that sort of deadline can be quite effective!

- After each small deadline, promise yourself a reward. Perhaps it could be a new paperback or a tennis lesson. After the entire project is completed, think on a little grander scale and promise yourself dinner out and a movie, or tickets to a football game.

- Try to do things as they occur to you. The more papers you process as they arrive in the mail or the more tasks you complete as you think of them, the less opportunity you will have to procrastinate.

- Ask yourself, "Is there a simpler way to do it?" Maybe you're making the task more difficult than it is. Do you really need to make dessert for the party from scratch or would a fruit platter do just as well?

- Ask yourself, "What's the worst thing that will happen if I *do* it?" (Perhaps you'll spend a beautiful Saturday afternoon inside finishing your project, but isn't that better than worrying all day Saturday whether you'll feel like doing it on Sunday?)

- Do nothing! Try sitting with the project in front of you for a full fifteen minutes. People generally become so frustrated by just sitting there that they dive into the project before the allotted time has passed.

- Listen to your moods. When you're motivated, use that energy to get the project done. Lots of people laugh at those who use anger as a motivation to scrub the floor or clean a closet, but what's so silly about it? It makes them feel better by burning off the excess energy caused by the anger, and they accomplish something they probably wouldn't otherwise.

- Plan an appropriate reason to be motivated. For example, if you have been procrastinating about getting the rugs and windows cleaned, host a Sunday brunch. Your friends may not care if your house glows, but it will make you feel good if it does.

- Be opportunistic. If your father calls and says he'll be a half hour late dropping by, take that thirty-minute block of time and make a stab at something you've put off. Or if a meeting that would have taken a full afternoon is canceled, consider working on a special project that needs your attention. With a full afternoon, you have a longer period of time to concentrate.

- Expect problems. The kids may get sick. You may be delayed coming back from your trip. If you anticipate that you really won't have "all of next week" to work on something, then you may be motivated to start a little earlier.

- If you tend to stall when you're almost finished with a project, maybe you fear being judged once you're finished. Go easy on yourself. At heart, you know it doesn't really need to be perfect.

- If you've promised to get back to someone about a decision but haven't made up your mind yet, call and tell him you haven't made up your mind, but you *will* get back to him. Then at least you don't add guilt (about not getting back in touch) to your indecision.

- Remember that you really are not the only one who can do the job well, so delegate to someone else what you would rather not do or hire someone to do it for you. You could also barter with a friend. If she'll organize your files, you can help set up her computer.

- Be sure to use your leisure time for leisure. Most procrastinators ruin much of their free time because they are worrying about whether "tomorrow" is really enough time to get something done. By learning to do things in advance, it provides the opportunity for worry-free leisure.

- Sometimes procrastination is a decision in itself. If you don't get around to sending for the travel brochures you promised your spouse you'd send for, think again. Maybe you really don't want to go away right now.

How to Help Procrastinators

Whether the procrastinator is your spouse, a coworker, or another family member, you can't make procrastinators do something they don't intend to do. However, you can encourage them. Here is some advice:

- Discuss the project with them, but make sure you leave them with a sense of control or they'll never do it. Open a discussion about the consequences of a delay. Don't threaten them, but be certain they understand.

- Help them be realistic. Is completing the report for work and going to the party a realistic expectation for Wednesday night? Help them realize that they may not be able to do it all.

- Suggest that they break down the project and establish small rewards for finishing certain steps.

- Whatever you do, don't do it for them. Give lots of support and encouragement instead.

- Offer an incentive—a night out, tickets to the hockey game, or a CD for family members; the promise of seeing that they get to go to a special presentation for a coworker.

It's sometimes said that certain people are so well organized they are even born on their due dates. Well, I had a client whose husband was born on his due date, but he certainly wasn't well organized! He put off everything: household chores, fixing things, paperwork, important phone calls. His wife even recalls asking him to fill out some information for her, and it took him two-and-a-half years to do it. Finally, she figured out how to motivate him. Money was his Achilles' heel, so she promised that if he didn't do certain tasks by certain dates, she was going to hire someone else to do them. The thought of paying someone money pushed him to action.

Now all *you* need to do is find the motivator for your procrastinator!

2

Managing Interruptions

- You never have the chance to take a nap, but this afternoon you're *so* sleepy and everyone is gone, so you decide to lie down for a few minutes. . . . The phone rings.

- It's Friday afternoon, and you're just packing up to leave work. . . . An "urgent" fax comes in, and now you're stuck doing the work the fax requires.

- Finally, you have an hour to work on that project that needs to be finished, and you've just gotten organized to begin when . . . a colleague decides to drop in for a visit.

Does any of this sound familiar? Probably. Interruptions are very much a part of our lives.

While some interruptions can be prevented, many are inevitable, and the best you can hope for is to manage them.

Planning

Most interruptions come about because the priorities of someone else come into conflict with what you've planned. A coworker comes into your office and sits down to chat; your child wants you to get her more juice; your husband thinks you must know where his blue shirt is; the list goes on and on. Here are some ways to minimize these types of interruptions:

- Ask friends and family not to drop by without notice.

- Group together interruptions that are within your control. If you are taking a day off from work so that some furniture can be delivered, for example, have the plumber come to repair the bathtub faucet and schedule the cable TV repair person to check your cable hookup. Narrow this block of time as much as possible by scheduling everything for morning or afternoon.

■ If you live in an apartment building with a doorman, ask him to hold packages and deliveries for you.

■ Help your family help themselves. Determine what they most frequently request from you. Food? Help in finding things? Try to arrange things so that they can do it themselves. For example, healthy snack food such as carrot sticks and juice can be provided in such a way that a four year old can get it himself. Or if your spouse has a particular weakness (e.g., losing things), try to establish a system so that you don't have to be the one who always figures out where things are. (If finding a pen when needed is a problem, for example, stock up on so many that he or she can't possibly not find one.)

■ Teach your family that a closed door or a Do Not Disturb sign means business.

■ Learn to say no. If you feel you've acted as family servant and kind neighbor one too many times this weekend, and you have no private time of your own, stand your ground. A simple no will sometimes make the interruption go away.

■ Set up rewards. If you have a half hour or an hour with no interruptions, promise the children a treat such as playing a favorite game. For your husband, you might prepare a favorite dinner or leave a card for him expressing your thanks.

■ The telephone answering machine and voice-mail are the greatest inventions since sliced bread. Turn one on when you need some quiet time. (See Chapter 3 for additional information about handling such interruptions.)

■ As a last resort, leave the house. Sometimes investing in a baby-sitter—or if children aren't the problem, just simply getting away—is the best way to have uninterrupted time. Go to the library, or a park bench in the summer, and enjoy your time there. At work, find a quiet conference room where you can accomplish what you need.

Managing Interruptions

- If someone over the age of four is interrupting you, try:
  - "How can I help you?"
  - "I'd love to hear about it, but could I come and discuss it once I've finished my project?" (For children, you need to speak of time in relation to something they understand. You might say, "Can I come and discuss it once you've listened to both sides of your tape?")

- Don't prolong a conversation or do anything to extend an interruption. Once you've been interrupted, it's tempting just to stop, but remember that this is the time you intended to devote to something specific (whether it was personal time or paying your bills), so see that you get right back to it.

- Plan for the fact that there *will* be interruptions. If the phone is your main interrupter, there will be times when you don't have your machine turned on, so keep small projects near the phone to work on during a conversation. A long cord on a kitchen extension can also permit you to dice food, fix snacks, or prepare lunches while on the phone. Make use of that time.

Don't Be Your Own Interrupter

- Don't use interruptions as an excuse to avoid your work.
- Don't make the mistake of initiating phone calls or visits to break the peace.
- Don't encourage unnecessary personal telephone calls from family and friends.
- Don't start another project before you finish the first one.
- Don't procrastinate. Once you have the time, use it!

3

The Telephone

How many times have you really gained momentum on a task only to be interrupted by a telephone call you really didn't want to take?

How often have you been stuck on the telephone, trying to get off, but were somehow unable to end the conversation?

And what about the times you have been put on hold for what seems like an eternity—especially the times when *they've phoned you!*

Or how many times have you phoned someone only to forget one of the reasons you called?

The telephone is a great invention and can be a terrific convenience and time-saver. But few people realize that you don't have to permit it to rule the household or workplace by allowing callers to interrupt meals, delay departures, waste your time with needlessly long calls, and otherwise cause inconvenience. Learn to control the telephone so it doesn't control you.

Establishing a Telephone Center

First you need to organize the area around your telephone so that you can efficiently make and receive calls.

- A pad and pencil should be kept by every telephone in the house. (Be sure to have these conveniently located near office phones, too.) Keep an extra pad nearby at all times so that you can restock easily. If your pens and pencils tend to "wander away," buy a pen-on-a-cord and attach it to the telephone.

- Keep your calendar, telephone books, area code map, and a directory of personal telephone numbers close to the phone used most frequently.

Before You Place a Call

Perhaps the easiest telephone habits to alter concern your outgoing calls, and these changes can result in substantial time-saving.

- Establish a "telephone time," during which you make all necessary calls. By making all the calls at one sitting, rather than throughout the day, you are more likely to stay with the task at hand rather than to digress and have a chat with someone.

- To avoid having to call a person back again, make notes about what you need to discuss. If you need to make just a few calls, with only a point or two to be discussed with each person, you can easily make such notes on your calendar. However, if you're doing lots of phoning (on a regular basis or even just on one day), use your telephone pad for some preplanning. On the top line of the page you can note the person's name, telephone number, and the date. Beneath that, note the points that need to be discussed. As you talk, you should write down any significant information from the conversation. A typical page might look like this:

JACK'S RENT A CAR
555-3331 6/3

- What is your daily rate?
- How many free miles?
- Where can the car be picked up and returned?

Record the replies on the bottom and then compare the information with other car rental services you are calling.

- When your calls are completed, transfer important information to your calendar (e.g., date you need to follow up with someone) or to your files (questions you asked your accountant regarding your taxes would go in your Tax File). Then throw away the sheet.

- As you dial, concentrate on the call you are making and what you need to discuss. When phoning several people at one sitting, there is a tendency to let your mind drift and forget whom you've called.

- Get to the point of your call quickly and stick to it.

- Take care of business before pleasure. If you need to discuss financial matters with your broker, make sure all business is taken care of before discussing the perils of the flu season.

- Don't let a person babble. If their reply begins to wander, don't hesitate to bring them back to the conversation with a polite but firm: "Do you have that information or could you suggest someone else for me to call?"

Ending Conversations

Sometimes getting off the phone can be an art in itself. Certain people—you know the type—ignore all the subtle signals you give; they must keep talking. Here are some tips on how to free yourself more quickly:

- Warn them in advance that your time is limited: "It sounds interesting, but I've got to leave here in five minutes. Can you tell me about it briefly?"

- Try inserting, "Before we hang up" as a mental warning to the other person that this call will end soon.

- At home, keep a kitchen timer near each phone, and when you want to get off, set it. When the bell rings, you can announce, "Well, I have to go. I've got to take something out of the oven."

- At the office, try pretending someone has arrived for a meeting, and for that reason, you've got to get off the phone.

- For the person who calls frequently, you'll soon run out of contrived exit lines. Try leveling with them: "I really can't spend a lot of time on the telephone. Let's make plans to meet for lunch instead."

If You Don't Know Where the Time Goes . . .

- Conversations last longer than you think. Time them by keeping a clock by the phone. One client limits all calls—not just those that are long-distance—to no longer than five minutes and uses a timer to remind himself.

- If you don't really know why the phone is taking up so much of your time, try logging your calls. Keep an $8\frac{1}{2}$" × 11" sheet near each phone and list the following: the time of the call, the name of the person with whom you spoke, who originated the call, your precall activity (so you'll know what the call interrupted), and the subject and length of the call.

Time	Person	Originator	Precall Activity	Subject	Length

A quick scan of the sheet after a week or so will tell you how your telephone time is spent. Then you can determine how to eliminate or shorten certain calls. You may find that you've been taking calls throughout the day when what you really needed was a block of uninterrupted time. Or there may be one person who calls you almost every morning (when you're jammed) just to pass the time. You can solve the problem by suggesting a better time to talk.

New Telephones That Extend Your Range

Like it or not, today, telephones can go with you almost anywhere. Though there may be days when you wish you could go back to a pretelephone era, for the most part, these new inventions add convenience and save time:

- *The cordless telephone* (distinct from a cellular phone because it still has to be within a hundred feet or so of a "home base") is perfect for at-home use. Because you aren't tethered by a cord, you can sit on your porch and make a telephone call, or you can take the phone with you while you do some picking up around the house.

- *The cellular telephone* started out primarily being used as a car telephone, and it is still terrific for emergencies or as a time-saver to make some calls when you're stuck in traffic. Today, everywhere we go, people are speaking on "cell phones"—on street corners, at airports, in shops, and at tourist attractions. Having one is helpful in an emergency and keeps you in constant touch with family, friends, and colleagues. (Remember to turn it off when you to go your child's recital. There are some things that really shouldn't be interrupted.)

Consider a Beeper

Beepers aren't just for doctors anymore. Today they are used in a wide range of businesses as well as by regular people like expectant fathers who want to be called at "the critical moment" and by teenagers whose parents want to be able to reach them at certain (usually late-night) times.

What's more, beepers are becoming much more sophisticated than the one-way pagers they were designed to be. Today you can buy a two-way model that offers the promise of becoming a sophisticated way to relay short messages. Not only will users receive a phone number and a simple text message, but they'll also be able to reply. Because beepers of the future will need keyboards to send lengthy messages, it is expected that most two-way systems will use the new palmtop computers as their basic tool. (You can read more about these in Chapter 9.)

Telephone Company Add-Ons That Make Sense

Telephone companies have developed a number of additional services that can make your life easier. (Some home phone systems now have these features built into the unit.) Here are some of the ones you might like to know about:

- *Caller identification* provides you with a screen display of the telephone number from which the call is originating. This allows you to pick up right away when it's your spouse and let it ring when it's a solicitor.

- *Call waiting* beeps you when you're on the telephone and another call is coming through—it's almost as good as having a second line. This way you no longer need to keep the line free if you're expecting another call. If you have kids in the house, set rules on whose call takes priority when call-waiting beeps.

- *Call forwarding* transfers an incoming call to whatever number you specify. You can forward calls to your vacation home or send them through to your voice-mail system if you're away and can't be reached.

- *Use *66 and *69.* If you hate redialing a number when it's busy, then *66 is for you. When you get a busy signal, just punch in *66, and the telephone company will keep dialing the number for you for a half hour and call you back when the line is free. You can use *69 when you've just missed a call or when you realize you forgot to tell your previous caller something. The telephone will redial the number of the last person to call you.

Special Telephone Features That Save Time

Today's programmable telephones have added features that would amaze and thrill telephone inventor Alexander Graham Bell. When you shop for a system, look for the following:

- *Speed dialing.* Many systems today have the capability of storing your frequently called numbers. Just program in numbers like the fire department, your mom, and your best client, and you'll find, in time, you'll hardly remember their full numbers.

- *Speaker phone.* For hands-free calling or for waiting while on hold, a speaker phone offers great convenience. Punch the "speaker" button, and you're free to do what you need to do.

- *Automatic redial.* If the number you're calling is busy, simply push "redial" on your telephone. The system will let you know when it's gotten through.

- *Mute button.* This is a vital addition to any phone being used in a home office. When the dog barks or the baby cries during a business call, just press "mute" for a moment.

- *Conference calling.* If you have more than one telephone line, then this feature will permit you to set up a conference call—very helpful for business calls and also nice when you'd like to speak to more than one relative or friend at the same time.

Answering Machines and Voice-Mail Systems: Maximizing Their Use

Answering machines have been around for a long time, and now voice-mail systems are becoming quite common. Today when you phone someone's office and the person isn't there, chances are you'll get a voice-mail message instead of a secretary.

The money spent on an answering machine or voice-mail system is well worth the investment. Here's why:

- The system can receive calls while you're not there, meaning that you get all the information people need to convey to you (appointment canceled, meeting changed).

- With voice-mail, you can send the same message to several people within a company, messages can be stored and retrieved selectively, callers can leave messages twenty-four hours a day, and you can add beeper capabilities if you're in a business where you may need to be reached instantly.

- Callers are now so accustomed to various voice-mail and machine answering systems that most will leave very detailed, explicit messages. A system with unlimited time for recording incoming messages can serve you and many of your callers as a "secretary." Lengthy messages can save both parties extra phoning. (A business associate of mine will often phone people *hoping* to get their machine so she can leave one efficient message and be done with it.)

- Get in the habit of recording new messages to keep them current; this is particularly helpful with a business voice-mail system. If you're out of the office for a few days, your message can tell callers that so they know they may not hear from you right away.

- Would you like callers to leave an "organized message" instead of a rambling one? Tell them that on your greeting. I do, and it works!

- You can use the machine as a way to screen calls. If you're working on a project or taking a break, you can leave the machine on to monitor who is calling. If it's urgent, you can answer it. If it's not, you can call them back later—at your convenience.

- If you have an assistant screen your voice-mail, ask that a log of all calls be recorded. Lengthy or detailed messages should be "archived" so that you can listen to those yourself.

- Receiving a call when you're trying to get out the door can be very irritating, because it often means you have to rush for what seems like the rest of the day. A solution? Turn on your machine or voice-mail system about fifteen minutes before you need to leave. That way you won't be delayed by any calls you don't want or need to answer. If you're on your way to an appointment, be sure to call and confirm in advance. That will keep you from missing a possible cancellation call.

Additional Ways to Control Your Calls

- Have someone else answer the phone for you at certain times. You can return the favor by doing the same for him or her.

- Turn off your home phone or unplug it when you don't want to be disturbed, such as at dinnertime.

Other Telephone Tips

- When you have *lots* of incoming and outgoing calls, keep a list of calls to make and a list of expected returns.

- Avoid "telephone tag." When you leave a message for someone to call you, give a time when you'll be available (and when it will be convenient) to receive the call.

- When leaving messages, provide as much information as possible, being specific and clear, so you can eliminate extra phoning later.

- Ask others when it's a good time to call them. If you haven't been able to reach them during your "telephone time," you'll now have some indication as to when they might be available.

- Return telephone calls. You'll increase your credibility if you do.

- If someone takes messages for you, ask him to repeat back the caller's name and number to ensure he gets the correct information.

- Put long extension cords on your telephone (or consider buying a cordless phone). Then if you need something from your files, you can retrieve it while still talking. It also helps in keeping track of family whereabouts.

- With so many fax machines programmed to dial numbers (and to dial repeatedly until the fax goes through), it is not unusual to get caught by a fax machine calling a wrong number that turns out to be your regular telephone line. Because of the re-dial capacity of most fax machines, you can find yourself receiving these annoying calls every five minutes for quite some time. Though at some point there will undoubtedly be a technological way to zap such calls, in the meantime, phone your operator who can interrupt the line and prevent the erroneous fax calls.

The next time you think: "I can't believe how much time I've wasted on the phone!" remember what you've learned in this chapter and see if there isn't a way to accomplish what you need to do in less time.

4

Getting Out of the House on Time

One day a colleague and I were to attend a meeting together, and about an hour before we were scheduled to be there, I had a frantic phone call from him. He'd been running late that morning and had forgotten all the papers for the meeting as well as his calendar, which gave the address of where we were to meet. It was too late to go back, so he had phoned me for the address and we had to do without the papers that day.

Another friend constantly forgets things but remembers them before she reaches the lobby of her building. She is constantly going back up to the apartment for her child's lunch, her calendar, or the dry cleaning she wanted to drop off that day. Of course, this often makes her late.

A common reason people run late is because they practice "at-the-door" planning. They don't consider what they need for the day until they are ready to leave. Or they get everything organized, but leave it in the kitchen or the bedroom where it is all too easily forgotten when they're running out the front door. Needless to say, this type of leave-taking sets off a poor chain of events all day. Here's how to smooth out your departure:

Do Ahead of Time

- Lay out your clothes the night before, which can be done quickly and easily if your closets are well organized. Don't hang up anything if it needs to be laundered, mended, or ironed. And, if necessary, shoes should be shined before being returned to the closet.

- To avoid a last-minute "key hunt," establish a place where keys are always kept.

- Set the breakfast table.

- Pack your purse or briefcase and leave it in a convenient spot by the coat closet.

- Think in advance about what you need to do in the morning. Add up how many minutes each task will take. To that, add travel time and an additional fifteen to twenty minutes for traffic and "surprises." This will allow you to plan exactly how much time you need to get out of the house on time.

- For an especially early departure (or for the person who needs all the help he or she can get in the morning!), leave out—and also group together—coat, scarf, gloves, hat, purse, briefcase, keys, transportation money, and anything else you need for a quick exit.

Set the Morning Routine

- Make your bed as soon as you get up.

- Use an answering machine to screen morning calls so you don't get bogged down by a conversation that could be held later in the day.

- To avoid congestion in the bathroom, schedule different shower times for family members. Bathing or showering in the evening can also reduce friction in the morning.

- Stay with the task you start. Don't hop from room to room as you get ready. As you leave each room, tidy up as you go, and take items such as your coffee cup with you.

- Call to confirm your appointment before you leave home and double check that the person you are seeing is running on time. Never assume that other people are as organized as you are.

- If you're really in a squeeze, ask yourself: "Okay, what must be done now to get me out the door, and what can wait?" (You must get dressed; the dishes can wait.) Just keep asking this same question until you're out the door.

Especially for Parents

- Have standing backup arrangements for what you'll do if one of your school-age children is sick or if the babysitter is late or doesn't show up at all.

- The night before:
  - Lay out children's clothing.
  - Make lunches.
  - Repack diaper bag, if needed.

- In the morning, get up and be dressed first so you can tend more fully to the children's needs.

- Leave extra time for last-minute occurrences.

For the Chronically Late

I'm sure you've heard people jokingly say, "He's always late—he'd be late to his own wedding!" Well, I've got a sister like that, and she *was* late to her own wedding! She applied her makeup at home but wanted to put on her dress at the place where the wedding was being held, and because she was running so late all her guests saw the bride arrive beautifully made up—but in blue jeans.

If you're like my sister, here are some tips that might help out:

- Put yourself on a tight and consistent schedule. Routines soon become second nature and make it easier to get moving and get things done.

- Have a clock in every room—even the bathroom.

- Set the clocks a few minutes ahead.

- In your calendar, mark your appointments a little earlier than they really are.

- Set a kitchen timer for fifteen-minute time slots. The bell will remind you how much time has passed.

- Ask a friend to call to get you moving or even stop to pick you up.

5

Preserving Personal Time

When I ask people about their personal time, they frequently answer, "Personal time? You've got to be kidding!"

There's no doubt about it. In today's fast-paced society, with so many things to do and so many things to attract our attention, it's very difficult to set aside time for ourselves. Some people spend their personal time taking a relaxing jog in the morning when they can let their minds drift. Other people read a good book. Still others think the best thing in the world is having time to call an old friend.

No matter how you spend such time, you've got to *work* to preserve it. Here are some tips:

Finding the Time

- The first thing you need to do is decide how you can best provide for some personal time. Some people like to schedule it—a workaholic might reserve Sunday afternoons for herself; a mother might schedule a regular babysitter once a week so that she can have time off. One couple I know has standing appointments with a sitter for every Thursday and Saturday night so they know they'll have time off together. Others find it satisfactory to take time as needed. When they are really feeling overwhelmed, then they work to carve out time for themselves.

- Some people steal their personal time from their "sleeping time" by getting up a half-hour or an hour earlier. (Set your alarm earlier by ten-minute increments to adjust gradually to the new wake-up time.)

- You can also borrow personal time from "waiting time" while in your doctor's office, or during a bus or train ride; or you can use the time gained from a canceled appointment.

- If you have children, make it clear you need time on your own. If you've organized a half-hour activity for them while you have a break, explain that this is *your* time. Or explain that you'll play or talk with them when their game or TV show is over.

- To have personal time you must guard your right to it, but sometimes you'll need to be creative. With my family's hectic schedule, I now find time to exercise before the household gets up. It's worth it to me to find this time by working around the family's schedule.

- Make a definite decision as to how you want to spend your personal time, or it will simply slip away from you. Do you want to spend it alone? With the family? With friends? And what sort of activity would you like to do?

Make a firm resolve to protect that time, just as you would guard a commitment you made in any other part of your life.

6

Twenty-Two Time Wasters to Avoid

Letting something or someone else waste your time means losing control of your time. If you let this happen, you will never find those precious moments to call your own. For each of the following time wasters, there is an obvious solution. In the list below, how often do you recognize yourself?

- Not having a plan; lacking direction
- Failing to set priorities; trapped by indecision
- Unable to say no
- Attempting to take on more tasks than you can possibly handle
- Failure to delegate; trying to do everything yourself
- Scheduling activities so that you have too much or too little time for something
- Putting off something that should be done today
- Focusing on how busy you are; avoiding priority work
- Suffering from personal disorganization; unable to find things because of clutter
- Jumping from one activity, project, item to the next instead of getting *one* thing done
- Leaving tasks unfinished and having to rethink what you were doing in order to finish up
- Getting bogged down by the details instead of keeping your goals in mind
- Starting a project without having enough information

- Lacking skills to accomplish what you intend (e.g., having to grope with the computer because you're not familiar with the program you need to use)
- Being kept waiting
- Being interrupted by the telephone
- Socializing during time you set aside for projects
- Being interrupted by visitors who drop in—and you let them take control
- Not getting to the point in a conversation; not saying what you mean
- Holding a meeting without an agenda
- Not using your commuting or travel time wisely
- Watching television when you had planned to do something else

Solutions to all of the above are found throughout the book, so please keep reading.

How to Use a Kitchen Timer to Manage Time

A simple kitchen timer can prove invaluable as a reminder system or as an aid in managing small blocks of time. Buy a portable timer so you can use it in various parts of the house.

Here Are Fifteen Ways to Use a Kitchen Timer:

- As a way to time (and limit) your morning shower. Aim for one that is three minutes long.
- As a reminder to make a telephone call.
- As a reminder to try a call again when you've gotten a busy signal the first time.
- To limit telephone conversations that tend to get lengthy. (Set the timer for five minutes.)
- As an incentive to start something. If you've been procrastinating on a project, set your timer for ten minutes and promise to work that long on what you don't want to do. Chances are you'll no longer feel blocked by the undertaking, but if you do, use the ten-minute system again the next day until you're comfortable with the project or until you're finished with it.
- As a way to get started exercising: "I'll exercise for just fifteen minutes."
- As a way to motivate yourself to organize your desk: "I'll spend only ten minutes sorting papers."
- Play "beat the clock" to get the chores done around the house: "I'll bet I can clean all the mirrors and windows in less than fifteen minutes."

- When working in blocks of time (such as spending half an hour setting up a library for your books). Stop when the bell goes off.

- As a reminder to turn off the stove, the sprinkler, and the like.

- To tell you when it is time for something (e.g., a television special or a favorite radio program).

- As a way to time a discussion or argument. Each person gets three minutes to present his side of the case.

- To free you from worrying about time. If you come home and have only forty-five minutes until you must leave again, set the timer rather than watching the clock. It frees you to focus on something else while guaranteeing that you'll know when it's time to go out again.

- As a way to help a small child cope with waiting time. If a youngster wants your attention when you can't give it, set the timer for when you'll be finished with your task. Tell the child to play until the bell goes off and then you'll read her a story.

- As a way to time "turns." When two preschoolers get into an unresolvable argument over whose turn it is to play with a certain toy, give each of them five minutes with the item. The ringing bell signals that the turn is over.

PART II

Paperwork

8   Books

9   Calendars

10 The Family Computer

11 Desk Organization

12 Filing Systems

13 Health Records

14 Mail, E-Mail, and Faxes

15 Resource File

8

Books

I have heard of sizable book collections, but the one belonging to one particular client was ridiculous. Her apartment was covered, wall-to-wall, with books. There were books used as end tables, books that supported a missing leg of a bed, and books that lurked in every nook and cranny of the apartment. My client literally had to create aisles in the piles of books so that there could be a path through her apartment. I got the feeling that part of the New York Public Library was housed in her living room.

Regardless of the size of the book collection, most of us have had occasion to refer back to a book we read a few years ago—and then can't locate it. You can't help but wonder: "Did I throw it out? Did I loan it to someone? Did I store it in a box? Or is it simply lost somewhere on my shelves?"

Here's a way to establish a logical system for your home library so you'll be able to find a book when you need it.

To Establish a System

- Have on hand a few empty cartons for books you may want to donate to charity or store in an attic or basement. Also have a stepladder available to help reach high shelves.

- If you have a modest number of books, gather them together to take an inventory.

- If you have a large library with books in several rooms, tackle this project on a room-by-room basis. Work in blocks of time: Monday the den, Tuesday the bedroom, and so forth.

- Divide books into categories. Typical ones for most home libraries include:

- Antiques
- Art
- Baby care
- Biography
- Business
- Children's books
- Cookbooks
- Education
- Fiction
- Gardening
- Health
- History
- Hobbies

- Interior decorating
- Music
- Mysteries
- Parenting
- Pets
- Photography
- Politics
- Reference
- Religion
- Science
- Self-help
- Sports/fitness
- Travel

- As you categorize, watch for books that could be donated to a charity, hospital, library, school, or nursing home. (When you deliver them, get a receipt from the organization so you can take a tax deduction.) You may even want to try selling some to places that buy old or used books.

- Next, group together books you want to save but that don't need to be accessible (those you're saving for your children, those you don't expect to refer to). You may want to store them in the attic, the basement, or in the upper reaches of a closet. Label clearly.

- Now take an inventory of the books you want to keep and have accessible. Do you have adequate shelf space for them? Perhaps you can build shelves in the kitchen for cookbooks, or you may want to buy a free-standing bookshelf for the living room. Whether buying or building, keep in mind that adjustable shelves are helpful because you can alter their heights.

- As much as possible, store your books where you will be using them. Cookbooks should be stored in the kitchen, children's books currently being used should be in the children's rooms, reference books should be near your desk, and so on.

- Select specific shelves where certain books will be stored. Frequently used books should be within easy reach.

- After you have decided where each book category will go, organize the books according to subcategory. For example, cookbooks might best be sorted by type of cooking (French cooking, vegetarian cooking, and so forth). History books might best be arranged by period.

- Alphabetize within each subdivision either by title or author, depending on which you remember first about a book.

- When putting the books away, consider placing some books horizontally, which can provide variation in the look of the bookcase and can make titles easier to read.

- If you have so many books that some must be kept out of reach (on high shelves, in closets, in double rows, et cetera), consider a catalog system. On 4" × 6" index cards, write the book's title, author, and subject, and where it is stored. Buy a file card box and 4" × 6" subdivider cards that you can label according to subject category. You can then organize each category alpha-betically by title or author. This could also be done on your computer.

Other Tips

- If people borrow books from you, create a system so that you'll know where your books are. Use a page in your Desk Workbook (see Chapter 11) to record the book's title, the date it was borrowed, the borrower's name, when he or she plans to return it, and his or her telephone number.

- If you're on the verge of having an unmanageable collection like the client I described earlier, then by all means consider using the public library. She would have been better off if she had made a few trips there herself!

9

Calendars

One year in early January I had dinner with a friend who was determined to get organized. She had made a New Year's resolution that *"this will be the year to reform."* As we talked, she started telling me that her new calendar system would be the key to her organization, and she proudly began pulling things from a huge bag she was carrying. Out came a month-at-a-glance calendar (so she could see a month at a time), a daily planner for personal appointments, another calendar for work only, and a large hardbound notebook for jotting down inspirations. I had to tell her I didn't think this "system" would ever get her organized— it was just a lot of extra baggage to carry around! As you'll see, she would have been better off had she purchased just one calendar. With the right one, she could have kept track of everything.

Calendars come in all sizes and shapes. Some have lovely artwork every few pages; others quote literature; still others are very businesslike. And, of course, you can now buy electronic calendars or computer programs that will do the job for you.

Regardless of the kind of calendar you use, it must be a convenient one, and you should feel comfortable with it. A calendar used regularly and effectively can become an important tool in a well-organized life.

- *Use only one daily calendar.* (Families will also want a wall calendar in the kitchen to keep track of family members' whereabouts.) The "single daily calendar" rule is vital, yet some people think they can't live without two or three. The problem with having more than one calendar is that you may forget to transfer information from one place to another. One businesswoman kept one appointment calendar at home and another at the office—a logical but unwise practice. She switched to a one-calendar system the morning she arrived at a restaurant for a meeting only to discover two different clients awaited her—she had set up two breakfast appointments for the same day!

- *Choose the type of calendar you feel most comfortable with.* Some people like week-at-a-glance styles, while others prefer to have a page or two devoted to each day; still others are ready to go electronic. In choosing, keep in mind that a good calendar should be large enough to provide space to record appointments and activities, to make notes (such as questions to ask at your next appointment), and to keep a list of errands and projects to accomplish that day. It should also be small enough to carry with you at all times.

A good calendar might also include:

- A telephone directory (for frequently called numbers).
- An expense record.
- Extra pages for notes (handy for jotting down ideas while you're on the go).

- *Record everything.* Don't trust yourself (or clutter your mind) with having to remember the dinner date with your neighbors next Tuesday. And even a standing Friday afternoon squash game should be noted so that when you glance at Friday, you have a picture of what the day holds for you. If appointments are not written down, you may unintentionally forget about one of them.

- When using your calendar to record an appointment, write down the address, telephone number, and directions in the space next to the appointment. The more information of this type you write down, the better your calendar will serve as a helpful record for tax purposes, or if you need to go back and verify something.

- Always review your activities at least one week in advance so you'll know what is scheduled and can make any changes if you need to.

- At the office, leave a photocopy or printout of the day's or week's appointments with your secretary so that he or she always knows your whereabouts. If your secretary keeps your calendar, he or she should leave a photocopy for you. (See below for additional ideas on scheduling via computerized calendar.)

- Spouses should periodically (daily or every few days) review each other's plans (especially when both carry a calendar) so that each knows when the other will be late coming home or will be going out of town, and also can be aware of and note places where they are to go together.

The Family Wall Calendar

- Purchase a large (I like 17" × 22") calendar to hang in a central location near a telephone. In most homes this is the kitchen.

- Have each family member write on it in their own predetermined color (choose a color for family activities as well), so that information about someone or about family activities is easy to spot.

- When children become old enough to start taking responsibility for their own plans, it's time for them to write them down on their own. Parents should write down plans they make that affect the children, such as "Sunday dinner at Grandma's" or on Tuesday, "Mom late for dinner." Children should record all their plans on the calendar so that if you arrive home one afternoon and find that your child isn't there yet, you can quickly check the calendar to see where he or she is. Also write down standing appointments such as religious school or gymnastics class.

- Make a habit of checking the wall calendar daily to see if there is information there that you need to add to your personal calendar. You don't want to schedule a meeting at the time you promised to pick up your daughter and her friends at the ice skating rink.

Computer Calendars

Calendar software for computers usually combines an appointment book, address book, to do lists, and space for notes. They offer terrific opportunities for organizational improvement.

- Rescheduling can be accomplished with a few key strokes—the entire appointment, complete with driving instructions, can be moved from Tuesday to Thursday with great ease.

- They inform you of your availability at a glance. If you need to know if you have any free time next week, a click of the mouse will instantly provide you with the entire week's schedule.

- They offer dual or group scheduling. Both boss and secretary can input into the same system, making it easy to coordinate and stay up-to-date. Group scheduling, such as a departmental meeting, can also be accomplished via computers on Local Area Network systems. (You choose how much of your calendar you want to make available for "public" scheduling. The rest can be kept private.)

- Standing appointments can be set to appear automatically.

- Your to do list can carry over from day to day until all tasks are complete.

- Search capabilities are a part of the package. Your computer can, for example, help you find the last time you went to the eye doctor.

- If you are hooked up to a modem, some systems feature auto-dial and auto-fax features. To fax a report to a coworker, you can look up the person's fax number in your online address book, highlight the report, and with a click on the "fax" icon, the report will be on its way.

- "Contact manager" versions of these calendar systems provide space to log phone calls and take notes on meetings. The next time you're in touch with a particular coworker or client, you can pull up the information and pick up right where you left off.

There are a couple of drawbacks to having your calendar on computer. If your computer is turned on for only a couple of hours a day, you may find that it's inconvenient to enter dates or check your address book. This can be partially overcome by working from a printout of your schedule when you're away from your computer, but you should keep this in mind if you're considering a switch. One fellow who loved the organizational aspects of having his calendar on computer finally went back to a paper-based calendar system after a couple of years: "I was in and out of the office so much each day that even with the information on my laptop computer, I just found that paper was more convenient for me."

Electronic Organizers or Personal Digital Assistants

Formerly considered an executive toy, today electronic organizers are used by a wide range of people. One style, the *personal information manager,* is a hand-held electronic device designed to keep phone lists, addresses, and appointments, but these systems generally are limited in capacity because they do not interface with a computer.

A more advanced style is actually considered to be a *palmtop computer* (also known as a "personal digital assistant"). It operates much like a personal computer, and it can be connected to a fax machine or to an online service or linked to your computer for information exchange. Palmtop computers function like organizers, keeping phone numbers and appointments, but they often include word processing and spreadsheet capabilities and sometimes wireless faxing and data reception.

If you decide some type of electronic organizer is for you, keep the following in mind as you shop for a specific model:

- Is the one you are considering a convenient size and not too heavy? You want it to feel portable.

- Does it require warm-up time, and if so, is the wait a reasonable one? If someone wants to book an appointment, you don't want to have to wait long to be able to access your schedule.

- How is the data entered? By keyboard? By pen onto the screen?

- If there is a keyboard, is it comfortable? If you are a touch typist or have large hands, some of the keyboards may feel too small. "Hunt and peck" typists seem to mind the shrunken keyboards the least.

- If it's a pen-based system, test to see if the organizer can decipher your handwriting.

- Compare screens. Make sure the one you select is easy to read. Those that feature backlighting tend to be more versatile.

- Ask about memory capacity, and be sure the model you're considering has the capacity for adding extra memory if you think you might need it.

- Is there a rechargeable battery pack available? Most burn through batteries quickly, so it's helpful to be able to charge a battery pack at night.

- Is there any risk of losing the information? You might want one that connects to your computer so that you can back it up on a regular basis.

- Does it provide ready access to your phone directory, schedule, and to do list? Do you like the format of each of these items?

- Ask if there are other software cards available. Companies have created software such as thesauruses, dictionaries, time and expense records, foreign language translations, city guides, financial planning programs, and games.

Keep an eye on these hand-held gadgets. The technology is changing rapidly, and soon most of them will have the capabilities of a small computer. A single command from this tiny instrument will send a wireless fax about Friday's 3 P.M. meeting, note the date in your calendar, and add "prepare for meeting" to your to do list, all at the same time.

In the long run, this invention is going to be hard to resist!

10

The Family Computer

If your family is not yet computer-literate, chances are you've been wanting to become so as you listen to friends extolling the benefits of computerization. Now is a good time to take the plunge. A computer is turning out to be as convenient to have at home as the microwave.

Here are some of the points to keep in mind as you enter—or expand your reach—during the computer age.

Buying a Family Computer

- If you're buying a new computer, purchase the most current model. Technology is changing so rapidly you need the latest machinery in order for the computer to do all the things you want it to.

- Be sure your computer has a warranty. If a problem is going to occur, it generally happens within the first few months.

- Most computers today come with a CD-ROM and a built-in modem. Buying an older model or a cheaper model without these features is being penny-wise and pound-foolish. Rest assured that you will use both.

- Watch prices on scanners. They are designed to scan pictures and text into your computer. At some point, these will be an integral part of home computers, too. As the technology improves and the prices drop, the home use of scanners will grow.

- Invest in an antivirus program, or download one from an online service. The odds of getting a virus on a home machine are low, but if it should happen, it can wipe out your entire hard drive in seconds.

- Fill out the postcard that comes with any computer program you buy so the company can notify you about updates.

■ Ask at the computer store for the name of a "wizard," someone who knows and understands computers inside and out. Getting a telephone number of a person you can hire on an hourly basis to help you set up your system or learn something new will be invaluable. (And don't be surprised when your wizard turns out to be nineteen years old and wears a baseball cap and sneakers. Some of the most knowledgeable computer experts are young.)

Becoming Computer Literate

■ Take a course.

■ Go to a bookstore or to a computer store and browse through the computer books, looking for ones that pertain to the programs you're using. Some of them are directed at helping even the most computer phobic, so watch for ones that look easy and useful. (Also ask store personnel for recommendations.)

■ Subscribe to one of the computer magazines. Purchase several at a newsstand and subscribe to the one that best meets your needs.

■ Anytime you invest in a new software program or add a feature to your computer, set aside time to become familiar with it. Many programs come with tutorials that provide some basic exposure to the system, and like anything else, you'd be amazed at what reading the operating instructions will do for you! If you're still stumped, an hour with a tutor can get you up and running.

■ If children will be using your computer, invest in one of the programs that prohibits them from entering your files. There are several that give children access to all material intended for them but let only the adult password-holders go beyond to information such as family finances.

Backing Up Is Vital

■ Invest in a good backup system that is easy to use. The single *biggest* mistake people make in using their computers is failing to back it up. You may not have a problem for years, but a breakdown can happen, and losing years' worth of data is devastating.

- Most home computers need to be backed up only once a month, so establish a schedule and note it on your calendar. You might make it one of the things you do on the first of the month, for example. If you use your computer frequently, you may want to back up weekly, or whenever you've entered a lot of information.

- Computers used for work should have three levels of backup: monthly, weekly, and daily (the daily backup can be selective).

- If you're working on something extremely important, make two backup copies. Store one in the desk where you've been working. Take the other one with you. (If you're at the office, take it home; if you're at home, take it to the office.)

Now for the Fun

Here are just some of the organizational tasks you'll accomplish more quickly on the computer:

- *Address Book.* Access information on friends and associates at the touch of a computer key. (See below for more information.)

- *Calendar Programs.* Your life at a glance. (See Chapter 9.)

- *Graphic Design.* Now you'll write the invitation and design it, too.

- *Health Insurance Forms.* These programs help simplify filing for reimbursement.

- *Home Design.* New programs let you design anything from a complete house to a decorating scheme.

- *Household Information.* Enter basic information into a computer once, and modify it as needed. Anything from a boilerplate instruction sheet for a nighttime babysitter to a checklist for closing up the house when you're going to be away.

- *Kitchen Know-How.* Cookbooks on computer offer the benefits of search-and-find. If you're looking for a chicken and oregano recipe and can't remember what it's called, the computer will find it for you.

- *Legal Needs.* There are programs on making a will as well as programs that give you boilerplate letters for leases, power of attorney, and so on.

- *Mailing Lists.* If your latest volunteer job involves sending out mailings, your problems are over if your computer is properly equipped.

- *Money Management.* Instant access to your finances. (See Chapters 16 and 17.)

- *Photo Storage.* At last, get those photos out of the shoebox. Now you have a fun place to put them—on the computer. You'll need a scanner (some are inexpensively priced and are created precisely for home use for photos), and you can place them in personalized documents, calendars, newsletters, invitations, or brochures. Or forget the printing process entirely and send photographs over the Internet to friends and relatives.

- *Résumés.* Type and retype no more.

- *Travel.* Some software programs become your driving guide, plotting how you can best get from point A to point B.

Address Books on Computer

To be well-organized, you may find that it's worth investing the time to put your address book on computer. Today we all come with so many "contact" points (address; e-mail address; office, home, and cellular telephone numbers; fax number; etc.), it's very hard to find a way to keep a traditional book or system up-to-date.

- Computerized address books permit you to sort people's names alphabetically, geographically, or by category. You may want to locate all your friends who live in Florida, or you may be looking for the telephone number of a restaurant on Fifty-second Street that you used to frequent regularly—enter the appropriate cues, and the computer will find the information for you.

- Create a printout of your computer address book and store it in a looseleaf binder. This gives you easy access to the information even when your computer isn't on. Updating is easy. Enter the new information into the computer and print out a new page.

■ Entering all the information into the computer can be tedious, so do it in chunks. Assign yourself the task of entering ten names per day. This will take only five to ten minutes, and over a period of a few weeks you'll be able to complete the entire job.

■ Once your address book is complete, get in the habit of updating it regularly. As soon as you receive a change of address card, put the information in your computer. This is the key to an up-to-date, efficient system.

Reaching the World Beyond

If you've purchased a modem (a telephone linkup that connects your computer to a vast network of computerized information) for your computer, then you know the world is at your fingertips. You may be transferring money around in your bank accounts or booking airline reservations from home; your high-school-age son or daughter likely is using it for library research (and probably spending some time chatting on an online service "party line"). You and your spouse may be using it to send and receive electronic mail. The possibilities are limitless.

■ If your computer does not already have a modem, invest in a high-speed one. Technology is constantly improving, and you want to start with the best available. Book your computer wizard to hook it up. If you don't know what you're doing, you'll waste a lot of time.

■ Consider adding an additional phone line for your modem. If you've got a fax, you could combine the two. Using one phone line for all telephone/fax/modem equipment will ultimately be very frustrating.

■ Investigate online services, and talk to friends and/or computer dealers about software that connects you directly to the Internet. You may decide direct Internet access (for which you still have to pay a fee) through a commercial "access provider" is more to your liking, or you may opt for some of the conveniences and features of the online services. The online services are user-friendly and offer attractions such as "chat rooms" and a wide variety of well-organized research material and files that are easy to access.

■ If you're using an online service, it can become expensive over time. Purchase an offline reader/navigator program that lets you more efficiently capture your mail, news, and messages from your favorite forum. It can decrease your online time considerably by letting you download and respond to e-mail and forum messages offline.

■ If you have children, investigate the parental control features that are available so that you can let your children enjoy the wonders of interactive exploration without being exposed to material in poor taste.

If You Are Considering a Laptop

As notebook (laptop) computers have become more functional, they've become more popular, too. Today there are dozens to choose from, and you'll want to take time to select the one that best suits your family's needs, whether it's one for your teen to take to college or one for you to use for work.

Should you buy a laptop instead of a regular computer? Not if you have the space and don't need the portability. Desktop computers are still cheaper and easier to use, but you can't take them with you. That's when you want the laptop.

■ You should be able to find a good portable computer that is about the size of a ream of letter paper ($8\frac{1}{2}$" × 11" × 3") and that weighs about six or seven pounds, though some of the more expensive ones weigh even less.

■ Notebook computers vary widely in price, and the difference is primarily in the speed of the computer and the size of its hard drive. Faster computers that have more disk storage space are the ones that command top dollar.

■ Compare screens when you shop. The larger screen can have up to 60 percent more viewing area.

- Check the "pointing stick" or thumb pad that replaces the familiar mouse. Is it comfortable? Easy to use?

- Make certain that the notebook computer you buy has built-in connectors so that the computer can be hooked up to a printer and other peripherals. This is becoming standard, but you ought to make sure your unit has it.

- Ask which software is already installed on the models you're considering.

- Though notebook computers are created for use in nontraditional circumstances, they are not designed to withstand being dropped or being used as a portable seat, so treat your new computer well. It's a powerful tool.

11

Desk Organization

For many people, their desks are where they live most of the day. And many of these environments are overwhelming disasters. I'm often hired to be a "desk doctor," and I can't tell you the number of times I've walked in and seen a desk that easily could have been mistaken for the home of a pack rat, yet the client assures me that he or she has "cleaned up" for my arrival. Referring to the magazine makeovers where a woman is transformed into the belle of the ball, one reporter whom I visited noted: "My desk looks like a 'before' and I want it to look like an 'after.'" She wanted her "hopeless mess" to become a model of efficiency. With dedication, it can be done, and that's what we'll work toward in this chapter.

I find that most of my clients' problems generally fall into one of three categories:

- *Poor space planning.* They have to keep jumping up and down to get the items they need.

- *Poor work habits.* Each day a few more papers become permanent residents of the to do stack.

- *Indecision.* They have no idea what to do with the stacks of paper on their desks.

Here are some ways to get your desk under control.

General Planning

- Whether you spend one hour or eight hours at your desk every day, careful thought should go into how you use it. Make it functional!

- At home, *try to establish a place that is solely for paperwork* (see building suggestions on next page). Though a storage unit on wheels can make working at the kitchen table bearable, it is not ideal to have to clear your work surface each time the family wants to eat.

■ It's preferable to have a desk of your own rather than sharing.

■ Know your work habits. If you like to spread out material as you work, provide yourself with enough space (such as a large desk surface or a long countertop).

■ A good chair is as important as a functional desk. Invest in one that is right for you. A chair on wheels is particularly handy.

Buying a Desk

■ Shop for a desk with enough surface space so you can spread out your materials.

■ Files and supplies should be very accessible. Some desks have this type of storage built into them.

■ Sit at the desk in a chair similar to the one you'll be using. The desk should feel comfortable to you, and there should be enough room underneath for your legs.

■ I prefer desks that are wider than they are deep. Deep desks lend themselves to pushing stacks of paper into the far corner, making it too easy for things to get lost.

Building New Desk Space

■ A practical, inexpensive desk can be made by placing a laminated board across two filing cabinets. Such an arrangement will provide a large work surface, with files that are close at hand.

■ If you're working with a carpenter, consider a U-shaped counter with storage underneath. It will provide lots of space conveniently within reach.

■ One compact way is to build work space in a closet. Then just close the door when you're finished for the day!

■ If you have a useless cubbyhole in a den, bedroom, living room, or even the kitchen, consider building a desk in that area. You can add shuttered doors to close off the area when not in use.

■ When space is at a premium, build a collapsible counter. But be sure to have shelves or a storage unit nearby for supplies.

Organizing Your Desk Area

■ You must be able to find what you're looking for quickly. "A place for everything and everything in its place" is an important principle to keep in mind.

■ To avoid having to jump up and down as you work, plan space nearby for:

- Address book/Rolodex
- Birthday Book (see Chapter 42)
- Calendar. (Though your calendar should always be with you when you're out on appointments, it should also have a "reserved" space on your desk.)
- Computer
- Dictionary
- Files
- Reference books
- Resource Files (see Chapter 15)
- Telephone and answering machine
- Trash can

■ Materials to have on hand:

- Calculator
- Canceled Checks Folder (see Chapter 16)
- Checkbook
- Clock
- Eraser

- Envelopes
- Household Affairs Folder (see Chapter 17)
- Labels
- Letter opener
- Notepads
- Paper clips
- Pens and pencils
- Rubber bands
- Ruler
- Scissors
- Stapler
- Stamps
- Stationery
- Tape

- Organize the above materials according to use. For example, you may use your letter opener more frequently than your stapler, so place it in a more convenient spot.

- A bulletin board is a terrific desk aid, but don't fall prey to putting up notes that stay up until they are yellow with age. The bulletin board should be used for reminders that need to be visible, such as zip code or area code maps you use frequently.

Additional Storage

- Any type of work area can benefit from a storage station on wheels with swing-out drawers, storage bins, and trays.

- Design and have built a shelving unit to go above your desk to store items such as those just mentioned. The unit should be in the proper proportion to your desk—close to it and low enough to reach without standing up.

- At a stationery store, look for desktop organizers that will store the items you won't be putting in drawers. There are units that can hold a few file folders for current projects; others have space for pens and pencils as well as miniature drawers or cups for items such as rubber bands and paper clips. But don't buy so many that you clutter your desk with unnecessary organizers.

Establishing Better Desk Work Habits

When it comes to desk organization, stacks of paper are the single biggest problem I see. You don't have time to finish a project, so you leave it until morning. . . . You're expecting an answer from XYZ Company by the end of the week, so you'll leave the file out until then. . . . You didn't finish reading the mail, so you'll leave it until Monday. And the only problem is that by the time Monday comes, it's too late because now there is pile after pile after pile, and it seems it would take weeks to ever untangle the mess.

Here are some tips to help you work better:

- The key is not to let paper and piles keep multiplying. *Process each paper as it comes in,* and get it off your desk (see Chapter 14).

- Make it a rule to *always refile* things. You can establish a special place (such as a desktop standing file) for current projects, but otherwise put everything away.

- Keep your desk free of clutter. It may tempt your eyes to roam, making time at your desk less effective. Put loose papers in clearly labeled files ("To Do," "To Read," etc.) or color-coded ones (purple = medical, green = legal matters).

- If you're concerned about remembering where you are going to put some notes you'll need for an upcoming project, note the location on your bulletin board or in the Tickler File (see Chapter 12) under the day or month the project is due.

- If you have taken files out of dead storage for a specific project, gather them up when the project is completed and take the time to put them back where they belong.

- Establish a Desk Workbook. Buy a medium-sized looseleaf notebook (you can easily keep the workbook current by simply taking out pages that are no longer relevant), paper, and dividers. It is invaluable for recording ideas in the working/developing stage. Instead of jotting down notes on scraps of paper and never knowing where to find them, you'll have one place to look when you want to refer back to that million-dollar idea you had the other night. Items found in a Desk Workbook might include: a clever paragraph for a sales letter; the punch line for a speech to be written at the end of the week; a new marketing idea; possible titles for a new project; anecdotes; meeting notes; details of a telephone conversation. Move this information to a file when appropriate. For example, the punch line for a speech should be moved to a folder labeled "Speech" once research and writing of the speech is underway. Use the dividers to break the notebook into categories ("Ideas," "Business Plan," "Meetings," or whatever you choose).

▪ Your Desk Workbook (or the bulletin board) is also a perfect place for an assignment sheet that will keep track of ongoing projects. List the date the assignment was given to you (or when you assigned it to someone else), a description, a progress report, comments, and the due date.

▪ To keep track of deadlines, use your Tickler Files (see Chapter 12), computer, or calendar. Be sure to note a project's deadline on a date earlier than when it is due so you will be sure to finish it in time.

▪ Set aside time daily for doing paperwork. Choose an hour when there are few distractions—if at home, in the early morning before the family gets up; or, if at work, before the staff comes in. During this time, use an answering machine or your voice-mail system to screen calls or have your secretary hold calls, or have a coworker answer your phone (you can return the favor at another time).

▪ Use your desk clock as an important ally. If you're procrastinating about something, tell yourself you'll work on it for "just fifteen minutes." And use the clock to help you stop early enough so you will have time to put things away at the end of the day.

▪ Clean up your desk every night so there's no chaos when you begin the next morning.

What to Do When Your Desk Is a Disaster

Many of my clients are truly frantic because their desks are such a mess. They can't find slips of paper on which they wrote important phone numbers; they know they received information they sent for, but now it's buried in a pile of paper; they were working on a chapter of a novel, but now the notes for the next chapter are gone. . . .

Here's how I counsel them when I make a "house call":

▪ Address your desk problems in blocks of time. You may be able to straighten out the clutter in a few hours, or you may need a weekend. Sometimes it's better to devote a couple of hours a day to the job until you're done.

▪ Have on hand a trash can, a pen, file folders, labels, and any other desk organizational aids I have discussed above that suit your needs.

▪ Clear the space you want to organize (the desk surface, one of the drawers, etc.). Then make a big pile of all the paper.

▪ Evaluate each item, categorize it, and put it away (in the desk drawer, in a file, in one of the desk organizers, etc.), throwing out as much as possible (see Chapter 12).

▪ Even when you are feeling overwhelmed, just keep sorting and categorizing. If you devote the necessary time, your desk can be cleared.

▪ Reread this chapter's "Establishing Better Desk Work Habits" periodically. The tips offer the key to keeping your desk clear once you're there.

12

Filing Systems

Most people have trouble with filing. I once had a client who was truly desperate because of an overflow of paper. She finally took to carrying all her important papers in a tote bag everywhere she went. "I didn't want to put them down at home because I was afraid I wouldn't be able to find them again," she said.

So much material bombards us in this information-filled world that it is often overwhelming to sort through it all and store it for future reference. The solution is a personal filing system that will store all pertinent information you and your family may need. I can help you create that system—I've done it for the desperate, and it will work for you, too.

So whether you've turned to this chapter because you're drowning in piles of paper or whether you have a fairly organized system that you just don't keep up, there is hope. It will take perseverance and some time, but there is a way to create a filing system for home or office where it will take you no more than five minutes to locate a piece of paper, no matter how long it's been since you saw it last.

Common Filing Mistakes

There are three common mistakes people make when filing:

- They fall into the "Now where would I have filed that?" syndrome. By not establishing a logical system, they have trouble remembering how to find what they've filed.

- They establish a workable system—but don't keep up with it. If you have more than ten or twelve pieces of paper waiting to be filed, you've fallen into the "I'll do it tomorrow" trap.

- People file "in perpetuity." Just because you thought a certain piece of paper might come in handy after graduate school, there may be no good reason to still have it on hand today.

Establishing a System

The most effective filing system is one that is:

- Simple
- Easy to understand
- Easily accessible to anyone

You don't want a system that is so complicated you or others will need written instructions to figure it out.

- First, set aside time to reorganize your system. If you have a limited number of items to be filed, it may take half a day. If you have extensive home files, plan to spend three days or so (or an hour a day for two or three weeks).

- Next, invest in a good, sturdy file cabinet. Whether it is a one- or a four-drawer unit depends on your filing needs. Allow room to grow!

- Finally, plan that your files will ultimately be stored near your work station.

Alphabetical or Color-Coded?

There are two simple systems for establishing a filing system. Both are quite workable:

- *Alphabetical.* The key element here is choosing appropriate titles so that the folder will be where you expect it to be. For example, if you're starting a file for ideas for a new career, should you call the file "New Job," "Career Ideas," or "New Career"? This will obviously make a difference in how the folder gets alphabetized. How to decide? *Title it as you most often think of it.* Monitor yourself for a few days and see how you refer to the subject. If you say to a friend, "I'm thinking of looking for a *new job*," then "New Job" would likely be the best title for the file.

- *Color-coding.* Here's how it works:
  - Decide on a color system that will work best for you; for example, pick a different color for each member of your

family. These colors should be consistent throughout the home; John's toothbrush, towels, et cetera—as well as his file folders—should be red. Or, you can use this system for different subjects: insurance is green, travel information is blue, and so forth. Color-coding speeds filing and acts as insurance against misfiling. Your memory responds to color first, so when you want the insurance folder, you automatically think "green."

- Apply this color scheme to the files themselves by using colored folders and file labels or tabs so you can easily pick out the proper color and category.

▪ Make a color key that will explain the system to everyone who wishes to use the file, and have the key within easy access.

▪ Some people do a combination of alphabetical and color-coding. The colored folders are filed alphabetically. It makes retrieval within the file drawer easier. In my filing system, any client-related information is stored in blue folders, and each folder is filed alphabetically by the client's last name.

Step One: Getting Started

▪ Have on hand a pen or marker, file folders, and file labels that match the color of your file folders.

▪ Choose a work area with plenty of space.

▪ Gather together all the miscellaneous papers you want to file as well as any existing files you may have.

▪ Evaluate the type of information you want to keep to begin developing file categories. Of course, the categories will vary according to your interest or work requirements, but they will probably include some or many that are listed below. (These categories are primarily for the home.) Following each category, I have included some of the items which might be filed there. (As discussed previously, the exact title you choose for each file is the one that will work best for you.)

- *Automobile*—payment book, leasing contract, owner's manual, mileage chart, consumer information.
- *Bargains*—listings of the best places to shop for certain items, articles about discounted items.
- *Cash Receipts*—receipts for major purchases such as appliances, jewelry, television, furniture, home maintenance equipment, as well as your New Purchases list for the year (see Chapter 22 for details).
- *Consumer Information*—articles on consumerism and listings of whom to contact for various problems.
- *Contracts*—agreements between you and people who work for you or for whom you work.
- *Correspondence*—letters you want to keep for reference (each family member should have a separate file).
- *Credit Records*—list of credit card account numbers with name, address, and phone number to contact in case the card is stolen; installment contracts.
- *Employment*—past and present résumés, personal benefits report, employee benefits information, pension records from previous employers.
- *Financial Planning*—budget-related items, financial goals, financial planning articles.
- *Gift Lists*—lists of gifts given in previous years as well as an ongoing list for the current year.
- *Guarantees and Warranties*—warranties, instruction manuals, lists of authorized service centers.
- *Hobbies*—articles or information about your interests.
- *Housing, Owned*—home improvement receipts, records of land transfer taxes, list of purchase price, closing and selling costs.
- *Housing, Rented*—copy of the lease rental agreement, pictures showing move-in condition of rental property.

- *Important Documents*—photocopies of documents such as birth certificates, passports, marriage license, divorce papers; originals should be kept in a safe-deposit box (see Chapter 23). Photocopies of family wills (originals are sometimes kept by your attorney); original copy of letters of last instructions. In addition, your social security number, driver's license; and information regarding the whereabouts of important documents and names and addresses of personal advisors—all of which are contained on your Financial Master List (see Chapter 19).

- *Insurance*—copies of all policies. List of policy numbers, names of insured persons and possessions, issuing company, agent, type and amount of coverage. Personal Property Inventory (see Chapter 22) including original purchase price of valuable items, model and serial numbers, and photos showing especially valuable or unusual possessions. (Keep another copy of this Inventory in your strongbox and one in your safe-deposit box.)

- *Interior Design*—names of recommended designers, articles about home design, photos of other homes you like.

- *Investments*—records of stock or bond purchases and selling prices; transaction slips (broker's purchase and sales statements); brokerage statements.

- *Medical History Records*—history of family illnesses (see Chapter 13). Each family member should have a separate, color-coded file.

- *Reviews, Restaurants, and Movies*—articles giving recommendations.

- *Trust Information*—Trust correspondence and copies of documents (original documents should be stored in safe-deposit box).

- *Volunteer Work*—material and correspondence pertaining to any volunteer organization with which you work.

Step Two: The Process

- Overwhelming as it may seem, go through the stack of papers you've collected piece by piece, making a decision about where to file each paper—try to handle each paper only once.

- As you evaluate each item, your first questions should be, "Do I really need to save this? If I needed the information, could I get it elsewhere?"

- Next ask "How do I plan to use this information?" and not "Where should I put this?" For example, a business card of someone you met from Atlanta might be filed in "Georgia Business Trip" rather than with other business cards because you hope to visit him the next time you are there.

- If you're stuck, put that piece of paper aside and review it again when you've finished processing the others. Where it belongs may be clearer later.

- Keep working through your papers until you're completely finished. It may take several hours or days, but it will be worth it! You'll have an organized system that will work well for you.

Step Three: Develop Good Filing Habits

- Depending on the file, there are different ways of organizing within it. For example, the information in a file of correspondence with one company (perhaps concerning a complaint) might best be filed *chronologically,* with the most recent letter on top. The information in a file of correspondence with many companies would best be filed *alphabetically* by company. Choose the system that makes sense for each of your files.

- Staple, rather than clip, relevant material together. Paper clips tend to catch on other papers.

- Store each ongoing activity and project in its own file folder, clearly labeled so you don't have to go through the file to see what's in it. Sometimes people make the mistake of assuming they can stack something on their desk since they'll be finished with it "soon." You'll be much happier if there's "a place for everything, and everything in its place."

- Divide larger projects into several folders to facilitate retrieval. For example, your work organizing a conference might be broken down into "Conference Publicity," "Conference Brochure," "Conference Mailing Lists."

- If you've had a difficult time deciding where to file a certain piece of paper, consider cross-referencing between two (or more) files. Put a reference slip in each file where the paper *could* have been filed, telling the exact location of the item. This is more efficient (and less bulky) than making multiple copies of something which might fit into one of several categories.

- If you must have the complete copy in another file (for example, something you want on file at home and at the office), make a photocopy.

- If you must remove papers from a file for any period of time, leave a note as to where they are.

- Keep frequently used files in an accessible spot.

Step Four: Maintain Your Filing System

- File regularly. Choose a basket or create a "To File" folder. Establish a set time to file—at least twice a week, and preferably daily. The more often you file, the less time it takes.

- Keep files lean and current by moving out information you haven't worked on in six months or more. Establish "Inactive" project files (appropriately titled) and store them in an accessible spot (bottom drawer of a file cabinet? cardboard file box in a closet?), but be sure not to mix them in with your active files.

- The easiest way to maintain a file is to sift through it every time you pull it and toss material you no longer need. This way you can easily maintain your files with little or no effort.

- If there are files you do not pull regularly, choose a time once every three months or so to look through them and weed out the items you no longer need. With entire files you won't be needing soon, place them in inactive storage.

Establishing Tickler Files

Tickler Files for items you want to be reminded of are invaluable to being organized. The files are designed to "tickle" your memory and keep track of details you don't want to think about or have on your desk until needed.

- You will need eighteen file folders. Of these, twelve should be labeled for each month of the year, five should be reserved for each day of the business week (Monday through Friday), and the sixth and final folder should be labeled "Weekend." (If you're setting up a system for your office, you'll want twelve monthly folders and thirty-one additional ones, one for each day of the month so that you can slip in notes and materials for meetings or conferences throughout the entire month.)

- The monthly Tickler Files will remind you of long-term items. You can date-file your ophthalmologist's business card in order to be reminded to make an appointment to see him in January. Or perhaps you've been told to follow up on something in six weeks—all these reminders should be placed in the appropriate monthly Tickler File. You may want to keep an index card reminding you of upcoming birthdays on file here (see Chapter 42). I also note down on a card when I should expect an insurance renewal, and I file it in the appropriate month. Other items to be date-filed here might include a pet's yearly vaccination schedule, a reminder to call regarding air-conditioning installation in May (before you really need it), a note about family checkups in September, a reminder to get winter coats out of storage in October, and the like.

- The daily Tickler Files will help you organize the papers you need for projects to be done on a certain day. A postcard you receive Saturday notifying you of a dental appointment you will have to change should be put in Monday's file to remind you to call and schedule a new appointment. An article you want to send to your mother might be filed under Wednesday—the day you plan to write her. A note about a question for your insurance agent whom you need to call on Thursday should go in that day's file. A marketing questionnaire you plan to fill out while waiting for your son to take his piano lesson Tuesday should be filed appropriately. Weekend files might hold such items as film negatives to be developed, photos to be framed, or a note about the kind of seeds you want to look for at the garden shop. As you take care of each item on the appropriate day, discard the reminder. If for some reason you are unable to process something, select another day in which to file it, and take care of it on that day. (Make it a top priority if you've had to delay it once).

Don't Bother to File

- All the business cards you receive. While you'll want to put valuable contacts in your address book, many people who give you their card you'll never see again. Bind such cards together with a rubber band and store the bundle in your Resource File (see Chapter 15). If you eventually do want to contact someone, you can retrieve the appropriate card and create a "Contact" card for them. Otherwise, you can look through the collection periodically and toss the ones you don't expect to need any longer.

- Papers or clippings you don't really need. If you're wavering, toss it. Chances are it really *won't* come in handy.

- Catalogs or bulletins that (being realistic) you know you won't refer to

- Duplicates of anything

- Information that is obsolete, such as real estate prices of three years ago or old restaurant reviews

- Chain letters

- Fliers people insist you take

- Old notes

13

Health Records

Everyone should keep a complete record of their health. (And, of course, parents must assume responsibility for their children's health records.) The history of the diseases you've had is important to any medical professional who serves you. In addition, you need to keep records about your reaction to various medicines. If a new doctor needs to prescribe an antibiotic for you, he or she will need to know which ones (if any) have caused negative reactions.

Establishing a System

- For filing purposes, each family member should have his or her own color (see Chapter 12).

- Buy 5" × 8" index cards in the appropriate colors or use white cards with appropriately colored file labels to denote each family member's color. This also could be stored on your computer, but be sure to create a printout and file it. You'd hate to lose your health records if your computer crashes.

- On each person's card, record the following information about significant illnesses or doctor's visits:

MEDICAL RECORD JOHN JONES			
Date/Doctor	Reason for Visit	Medication (and Instruction) or Immunization	Reaction

- For adult family members, keep an accurate record of illnesses or health problems severe enough to merit a visit to the doctor. For your own information, note frequent colds or headaches and your reactions to various types of over-the-counter drugs. If you need to see a doctor for persistent headaches, you'll have accurate information, or if you want to know which cold remedy doesn't make you sleepy, you can check your notations.

- For children, note immunizations and major illnesses such as chickenpox so that later in life your children will have a medical history to which they can refer. While you may not want to keep track of each time your child goes for a checkup, it will be helpful to note the date of an ear infection and what medication was used. That way if the illness recurs you'll know what medicine your child was given and how effective it was. If you have more than one child, a written record of this information is vital! There's no guarantee that you'll remember who reacted badly to a certain antibiotic or who had chickenpox five summers ago.

- Store these cards or the computer printout in your Health Records File in your file cabinet for easy access.

14

Mail, E-Mail, and Faxes

Mail Quiz

- Are there stacks of magazines and newspapers in every room of your home?
- Has personal correspondence been lying around for so long that it's begun to collect dust?
- Do you sometimes RSVP to an event after the date specified?
- Do you forget to make note of upcoming meetings or social engagements?
- Do you occasionally get bills stamped "Third Notice—Payment Overdue" and realize you must have misplaced the first two bills?
- Do you have a pile of junk mail you are saving "until I have time"?
- Have you ever found uncashed checks lying around?
- Do you hate to throw things out?
- When you return from vacation, do you have so many e-mail messages that you just can't imagine finding the time to answer them all?
- Do you sometimes find that you spend valuable work time answering an unending amount of e-mail?
- When you hear the fax machine click on, are you often inclined to drop what you're doing to go find out what's being transmitted to you?

If you answered "yes" to one or more of these questions, read on.

The Mail

I've nicknamed the daily arrival of the mail "information blues time." It's the major reason so many people feel as though they are drowning in paper. What's more, there's no stopping it. Through rain, sleet, snow, and hail that letter carrier is going to continue to contribute to your growing pile of unread mail. When it comes to mail management, remember:

Rule number one is you must deal with the mail daily. As few as fifteen minutes each day is painless compared with what you may face if you let it pile up.

Rule number two is don't shuffle the mail. Make a decision about each item as you handle it and then follow through.

In addition, following are the specific ways you can successfully fight the daily deluge:

To Start

- Choose a specific time and place to process your mail, and have a large wastebasket handy.

- At home, sort the mail according to family member. Your stacks will be more readily manageable if you go through the magazines and catalogs first and then add letters to the top of each pile.

- Establish a set spot for leaving each person's mail so he or she will know where to look for it each day.

- If a family member is out of town, store his or her mail in a manila envelope so there will be no chance of misplacing anything.

- Next, sort your own mail using the following categories:

  - To Toss
  - To Ask About
  - To File
  - To Call
  - To Do
  - To Read

Here are coping strategies for items in each category:

To Toss

- Instead of asking yourself, "Could I possibly use this one day?" ask, "What's the worst thing that could happen if I throw this out?" If the answer is "nothing," then toss it.

- Make a game out of seeing how much you can toss before you reach a certain spot. If you live in an apartment building and pick up mail in the lobby, try to pull out as much "junk" as you can before you reach your apartment door. Home dwellers could try to pull out as much as possible before reaching a designated spot such as the kitchen wastebasket.

- At the office, go through your stack quickly, tossing everything that isn't even worth opening.

- Tear up the letters you throw out so that you won't be tempted to retrieve them. I haven't had a client yet who hasn't gone back into the trash to rescue something he or she couldn't live without. Should you ever throw away something you later need (a rare occurrence in my experience), chances are you'll be able to get another copy.

To Ask About

- Place items that require the comments of another person with the rest of that person's mail. At home, you may want to check with your spouse regarding a dinner invitation; at the office, you may need to pass a letter on to your boss or a coworker.

- Attach a sticky-backed note (the type that removes without leaving a mark), and write down your thoughts about the item (e.g., "Is the March 26 store charge yours? If not, there's a billing error," or "This business luncheon looks interesting. Do you plan to go?") so that you won't have to reread it later.

- Staple all pertinent information from the envelope together (travel brochure, agent's business card, price list, etc.) so nothing will get lost.

To File

- Papers that do not require immediate action (insurance policies, tax forms you receive in advance, some legal documents) can be filed.

- Bills should be filed in your Household Affairs Folder under Unpaid Bills (see Chapter 17) so they can be paid all at once or just prior to their due date.

- Establish Tickler Files (see Chapter 12) for those items that can't (or needn't) be resolved immediately. If you're thinking of registering for a class that starts in a month, put the course information in the folder for the appropriate month so that you can consider it as the registration date gets closer. If you've received a flier about a free event that you'd like to attend on Wednesday night, put the notice in Wednesday's folder.

To Call

- Can a matter be handled more quickly by phone than by letter?

- If the place you need to contact is closed for the day, put the item on your list of things to do for the next day.

- Remember to group the calls you make. It wastes time to scatter them throughout the day.

To Do

- The items on your list of things to do are the ones that require *action,* and several steps may be involved. Start with the most important items first. For example, notice if a returned check or an invitation requiring a written RSVP should be acted upon as soon as possible, while renewing a magazine subscription or answering your aunt's monthly letter can wait a little.

To Read

- Be selective. Read only what is important or what interests you.

■ Thumb through incoming publications and tear out information of special interest. Toss the journal or magazine, and keep the articles in a file marked On-the-Go Reading. Every day select several articles to carry with you. When you find yourself waiting—in line, at the dentist's office, or commuting—pull out your reading. When finished, toss the item or mark where it should be filed.

■ If catalogs and junk mail are the source of your mail overload problem, write to any companies with whom you correspond (mail-order houses, credit card companies, magazines) and request that they not give your name to others. You can create your own form letter to save time. (Many catalogs now have a special box you can check if you don't want your name given to other companies.) You can also write to Mail Preference Service, Direct Marketing Association, P.O. Box 9008, Farmingdale, NY 11735-9008 and ask to be removed from their mailing lists. Provide them with variations of your name: John J. Jones, Jack Jones, J. J. Jones, et cetera. Your name will be put on a Mail Preference Service list that is circulated among national direct mail companies, who will then remove your name from their lists. If you are a regular mail-order customer, this may only reduce your mail slightly as your name will remain active on lists belonging to companies with whom you do business. Put an end to annoying phone calls by writing to the Telephone Preference Service, P.O. Box 9014, Farmingdale, NY 11735-9014.

Sample Mail Call and Solutions

Below are some other typical items that arrive in the mail and advice on how to handle each one.

■ *A reminder of a six-month dental checkup.* Make certain the appointment is marked in your calendar. Confirm the office address and phone number, and note them down in your calendar next to the appointment. Toss the notice.

■ *A schedule for the upcoming concert season—but you're not sure you want to attend.* Even though you're still debating whether or not to go, note in your calendar (in pencil) any of the dates that interest you. Otherwise, you may book something else for those times. Then put the schedule in your Tickler File where you can review it again at a later date. If you need to order tickets by the end of the week, file the schedule in your Friday Tickler File. Otherwise, file the schedule in an appropriate monthly Tickler File. Just be sure to file it where you'll be sure to see it before your order needs to be in. (If orders must be in by October 1, for example, file the schedule in the September folder.)

- *Business correspondence that requires a reply.* As you read the letter, circle specific questions as a reminder to answer them. Then jot down key points on the letter itself for you or your secretary to draft a response. Put it on your to do list for the next day.

If you have lots of standard business correspondence, you may find that making a correspondence book will save time. Take paragraphs from the best of your recent correspondence, organize them by subject, and number them. Then you need note only the paragraph numbers you want and your secretary can use his or her copy of the book to write the letters. If your secretary has all the paragraphs on computer, he or she ought to be able to "build" a letter in just a few moments. It's a fast way of producing accurate, well-written replies!

- *Personal correspondence.*
  - Phone a reply.
  - Carry notepaper or postcards with you, and write a note when you have a spare moment or while waiting for an appointment.
  - Write one letter and make copies. On the computer you can add some personalization to a basic letter. Some people do a family update letter during the holiday season. One woman who was inundated with kind words from many people during a long illness found this was the only way to keep up with her correspondence.

- *Change of address note from someone you know.* Enter the information in your address book right away and toss the card.

- *Notes informing you of an upcoming meeting you need to attend.* Write down the date in your calendar and toss the letter. Keep the agenda, if there is one, in the appropriate Tickler File.

- *A piece of mail that gives you a good idea for a new project.* If you're inspired, start on it now. Otherwise, file it in your Tickler File.

- *Catalog from a company you like.* Thumb through it and mark the pages with items of interest. Contact the company by mail or phone. If you prefer to give your potential purchase a little more thought, put the catalog in your Tickler File under the day or month when you might be better prepared to decide (e.g., after paying your bills).

- *New catalog from an unknown company.* Scan the first few pages. If the information doesn't catch your interest immediately, toss the catalog out.

- *Business magazine.* Use the "rip and read" method. Scan the contents (or the magazine) for articles of interest. Tear them out and file them in your On-the-Go Reading file (described above).

- *Other magazines* (fashion, sports, architectural design). Save these for when you have some spare time. Put them with your leisure reading.

E-Mail

In today's world, it's hard to find anyone who isn't using electronic mail. Chances are your office depends on it, and if you've got a home computer and subscribe to an online service (see Chapter 10), then you're learning the benefits of using electronic mail for communicating with friends and family.

E-mail is an easy, fast way to correspond, but despite its time-saving efficiency, you've got to guard against it becoming an activity that eats up your time. Because it's so easy to use, many people are using it to chat—"Hi Johnny! It's hot here. What's new with you?" Obviously, answering these types of e-mail messages from people you barely know can waste a lot of time. In addition, follow these tips to use e-mail effectively:

- Set aside a specific time each day to answer your e-mail (just as you should your regular mail). Scan the incoming messages by order of importance, using the subject line or the sender to make a judgment. If you're running low on time and have not answered all your messages, skim through the remaining list, and do these three things:

  - Answer the more important immediately.

  - Save the significant for the next day.

  - Delete everything else.

- Keep your own messages clear and to the point. Be specific about what you need to know so that the message you get in return will also be concise.

- If you've been away for a few days and are staring at 200 to 250 messages, scan the list and answer in order of priority. You can work on it over a period of a couple of days, or you may decide that some messages aren't worth answering.

Junk mail exists in e-mail form, too. Here's how to stay off the lists:

- Be cautious about giving out your name and e-mail address.

- Check out special mail preference services through online services and the Internet to specify that you don't want to be on general mailing lists.

- If you receive unwanted e-mail, notify the senders. They are supposed to remove you from their lists.

- If you're on a cc: list at work and it's not really necessary that you receive all the mailings, tell the sender to remove you.

- E-mail addresses should be kept in your online address book so that you can click and send easily, but also note e-mail addresses in your personal address book so that you can stay in touch even when you're not on your own PC.

Faxes at Home and at the Office

Another wonderful invention of the past few years has been the fax machine. Like e-mail, messages travel quickly across telephone wires but instead of going into your computer, they materialize on paper—exact replicas of the paper that was sent on the other end of the wire.

In all likelihood, your office fax machine has been around for years, so you're well accustomed to having one around. If you're considering adding one at home, then here are a few points to keep in mind:

■ What type of paper does it use? The less expensive machines use thermal paper which comes on rolls and tends to curl. This may be the perfect choice for a family who is reading and tossing interfamily faxed communications. If you plan to use a fax machine for business purposes, you're better off selecting a more expensive model that uses plain paper. This will provide you with a better quality of fax to save and refer to over time.

■ Ask about other features. All can be used for low-volume copying; some have speed-dialing; most have memory so that an incoming fax can be stored if you are low on toner or out of paper, and many have a "broadcast" feature that permits you to send one fax to several different numbers. New machines being created for the home market are also designed to serve as answering machines, so keep shopping and comparing. They are getting better all the time.

Here are some additional tips for better fax management:

■ If you've also got a modem (see Chapter 10), consider getting a dedicated phone line for the fax and modem. Unless you live alone, trying to manage a telephone, a modem, and a fax machine on the same line may lead to a real communications jam-up.

■ Fax during off-hours. It's cheaper.

■ If you're faxing to another time zone, consider the hour there. The relative with the fax machine in her bedroom/office may not be thrilled to get your fax at midnight.

■ Just because a fax arrives instantly doesn't mean it needs to be answered instantly.

■ If junk faxes start arriving, fax back to the sender to remove you from the list. (The sender's number should appear on the fax that comes through to you.)

15

Resource File

Can you identify with any of the following comments?

"I remember that tailor I used a few years ago—he'd be perfect to repair my suede jacket, but I can't remember his name . . ."

Or: "I'd really like to get back in touch with that man I met at last year's conference to talk to him about a career change, but I have no idea how to contact him . . ."

Or: "The Jones family has moved, but who was that doctor they said was such a good allergist?"

Or: "Who was it that Mom used to repair her china? She probably doesn't even remember . . ."

A resource file can solve all these problems and more by providing you with a total system for keeping track of people whom you might like to contact again. Unlike names in a personal telephone directory, these people aren't necessarily individuals you contact regularly—just people you might need one day.

Some people like to integrate this information into their Rolodex system, making notations regarding the services on the back of the cards. Or see Chapter 10 if you'd prefer to put this information on your computer.

Otherwise, here's an efficient way to keep tabs on people and services you may want to contact again.

Establishing a Resource File

You'll need:

- 4" × 6" index cards in different colors (green for personal contacts, red for home resources, blue for medical, etc.).
- Index card dividers.
- Container for holding index cards.

I like using a card catalog system because each index card provides plenty of room for writing complete information about the person or the service. The system is also easy to update, because you simply add another card if you find someone new, or throw out a card if someone moves or a service goes out of business. In addition, there's always room on the card for adding new details.

- As noted in Chapter 10, an address book on computer offers many of the same advantages of this system. If you're looking for the printer whose name you can't remember, you can punch in "printer," and your computer will do the searching for you.

Contact Resource Cards

- Part of your resource file should consist of cards you make with the names of your personal contacts—people whom you've met at parties or conferences or to whom you've been referred by friends. Whenever you need advice, help, or special treatment, you can check the cards to see who might be of help. Update your cards with additional information you get about the person. Add new cards when you make new contacts.

- A typical contact resource card night look like this:

Mary Jones	Met at ASPW Conference	11/96

1234 Brill Ave., N.E.
Seattle, WA 98115

(206) 555–3311

Special knowledge of personnel job market; worked at XYZ Corporation for twelve years

Consultation fee: $150/hour

Husband: Mark
Children: Sam and Alex

12/20/96: Phone conversation: discussed training I would need to work in personnel field

- List why this person is of interest to you; include special knowledge and skills.

- Be sure to write down how you met the person or who referred you to him or her. Also note the date of the first meeting or referral.

- List fees.

- Record the names of spouse and children in order to facilitate personal conversations.

- If the person seems like someone you will get to know better, you may want to find out his or her birth date and make a note of it here.

- List dates and notes about conversations and meetings.

- As you prepare to put your cards into the index card container, you will need two of your card dividers. Label one "Contacts" and the other "Home Services" (information to follow). Some people file their cards alphabetically by name within each of these two groupings. Others find that they forget names, so filing by category makes the information more readily accessible. For example, suppose you have some work to be done that soon will require the services of a photographer. You meet one you like but know that you'll never be able to remember his name two months from now. Label an index card divider "Photographers" and use it to file the card on this fellow and on any other photographers you hear about or meet. If you decide to file by subject rather than by name, be consistent. (An index card divider labeled "Contacts—General" can be a catch-all for those for whom it isn't worth creating a category.)

Home Service Resource Cards

- On each card, list the company (or person), the address (and suite number), the telephone number, exactly what you used their services for (if you have), the date, and what you paid for the service.

- A sample card might look like this:

REPAIRS—CHINA AND GLASS

AAA Company   Referred by: Mother 12/96
100 Park Avenue, Room 5
New York, NY 10017

(212) 555–1776

Repairs glass and china; antique porcelain and ceramics are specialties; work takes minimum of two weeks

Repaired chipped goblet, 1/97, $25

- If a resource has come through a referral, note from whom you received the referral and the date.

- As you note details, be very specific. For example, one shoe-maker may be great at replacing heels; or one cleaner may be good at knits, while another does the best job on tuxedos.

- Additional resources can be gained by reading the "service" articles featured in many magazines. You can note information about those that might be of use and add them to your file.

- Use card dividers to create appropriate categories for your needs. Typical categories of home resources might include the following:

  - Babysitters or Child Care Services
  - Books (out-of-print shops or places to donate books)
  - Cabinetmaking
  - Carpentry
  - Charities (clothing or furniture donations)
  - Cleaners (some may have specialties)
  - Cleaning Equipment
  - Cleaning Services
  - Closet Aids
  - Clothing, Children's Resale

- Designers, Interior
- Desk Supplies
- Dressmaker
- Gutter/Roof Company
- Handyman
- Kitchen Supplies
- Pest Control
- Yard Services

Once you've set up a Home Service resource file, you will soon find it invaluable. Being able to rapidly locate all the home services you need will save you hours of telephoning and searching for the right person to fix your iron or the right store to go to for a certain type of cleaning liquid.

But when it comes to the Contact resource cards, you may one day astound your friends as a client of mine has done. Acquaintances would call him, and he would immediately place who they were and launch into a very friendly conversation: "How's Sue? What about the boys? Are they still enjoying Little League?" and so on. He was never at a loss as to who had called him. His secret? His resource file was always close at hand, and as soon as he heard the name of who was calling, his fingers were searching for the right card to tell him *exactly* who it was!

PART III

Financial Records

16 Banking

17 Bill-Paying

18 Budgeting

19 Financial Master List

20 Investments

21 Medical Payments
    and Insurance
    Reimbursements

22 Personal Property
    Inventory

23 Safe-Deposit Box and
    Strongbox

24 Income Taxes

16

Banking

From an organizational standpoint, there are two major difficulties when it comes to banking. The first concerns the chaos that can ensue if your checkbook and records are not kept up-to-date. An accurate, well-maintained checkbook can reduce your risk of a bank error going unnoticed, and it can save you a lot of aggravation at tax time.

The second type of difficulty involves the time that can be wasted while trying to get your personal banking done. How often have you fumed because the line at the bank was so long? I have some tips to help you with that, too.

Today your life can be greatly simplified by taking advantage of the various automatic services your bank offers, and you should also know about electronic banking. It's the way of the future.

Establishing a System

- When it comes to efficient record-keeping, one of the most important decisions to make is your choice of checkbook. I recommend using a larger desk-style checkbook simply because it provides more room for explaining each check or deposit.

- Clients frequently protest: "But what about the checks I need to write when I'm away from home?" The solution is simple. When you order your desk-style checkbook, also order a small number of checks in the portable checkbook format. The small checkbook should be used when you are on the go. Because you have an entire checkbook with you, you are automatically reminded to record the check. Then make it a habit to note the date, check number, to whom it was written, and the amount in your main (desk-style) checkbook when you do your daily paperwork that evening. I find that people who carry a single check with them forget to record it when they get home because the lone check provides no system to remind them. One man I know takes a check with him in the morning and then forgets to write down the amount for which he wrote the check. His wife says he regularly wastes time bemoaning the fact that he can't remember how much the check was for. The auxiliary checkbook will solve all that.

- Have checks imprinted with your name and address only. Some businesses won't honor checks without addresses, but there's no sense in providing them with other information, such as your telephone number or social security number, as well.

- Buy a special Canceled Checks Folder for each bank account you maintain. Each folder is sectioned off by month so that bank statements can be organized easily.

- Label each with the current year. On each folder list the account number, type of account, and the name in which it is held.

- Be sure to note *every* check you write in your main checkbook. (You must be equally diligent with your auxiliary checkbook, but there you need record only those checks you write while you're away from home.) Record the number of the check, the date, to whom it was written, and the reason for the expenditure. This will help substantiate tax deductions as well as clarify budget expenses.

- Deposits should also be carefully noted, and on each deposit slip, be sure to note the source of the income. The Internal Revenue Service may want to know whether that $100 check you deposited was a check cashed for a friend or whether it was income you failed to report.

- Balance your main checkbook after each entry so that you have an accurate view of your bank balance. (You need not balance your auxiliary checkbook since it reflects only a portion of the checks you write.)

- Keep all your deposit and withdrawal slips in one section of the Canceled Checks Folder until you need them to balance your checkbook. When your statement arrives, you will compare your slips against the bank's record, and once each deposit is verified, you can then put the slips with the appropriate bank statements.

■ When your statement comes, balance your account right away. The longer you wait, the more complex it will become because you will have to account for additional checks and deposits.

■ Make check marks next to checks and deposits that are verified and make a circle by those that have not yet appeared on the bank statement.

■ At the end of the year, the Canceled Checks Folder(s) should be stored with your Household Affairs Folder (see below) where they will be easily accessible yet out of the way.

■ It is generally recommended that you keep such files for at least six years—you may need to keep business-related records longer.

Personal Banking

If you are shopping for a new bank, you'll naturally be considering what services are offered and what rates are charged. But, in addition, consider how efficiently your transactions will be handled. Whether or not the bank will make life easier for you is almost as important as the services performed and the rates charged.

■ Is the bank part of a large network of banks so that you'll have access to automatic-teller machines almost everywhere you go?

■ Are there always long lines at the teller windows? How quickly can you see an officer if you have a problem? Does the bank have a drive-through window?

■ If you need to do banking in person, visit the bank during periods of least activity, which vary according to the bank and the neighborhood. Generally, it's best to avoid lunch hours (11:30 A.M. to 2:00 P.M.) as well as paydays, which generally fall on Thursdays and Fridays. Monday mornings can be busy because people come in to take care of financial matters after the weekend.

- Most companies can arrange to have your paycheck deposited directly into your account. If you can arrange it, you get the money instantly, and you needn't go to the bank to deposit it.

- Have your deposit and withdrawal slips already made out—and handy—before you go to the bank. You will save time and perhaps be more accurate since you've made them out in the privacy and quiet of your home or office.

- Banks are beginning to charge for more and more services. If your bank is among those who are charging for the use of a teller or an ATM machine, try to plan ahead to limit the number of times you need to use these services. This will also save time.

Taking Advantage of Bank Services

- Arrange for your bank to make recurring payments (such as mortgage or insurance payments) for you via their automatic fund transfer program. This is also terrific for savings. Leave instructions with the bank as to how much money should go directly to your savings account or brokerage firm, and that way you'll be guaranteed the money goes where you want it to.

- Are you interested in banking by phone? Many banks are using systems by which you can check your balance, verify deposits, confirm check payouts, stop payment on a check, get a summary of transactions, and pay bills, all by making a simple phone call. Ask about these at your bank or pick up a brochure.

Online Banking

If you've got a home computer with a modem hookup, you may be able to do a great deal of banking from the comfort of your own home. (Your computer can do almost everything that an ATM does, except spew out cash.) The at-home banking services make it easy to download bank transactions, transfer funds, reconcile checkbooks, and pay bills online using your PC and modem. Some are offering the availability of credit card account review, and some have facilities for you to buy and sell stock as well. Thus far, prices are low; banks foresee a day when cyberspace banking will replace the need for a "bank on every corner."

This new style of banking is particularly popular with people who are already computer literate, and with frequent travelers, who appreciate the convenience of being able to monitor their finances while they are on the road.

- If you opt for online banking, presently there are two variations to the services:

  • Some services are offered through banks, and to operate them you generally need to obtain the banks proprietary software (sometimes made available free of charge to encourage you to use the service). This permits you to see account information, make transfers between accounts, and pay bills.

  • Another type of online banking is available through some types of personal finance software. By entering your checkbook expenses and miscellaneous cash expenditures, this software will track your cash flow, help plan a personalized budget for your family, and provide you with helpful data for tax purposes. However, to use it for online banking, your bank must offer an interface with the software you've selected.

- Before purchasing any software, talk to a bank officer about your bank's electronic capabilities.

- Keep in mind that, at this writing, there is a twelve- to twenty-four-hour lag time between any banking transaction you perform (paying a bill, transferring funds, etc.) and when it's actually posted to your account, so don't expect to do anything at the last minute.

I have a friend Laura who is as casual as I am precise, and when I think of organized banking, I *don't* think of her. Right after her wedding reception, Laura ran to her bank's nearest ATM—in her wedding dress, mind you—to deposit wedding gift checks before leaving for her honeymoon. After counting up the checks and filling out several slips, she deposited her checks. Later, fear clutched at her when she realized that if the machine made a mistake, she and her new husband would be out their nest egg. The next morning she phoned a bank representative who assured her that if she deposited the checks, everything would be all right. Well, Laura spent the next two weeks of her honeymoon frantically worrying about her deposit. When the couple got home, they found their account credited for more money than she had listed. She had forgotten to enter a check, and the bank corrected her error! Her finances may have ended up in order, but what a chaotic way to start off a marriage. If she'd only signed up for online banking or opted for banking-by-phone, she could have checked her account while they were away and saved the mental wear and tear she went through worrying about it.

17

Bill-Paying

Perhaps you can identify with my friend who remarked how much he enjoys a good meal or a fun night out, "But it's so depressing when it comes time to pay the bills . . . ."

Owing others is nothing new. Early settlers may have paid off their accounts at the general store in goods or services rather than money, but the process was the same. They probably didn't like it any better then than we do now.

As you know, the only thing worse than paying a bill is discovering that you *didn't* pay it and are now being billed for a finance charge. Time and again, I visit clients who have left their bills in stacks of unopened mail; others have thrown out store invoices thinking they were junk mail. One woman simply stuffed her bills under a couch cushion. Needless to say, these bill-paying "methods" can be costly.

This chapter provides you with a simple and effective system for paying your bills. You'll even learn how to do it electronically. The organizational tips provided or the possibility of doing it online should make bill-paying somewhat less painful.

Setting Up a Household Affairs Folder

- Visit a stationery store and purchase a Household Affairs Folder. Here you will store your yet-to-be-billed shopping receipts, your unpaid bills, and your copies of the bills you have paid. (These are collected month by month. After they are used for tax purposes they are added to your permanent file or simply stored away in the Household Affairs Folder for that year.)

- Mark the outside of the folder with the current year.

- The folder is already divided into sections with preprinted categories such as: Automobile, Bank Records, Income Taxes,

Insurance Records, Medical/Dental, Real Estate Taxes, Receipts, Rent and Mortgage Records, Utilities, Unpaid Bills, and so on. But if the titles don't suit your needs, simply relabel them with stick-on file folder labels.

Sorting Bills, Receipts, and Solicitations

- Keep store receipts for items you have charged in a small envelope within the Receipts section. The envelope keeps everything together for eventual cross-checking with the bill and allows you to thumb quickly through the envelope to find out just how much you have charged at any given time.

- When a bill arrives in the mail, open it. Pull out your receipts and be sure that all charges are correct. If not, you have time to straighten it out before the bill is due. If action is necessary, phone or write the company. If all is in order, check the due date and put the bill back in its original envelope. Mark the due date on the outside of the envelope. File it in chronological order in the Unpaid Bills section of your Household Affairs Folder.

- When you receive solicitations for charitable gifts, file those that interest you in the Unpaid Bills section as well. (After covering other costs, you will have the opportunity to better evaluate to whom and how much you want to give.)

Establishing a System

- Assign one member of the family to be in charge of bill-paying. My husband and I take six-month stints at the job, but most families find it works better if just one person pays the bills all the time.

- Choose a set time twice a month for bill-paying and allow approximately thirty minutes for it. You may be wondering why you can't do it just once a month. There are three reasons. First, bills arrive throughout the month, and if you've only established one bill-paying period, you may find that you'll end up with finance charges for late payments. Second, by paying once every two weeks, you can pay closer to the date that the money is actually due. That gives *you* the use of your money for a longer period of time rather than letting the company earn interest on it. And finally, it is the rare checkbook that can withstand one major bill-paying assault. By paying twice a month you have allowed a little cash to flow in before it needs to flow out again.

- Establish a set place (your desk or the kitchen table, for example) for paying your bills.

- Have on hand a pen, your checkbook, a few extra envelopes, return address labels, stamps, a wastebasket, and your Household Affairs Folder.

The Process

- Remove all the bills and solicitations from the Unpaid Bills section of the folder. Pull out the ones that you need to get in the mail soon.

- If you did not do so when the bills arrived, you will need to cross-check the bill with your store receipts. Take out the envelope of store receipts from the Receipts section of the folder. For all bills, compare your shopping receipts with the actual charges. Make sure that all amounts charged are correct and that there are no extra charges about which you have questions.

- As you write the check, be sure to date it, correctly identify the payee, fill in the correct amount, and sign it with your legal signature. In addition, every check should carry some additional identifying information: A check to a department store should have your charge account number; a payment to the phone company should have your phone number; a major credit card payment should have your credit card number.

- When it comes to payments such as insurance, be sure to note your policy number, the type of insurance (auto, fire, health) and the time period that the payment covers on *both* the check and in your checkbook. Sometimes the computer continues to spew out bills despite the fact that you've paid them. This record will tell you whether you're up-to-date on your payments for different policies.

■ Mark "Tax" (or make a check mark) with a colored pen by any items in your checkbook that are deductible so that at tax time, a quick scan of the checkbook will give you accurate records from which to work.

■ Once the bill is paid, send off the check and the company's portion of the invoice in the envelope provided (or use one of your own, if necessary).

■ Mark your portion "paid" and put the date of payment and the check number on it. If you aren't paying the entire amount, note the amount that you did pay. Then transfer your part of the invoice or billing statement to the appropriate category in the Household Affairs Folder. (Utilities, Medical/Dental, etc.)

■ For insurance purposes (see Chapter 21), it is helpful to create a list of major purchases such as jewelry, cameras, electronic equipment, and other household items of value; bill-paying time is a good opportunity to tend to these records. You may want to check with your insurance agent regarding what constitutes a major purchase. On a sheet of paper or in your computer, write "New Purchases" and the year. As you make purchases throughout the year, note those that are over a certain amount (the figure recommended by your insurance agent), and after you've paid the bill, take the receipt for each item and store it in an envelope along with your inventory list. These records should be placed in your Cash Receipts file in your file cabinet for the rest of the current year; at the end of the year they should be moved to your strongbox. The records should be retained for the life of the items.

■ Information and receipts pertaining to the purchase of your home and/or any home improvements should be retained until you sell the home. Thus it is advisable to move these receipts into a permanent file rather than leaving them in your Household Affairs Folder. After paying house-related bills, remove these records and receipts and file them in your Housing file in your file cabinet (see Chapter 12).

- Now take a look at any charitable solicitations you may have received. Do you have fifty dollars to send to XYZ Charity? If so, write out the check and send it to them.

- File charitable donation confirmation slips and pertinent correspondence in the Income Taxes section of the folder. If you donate clothing or other material goods, store the appropriate confirmation slip here as well.

- Keep a running total of your bank balance. (If you've computerized your personal finances, this is taken care of for you.) Too many people enter the amount of the check but neglect to do the math to keep the total current. This makes it all too easy to accidentally overdraw your account.

- Seal and stamp your envelopes. If they should be mailed the next day, put them with your outgoing items near the front door.

Electronic Bill-Paying

If you've ever paid a bill just before the due date, you may have wished there were a way you could zap the money to the company electronically. Well, today that wish can almost come true. (The zapping is easy, but it sometimes still takes a couple of days for your money to appear in a company's account.)

Electronic bill-paying dispenses with the stamps, envelopes, and checks you've long used for bill-paying by giving you the ability to pay your bills through your computer and modem if you have special software. The software that is dispensed by your bank, or a type that interfaces with the software your bank's computer uses, provides you with check-writing capabilities. Once the electronic check is sent via modem, your checking account is debited and the money is deposited to the company you owe through an electronic transfer. (If computerized bill-paying is not available through your bank, there are also online bill-payment services that provide the access you need to pay bills electronically.)

Programs have been designed so that writing a check on your computer is very similar to writing out a paper check. The difference is in the sending; one check leaves your household electronically, while the other must be taken to the mailbox.

- Before signing on with a bill-paying service or deciding to utilize the service offered by your bank, check on the service's track record and reliability. Though most companies promise to resolve any problems and cover any late fees, you don't really want to have to deal with a service that isn't processing your payments on time.

- Contact your bank or the online bill-payment service, and ask for an application. You'll need to choose a personal identification number and send in a voided printed check for verification. In return, you'll get an account number and a local modem access number to use for transmitting payments.

- When you're ready to make a payment, you'll feel at home because software designers have created the system so that you enter information much as if you were writing a regular check.

- The first time you make a payment will be more time-consuming than later sessions because you'll need to provide the address and account number for each payee. Once the payee is part of your permanent record, you'll need to enter only the payee's name and the amount you intend to pay.

- If a company to whom you owe money does not accept electronic payments, your service will take care of preparing and mailing a real check.

- This system provides you with more control over your money than the traditional method of bill-paying because you specify the day on which you want the money transferred. You can keep the money in your account for as long as is reasonable and then release it. Experience shows that you need to allow from two to six business days for the transaction to occur, so don't wait until the day the bill is due to pay it.

- Keep watching for new developments in this area. The possibilities are quite intriguing, and ultimately, the systems are going to be easier and easier to use. Eventually you'll find it hard to believe that you ever wrote out checks by hand.

What to Do at the End of the Year

Your Household Affairs Folder will serve as a perfect record of your expenditures during any given calendar year and should be saved. Here's what to do:

- In early December, buy a new Household Affairs Folder.

- At the end of December, take out any materials from the old folder that should be transferred to the new one (unpaid bills, loan information, medical payment reimbursement cards, etc.).

- Close up the old folder and put it in an oversized envelope or expandable folder along with your Canceled Checks Folder (see Chapter 16), your check stubs for the year, and any other pertinent information. Label the folder with the appropriate year, and place it in temporary storage. You will need some of the documentation for filing your taxes. Once April 15 has come and gone, you can move the folder to dead storage in your attic or basement.

- While some items need to be kept for only three years, tax-related receipts and information need to be kept for six—so I recommend waiting the full six years before cleaning out your Household Affairs Folder.

18

Budgeting

For many months I had a client who would frantically call me week after week because she couldn't remember how and where she had spent her money. "I know I started off with $125 yesterday. Today I only have $20 left. How could I have spent so much money?" Each time we would reconstruct the errands she'd done and the places the money had been spent, and each week there was an explanation; but her feelings of being out of control were so painful that over time she finally adopted a more sensible approach and started budgeting.

How often have *you* said, "I just don't know where my money goes"?

The purpose of this section is to help you establish a simple record-keeping system that will give you a better understanding of the whereabouts of your money.

If you're using a computer, most personal-finance software provides everything you need to categorize your cash flow for better budgeting. However, the financial goal-setting and entry of the information are still up to you.

Setting Goals

- Set a long-term goal. When it comes to budgeting, most people want a long-term reason why they should do it. "I want to get ahead so that I'm not always worrying about how to pay the next bill. . . ." "I want to start saving for my children's college education. . . ." "I want to start preparing for retirement. . . ." "I want to buy a house in a couple of years. . . ." A long-term goal will give you a reason for sticking with budgeting.

- Establish short-term goals, with rewards. Sometimes people make the mistake of setting only a long-term goal. The problem with this is that it's easy to get discouraged—it can take months or a year or more before you begin to reap any rewards from it. Instead, establish short-term goals with rewards: "If we maintain our budget for two consecutive months, we'll treat ourselves to a special dinner at a restaurant" (one that is within your budget); "If I save $500, I'll buy myself a new sweater for $50." Such goals make budgeting easier in the short run.

Establishing a System

- *Income.* Surprisingly, many people don't know exactly what their actual income is. The following chart can help you document your monthly income (both income and expenses are figured on a monthly basis). Note take-home pay for both husband and wife, part-time income (moonlighting), and all other money your family receives regularly. For amounts that come in annually, such as a company bonus, divide the amount received by twelve months to arrive at a monthly figure.

- *Expenses.* Next, you need to determine your expenses. For our purposes, *fixed expenses* will be defined as unavoidable monthly costs, those you must pay each month. *Variable expenses* include items such as clothing, holiday expenses, and entertainment—costs that are often necessary but that you may not incur every month. Note that some expenses might be fixed for one family and variable for another; for parents who work outside the home, child care is an unavoidable expense. If, however, only one parent works and child care expenses consist of paying for babysitting a few times a month, that cost might be considered variable. Be sure to average in quarterly or annual payments such as insurance premiums, taxes, or yearly visits to the doctor. For example, if one of your insurance premiums is $200 per year, you need to set aside $16.67 ($200 divided by 12 months) in order to cover that expense.

- *Personal Allowance.* Note that this is listed as a fixed rather than variable expense. Each family member should be allotted a reasonable amount of discretionary money if family budgeting is to be successful. If you begin to feel deprived, you might be tempted to dip into money you're earmarking for other things. For children, having a personal allowance introduces them to some of the challenges of managing money.

- *Savings.* This is also listed as a fixed expense. For everyone, saving something (even fifty dollars per month) should be a top priority. Most everyone encounters a "rainy day" at some point, so don't put yourself in the position of saying, "I *wish* I'd saved!" When you pay your rent or mortgage, you should get in the habit of automatically writing a check to your savings account. By treating savings as a fixed expense, you can be guaranteed that you'll have money for something special or for when you need it.

- Now work through the budget on page 99, adding items as necessary.

Identifying Trouble Spots

- Now that you have one total for your spendable income and another for expenses, subtract your expenses from your income to see how you come out. If you're fortunate, your income will exceed your expenses and you will have a "surplus," which you can divert to savings. However, for many people, expenses exceed income, which means they must trim their budget. For example, perhaps your food budget includes bringing home food from a gourmet take-out shop one night a week. Consider bringing in dinner just once a month until you get expenses more in line with your income. Also review each item under expenses and see where you can save. But be realistic! Don't cut out all money for magazine subscriptions if you have one or two publications you really enjoy—just cut the costs of the ones you don't read so eagerly anymore. We cut down on two subscriptions when our twins were born because we never had the time to read them anyway, and we knew that extra time was going to be at a premium once we had two babies.

MONTHLY BUDGET

Income		Expenses	
Income		*Expenses*	
Husband's take-home pay	———	*Fixed*	
		Savings	———
Wife's take-home pay	———	Housing (rent or mortgage payments)	———
Moonlighting	———	Taxes, income (if not withheld)	———
Company bonus (as it would average into monthly income)	———	Taxes, property (money set aside for annual payments)	———
		Insurance	
		Auto	———
Dividends	———	Disability	———
		Health	———
Interest	———	Life	———
Other (profit-sharing, pension, royalties, trust, etc.)	———	Utilities	
		Gas and electricity	———
		Water	———
Total:	———	Telephone	———
		Food	———
		Transportation	———
		Child care	———
		Medical/Dental	———
		Education	———
		Debts or loans (car payments, etc.)	———
		Personal allowance	———
		Variable	
		Drug items	———
		Clothing	———
		Home maintenance and furniture	———
		Entertainment/ recreation	———
		Domestic help	———
		Charitable donations	———
		Vacation savings	———
		Holiday expenses (gifts)	———
		Other	———
		Total:	———

- If you are significantly overextended, you may need to seek out a financial counselor who can help you consolidate your debt. In the process, you should also think long and hard about how to bring your lifestyle more in line with your income.

- Watch your cash. For many people, weekly cash expenditures are a real problem, primarily because they just don't know where the money has gone. . . . Maybe you've allotted yourself seventy-five dollars personal spending money for the week, but somehow by Friday or Saturday, you're dipping into next week's allotment because you just don't have anything left. Try this: Slip an index card into your purse or wallet. Every time you spend cash on an item, note down how much you spend and on what. At the end of the week, most people discover they have a weakness for something that they have totally forgotten about: Perhaps it's paperback books or CDs, or lunch in a restaurant a couple of times a week. Whatever it is, once you're aware that your habit is proving costly, you'll be able to cut back on those expenses *if you want to.*

Charting Monthly Expenses

With this system there's no more "sneaky spending." I've visited many clients who buy major items (purchases they don't want their spouse to find out about) using what I call the "I'm-going-to-fool-you way." They put part of the expense on a charge card, pay for part of it in cash, and write out a check for the rest. Other clients sometimes buy things on the "I'm-going-to-fool-me way" by putting a big purchase on a time payment plan so that it doesn't seem so costly month to month. Of course, in both cases, the money is spent (and with the second method, it's spent and you have to pay interest in addition). This system of tracking expenses will keep the whole family honest and help you come to terms with exactly where your money goes each month.

JANUARY 1997			
Expenses	Date	Check # (if applicable)	Amount
Fixed			
Housing			
Taxes, income			
Taxes, property			
(money set aside			
for annual			
payments)			
Insurance			
Auto			
Disability			
Health			
Life			
Savings			
Utilities			
Gas			
Electricity			
Water			
Telephone			
Food			
Transportation			
Child care			
Medical/Dental			
Education			
Past debts or loans			
Personal allowance			
Variable			
Drug items			
Clothing			
Home			
maintenance			
and furniture			
Entertainment/			
recreation			
Domestic help			
Charitable			
donations			
Vacation savings			
Holiday expenses			
(gifts)			
Other			

Keeping It Up

With some practice, you'll find that budgeting can become a matter of habit, and you'll likely find that paperwork will be unnecessary. Until then, keep a monthly record (like the one above) of exactly what you're spending in each category. Later, a quick glance through your checkbook will show you where the money for that month has gone. And by the way, even cash withdrawals should note: "$50 groceries"; "$25 spending money."

- Be sure to budget for the unexpected. While the children may not need to visit the doctor as often as they did last year, plan that they will. It's better to have extra money at the end of the year rather than be caught short when extra bills come in.

- Review your budget every six months to be sure it is still serving your needs.

- Keep your goals and your budget realistic, and you'll find that budgeting is well worth the effort.

19

Financial Master List

There are two occasions when having a master list of your financial information is especially helpful. The first occurs when certain items are lost or missing (credit cards stolen, personal papers and insurance policies destroyed in a fire). The second happens in the event of death or incapacity. And, of course, at the time of such a stressful event, loved ones should not have to worry about locating items that may be needed immediately (power of attorney, letter of last instructions, will) and those that will be needed shortly (financial papers, insurance policies).

Gathering Important Numbers

If documents are lost, it is much easier to replace them if you have a list of identifying numbers. This information is also helpful to an executor settling an estate. Such numbers should include:

- Armed forces identification number (for discharge purposes), if appropriate
- Bank account numbers, name and telephone number of your banker
- Each credit card number and the telephone number to call if the card is lost or stolen
- Driver's license number
- Individual Retirement Account or Keogh number, location
- Insurance policy numbers, the insuring companies, and the name and telephone number of insurance agents
- Savings bond numbers
- Social security numbers for each family member
- Stock certificate numbers (if kept in your possession)

Preparing Additional Information for Your Executor

This information should round out the above to provide a complete reference sheet to your financial affairs. Include on it:

- Accountant's name, address, and telephone number
- Employee benefits, the company telephone number, and the extension of the individual in the company who handles benefits
- Financial obligations, such as your mortgage and any other outstanding loans as well as any money owed to you
- Investments—list them and the name and telephone number of your broker (who can provide information on short-term investments since it is difficult to keep an up-to-date record)
- Power of attorney—name, address, and telephone number of the person(s) who have been given power of attorney and what the power covers (signing checks, selling property, etc.)
- Properties owned, property locations, and the whereabouts of the deeds
- Safe-deposit box—its location, an inventory of its contents, and where you keep the key
- Whereabouts of:
  - Personal papers
  - Bank records
  - Tax records
- Will—its location and the name and telephone number of the lawyer who wrote it

Maintaining the List

- You'll need three copies of your Financial Master List. One copy should be kept in your safe-deposit box; another should be in your Important Documents file; a third should be in your strongbox (see Chapter 23). Even if you've drawn this up on the computer, be sure to make a printout so that it will be available and accessible to those who need it.

- Update the list as needed. Whenever you visit your safe-deposit box, check the contents against the list to make sure that it is up-to-date.

20

Investments

If you regularly comb the financial pages checking on the day-to-day fate of your stocks, then you probably have a system for watching your investments. Or perhaps you are more of a dabbler, or your great-aunt Milly left you some stock, and now you must become more knowledgeable. Whatever the case, you will benefit from using this basic system for tracking your portfolio.

While a paper-and-pencil system will always work, your investment life will change if you have access to the Internet or to online services. Keep reading to find out how you can benefit.

Establishing a System

- Gather together any material you have received from your broker. This would include brokerage statements, as well as buy and sell confirmations. Because this information needs to be kept with your annual records, it will eventually be stored in the Investments section of your Household Affairs Folder, but first you need to make a list of your holdings. Having these records will save you time during tax season.

- Establish a separate sheet for each type of brokerage account you have. (In addition to your own account, you may have a joint or custodial account you control.)

- Here's the information you will need to record: name of the stock or bond, the number of shares/amount you own, date acquired, total cost of purchase including commission. When you sell, note the date sold and total sale price. You'll then want to note your profit or loss. Your charts might look like this:

CHART 1

Stock	No. of Shares	Date Acquired	Cost or Other Basis	Date Sold	Sale Proceeds	Profit/ Loss

CHART 2

Bond	Amt. Bonds	Date Acquired	Cost or Other Basis	Date Sold	Sale Proceeds	Profit/ Loss

- If any of your holdings are gifts or inheritances, you'll need to ascertain what date to use as your acquisition date and the amount that should be your cost basis. The executor of the estate or the person who gave you the gift can provide this information.

- Note that if you hold long-term bonds (e.g., for your children's education), you should indicate the date they will come due. This will aid you in planning and organizing for that time.

- If you participate in mutual funds, employee stock funds, or an investment club, you should keep track of those investments in a similar manner.

- All records of purchases and sales of the same security should be kept together.

- Save all the transaction confirmations you receive, and file them in your Household Affairs Folder under Investments. They will be an important validation of your list.

Tracking Income

- If the securities are income-producing, you will need to track these payments as well. Some people have the checks sent to their homes; others have the income deposited directly into their brokerage accounts.

- To track income, set up a simple list that notes the name of the company, the amount of the dividend or interest payment, and the date. (When you buy or sell a bond there will be interest income or interest expense on the confirmation that should be included on this list.)

Stock/Bond	Date	Dividend or Interest Received	Taxable	Nontaxable

- Keep this list in your Investment file in your file cabinet since it is a permanent record you may refer to frequently.

Tracking Performance

- Track the performance of your portfolio regularly. Financial advisers recommend doing it at least quarterly, if not monthly or more frequently.

Date	Stock/ Bond	Original Cost	Price Now	% + or -	Action?

- To see how your investments are doing, note the date and the stock price. Then compare your original investment cost with the current price to see whether you have a profit or loss. Also compare the current price with the price the last time you tracked performance to see how they compare. As you check each stock, make notes as to any action you might want to take. (Buy? Sell? Watch closely?)
- Check your investments regularly to make sure they are in line with your financial goals and are performing well for you.

Investment Watching Made Easy

If your home or office computer has access to online services or to the Internet, you're going to find that the work of tracking your investments has suddenly become easy.

Online services offer the capability of tracking your stocks for you—as a matter of fact, they'll keep you up-to-date (within fifteen minutes) of the daily happenings of the stock market as well as your own portfolio. All you have to do is enter your stock name, the purchase price, and the number of shares you bought, and each time you click "quote," you'll find out whether your stocks are up or down. Investment tracking made easy.

Online services and the Internet also offer a wealth of information to make you a more knowledgeable investor. You can find Web site pages for individual companies or, through an online service, ask for an information sheet on a company in which you might invest. You'll find everything from global business news stories to minor—but helpful—details such as a listing for various companies and their "ticker" symbols (how they are listed and in which market the stock is traded).

The interactive world has opened up countless opportunities for keeping current and learning more about investments. Once you have a taste of it, you'll never turn back.

21

Medical Payments and Insurance Reimbursements

While some managed-care health plans now pay the medical establishment directly and reduce your paperwork of submitting claims, there are still a good number of people who need to keep track of which medical bills they've submitted to the insurance company and whether or not they've been paid. If you're in charge of this for your family, this chapter will offer helpful guidelines.

One normally well-organized couple ran into trouble with one set of bills when the wife paid the doctor directly, expecting to be reimbursed by the insurance company. In the meantime, her husband arranged for the insurance company to send the check to the doctor. The result was that the doctor owed them—not an easy tangle to straighten out.

Careful record-keeping—and assigning one person to the responsibility—will help prevent such incidents. Here's the system I recommend.

If you use a personal computer, stop by a software store in your area and ask about any programs that help with health claims submission. If there is one that is compatible with the forms you're filling out, it can save you a lot of time. Otherwise:

Establish a System for Reimbursement

- On 5" × 8" index cards (using a separate one for each doctor), note the following:

NAME OF DOCTOR					
Date of Visit	Amount Charged	Date Bill Paid	Date Info. to Insurance Company	Date and Amount of Reimbursement	Remarks

- On a separate card, list your insurance policy number (have a card for each policy), including your group number if applicable, addresses, telephone numbers, and anything that will expedite filling out the insurance forms and receiving your reimbursements. Store this data under Insurance in your Household Affairs Folder (see Chapter 17). At the end of the year, the cards should be moved to your new Household Affairs Folder.

- Prescriptions for which you can be reimbursed should be noted on the card for the doctor who prescribed the medicine.

- Health insurance policies should be stored in the Insurance file in your file cabinet.

22

Personal Property Inventory

If your home was ransacked by burglars or destroyed by fire, would you be able to provide your insurance agent with itemized bills of sale (receipts) for your more valuable possessions? For most people, the answer is no.

In this chapter, I will provide you with a system so you will be able to say yes. In addition to creating a record-keeping system for bills of sale, a Personal Property Inventory—which provides a record of your possessions—will help you get the full value from your property insurance should a disaster ever befall your home.

Taking Inventory

- You are going to need to take an inventory of your home, but before doing so, call your insurance agent to ascertain what type of information (and proof of possession) is required under your policy.

- Set aside time for this project. Some people prefer to devote a Sunday afternoon to it; others prefer to do it a room or two at a time—a simple room might take five minutes while a more complicated room might take up to an hour. Though the project may seem overwhelming, it will seem to go more quickly if you think of it room-by-room.

- Have on hand:
  - Pen
  - Pad of paper. (Or ask your insurance agent to provide an inventory booklet—most companies can supply them.)

- Camera with several rolls of film. (Some people prefer to document using a video camera.)

- Strongbox (fire-resistant file box available at most office supply stores). This is a sensible place for storing the Inventory once you've finished it.

■ Choose a room, such as the den, to begin. Note down the major items you have there.

■ After each item note the year of purchase and the price. (If you don't know the exact price, you'll have to estimate.)

■ Your inventory list might look like this:

DEN		
Item	*Year Purchased*	*Cost*
Color TV - 19"/Sony	1995	$300
VCR/Sony	1994	$250
Hide-a-bed Sofa/Sears	1997	$1000

■ Next, take a photograph or videotape of each of the different sections of the room, showing as many items as possible.

■ Proceed to the next room, remembering to check the kitchen, bathrooms, and hallways for items of value.

■ Don't forget drawers. Check each one, and itemize and photograph valuables.

■ Items of particular value such as jewelry or furs may need to be covered under a rider to your homeowner's or renter's policy and will also need to be carefully documented.

■ When the film is developed, order two copies of the prints you need. Arrange to have three copies made of the Inventory. (If you've videotaped, make copies of it as well.) One set of photos and an Inventory will be stored in your home strongbox; another set and an Inventory should be stored in your safe-deposit box; the third copy of the Inventory should be kept in your Insurance file in the file cabinet.

Updating the Inventory

If you ever need to make an insurance claim, your agent would much prefer it if you could provide her with sales slips for all the major possessions involved. Thus, sales slips or appraisals are the key to the future maintenance of your Personal Property Inventory.

- For claim purposes, you need to decide what dollar amount constitutes a large purchase. You may want to check with your insurance agent, or perhaps you're comfortable working with a figure such as $400.

- If you have not already done so (as suggested in Chapter 17), you will now need to create a list for these items. On a sheet of paper, write "New Purchases" and the year. File it in your Cash Receipts file.

- As you make purchases throughout the year, note those that are over $400 (or the figure you selected) on this sheet; after you've paid the bill, take the receipt for each item and store it in an envelope along with your Inventory list.

- On January 1 when you are packing away old household records to make way for new ones, transfer the past year's Inventory list *and the sales receipts* to your strongbox. This will provide a safe place for these documents.

- Create a new "New Purchases 199_" sheet for the upcoming year. (Put a reminder slip "Start new inventory sheet; move old one" in your January Tickler File to be sure the job gets done.)

23

Safe-Deposit Box and Strongbox

You may *think* you don't need a safe-deposit box. . . . Your papers are "fine where they are," and you have the perfect place for hiding your valuables. . . . Do you:

- Hide your money in a book?

- Keep money or jewelry in canisters or aluminum foil in the refrigerator or freezer?

- Freeze small pieces of jewelry inside ice cubes?

One woman I know is so untrusting of institutions (and people) that she carries her entire savings—thousands of dollars—with her every day!

The problem with all of these methods is they are unreliable. The best place for important papers and valuables is in a safe-deposit box.

When it comes to having one, there are two main problems people encounter:

- They don't know what to keep in it: "Should I keep the original of my will there? Do my insurance policies need to be stored in a safe-deposit box?"

- They don't know a good system for keeping track of what is in the box: "Is my passport there, and where is our marriage license?" "Did I put my gold pendant watch in the box, or is it missing?"

This chapter will help you organize the contents of your safe-deposit box. You will never again need to worry about what you're keeping in it. We'll also talk about strongboxes, and I'll list for you what should be kept there.

Selecting What Goes in Your Safe-Deposit Box

Anything that is too valuable to be accidentally misplaced or destroyed by theft, fire, or natural disaster should be stored in your safe-deposit box. Typical items include:

- Certificates of birth, death, marriage, and divorce.
  - A copy of your will with a note specifying the location of the original—usually with your lawyer; another copy should be kept in your file cabinet. (The original should not be kept in your bank box because many states seal the box at the time of death.)
  - Financial Master List (see Chapter 19) for your executor noting the exact location of important documents; names and addresses of personal and legal advisers (original in safe-deposit box; one copy in Important Documents in file cabinet; another copy in strongbox)
  - Legal documents
  - Letter of last instructions (original in file cabinet; copy in safe-deposit box)
  - Military discharge papers
  - Mortgage papers
  - Passports
  - Pension plan
  - Personal Property Inventory (one copy in safe-deposit box; one copy in file; one copy with receipts in strongbox)
  - Stock certificates, bonds, and certificates
  - Titles to property (boat, etc.)
  - Titles to real estate
  - Trust documents
- In addition, you may choose to store small valuables such as jewelry or valuable collections such as coins and stamps here permanently or while you are on vacation.

■ The rental fee on your box is tax-deductible if it is used to store income-producing property such as bonds or stock certificates.

Box Maintenance

■ Make a list describing all items in your safe-deposit box and keep it in your file cabinet under Important Documents.

■ Arrange the contents in the safe-deposit box neatly. Store the documents in clearly labeled envelopes.

■ Not even safe-deposit boxes are 100 percent safe. If the vault is robbed, banks generally do not have insurance covering the contents of safe-deposit boxes. If you are storing items of exceptional value, you may want to add a rider on your homeowner's or renter's policy providing the coverage you need.

■ Visit the box at least once a year to check the contents, and update your list as needed. (Put a reminder note in your Tickler File.)

The Need for a Strongbox

A strongbox is a small, fire-resistant file box that can be purchased at most office supply stores. Most strongboxes will survive all but the most devastating fires, so they offer you a relatively safe place to keep important documents that don't really need to be in your safe-deposit box but would be inconvenient to lose in a fire or other natural disaster. Strongboxes are not burglar-proof, so valuables should not be stored here.

Items you might keep in your strongbox include:

■ Financial Master List

■ Personal Property Inventory

■ New Purchases sheets for each year along with sales slips

■ All papers in your Important Documents and Insurance files that would pertain to reconstructing your life after a fire or other property disaster

24

Income Taxes

My brother-in-law is an attorney, and his work sometimes has involved assisting clients with income taxes and planning. He has seen more than one client bring in cartons containing every shred of paper from throughout the year that has *any* financial information on it—supermarket tapes, receipts for clothing, a scrap of paper indicating that twenty dollars was given to the building superintendent as a Christmas gift. All of this is thrown into the carton in no particular order, and the client arrives saying, "Here. I hope you have everything you need to figure out my taxes."

Preparing for tax season should be a year-round, ongoing process. If you do your part daily, you will considerably lessen the work (or the accounting work you pay for) that must be done prior to April 15.

Keeping Up-to-Date (Day-to-Day)

- Pay deductible expenses by check.

- Always get and save receipts, which should be filed by category in your Household Affairs Folder (see Chapter 17).

- Highlight deductible items (charitable donations, medical and dental expenses, business expenses, interest, educational expenses) in your checkbook using a colored pen, or mark the appropriate column in your check register with a check mark or the word "Tax."

- If you're keeping your finances on computer, your workload will likely be greatly reduced because the program will do much of the categorizing and figuring for you. (Just be sure to back up your computer regularly.)

- Use your calendar to keep an ongoing diary of unreimbursed business expenses. You *must* detail who, when, and where you entertained, and why and where you traveled.

- Keep detailed checkbook entries for identifying deposits. It's important to differentiate nontaxable income (gifts and loans, municipal bond interest) from taxable income (salary, dividends, interest).

- If the law requires you to pay estimated income tax on a quarterly basis, keep a record of all taxes paid.

In December (Year-End Planning)

- Estimate your taxable income for the year by using payroll records and checkbook deposits.

- Estimate your deductions for the year by using checkbook records and receipts.

- Figure approximately what your federal, state, and local income taxes will be. Or schedule an appointment with a tax professional for advice:

  • Compare approximate taxes with taxes withheld and/or paid during the year to arrive at how much you may owe.

  • If you are going to owe a considerable amount of money, you may decide to pay some of your deductible expenses before the year's end to gain the deduction for the current year.

  • Based on this early planning, you may decide to defer income (bonuses, stock profit) until January 2 of next year.

In January

- File your checks by month (with your bank statements) in your Canceled Checks Folder.

- Watch for your tax forms in the mail. If they don't arrive, pick them up at your local tax office, bank, or post office.

- Make an appointment with a tax professional, or schedule time to do the following yourself. Gather together and read or review:

  • Tax return from last year

- Tax literature pertaining to you
- Tax return instruction booklet

▪ Plan your tax strategy:

- Magazines, newspapers, and radio and television programs feature tax advice starting at about this time of year. Read or listen to what pertains to you, and see if there are ways to benefit.

- Discuss with colleagues and business associates their tax strategies for the year.

Organize

▪ Itemize the deductions you have in each category by reviewing your checkbook, calendar diary, and other records.

▪ The receipts to substantiate these expenses should already be organized by category in your Household Affairs Folder (see Chapter 17).

▪ Remember that your canceled checks offer additional substantiation and are kept in your Canceled Checks Folder.

▪ List your sources of income such as salary, interest, dividends, capital gains, professional fees, and pensions.

▪ If your taxes are being prepared by a professional, he or she will need the above figures. Ask the tax preparer what other information you should send.

▪ If at any time it looks as if you won't make the April 15 deadline, obtain from your local tax office or tax professional the IRS form for an extension to file.

If Doing the Taxes Yourself

▪ Complete forms. Have a calculator and scratch pad handy.

▪ Check all totals twice. Round off all numbers to the nearest dollar to eliminate having to do two columns of addition.

Wrapping It Up

- Get completed forms back from the tax professional. Review for errors and omissions.

- Place social security number on forms and checks.

- Sign all forms.

- Photocopy finished forms.

- Enclose a check for the appropriate amount of taxes due.

- Mail on or before April 15 or send your time extension form together with the taxes due.

- Gather together your W-2 forms, interest statements, and dividend slips, and file away with your copy of the return.

The latest thing in tax preparation is the possibility of filing your tax return electronically. If you're expecting a refund, you might like to investigate it as the IRS is processing the computerized filings quite quickly because their computers are doing some of the return checking. Otherwise, it's still a brand-new process, so ask your accountant or tax preparer about it.

PART IV

Household Matters

25 In Case of Emergency

26 General Household

27 Closets

28 The Kitchen

29 The Refrigerator

30 Supermarket Shopping
    and Inventory Control

31 The Laundry

32 The Medicine Chest

33 Hiring Household Help

In Case of Emergency

Whether it's a power failure or a serious injury, readiness is your best protection when there is an emergency.

To Post

Post an "emergency procedures" card by all telephones and near the place you choose to keep your first-aid kit. The card should include the following information (type the names of the places and persons in capital letters to make the card easy to read):

- Your community emergency telephone number, usually 911
- Telephone number of poison control center
- Address of nearest hospital emergency room and brief instructions on how to get there
- Name and telephone number of family doctor
- Telephone number of police
- Telephone number of fire department
- Telephone number of ambulance service
- Address and telephone number of pharmacy
- Name and number of nearest neighbor who would help
- Name and telephone number of family member (mother, brother) to call for backup help
- Address of your home, in case a flustered babysitter or cleaning person is making the call. (In an emergency, *you* might even forget!)
- Name and telephone number of veterinarian

- If there are children, the card should also include:
  - Child's full name
  - Name, telephone number, and address of pediatrician
  - Parents' full names and work telephone numbers
  - Child's blood type

- Family allergies, chronic illnesses (epilepsy, asthma, etc.), and any medications taken regularly that might affect emergency treatment

- Make photocopies of the above information, and put them in accessible, logical places: One should go in the diaper or stroller bag; a regular babysitter should have one in his or her wallet; a third should be in your Household Notebook (see Chapter 26). In addition, keep a supply of extra copies in a kitchen drawer. A new babysitter should be shown where the emergency numbers are posted and also instructed to take a photocopy from the drawer if he or she must leave with the children under emergency circumstances. The address of the emergency room and your child's blood type will be of little use if the sitter doesn't have the information with him or her.

Additional Telephone Numbers

In addition to the emergency numbers suggested above, you should also keep the following on hand in your Resource File (see Chapter 15) among your Home Service resource cards.

- Telephone number of gas/electric company in case of power failure or gas leak
- Telephone number of appliance repair offices in case of malfunction

Have on Hand

- Fire extinguisher
- Flashlight and batteries (check batteries periodically) or lantern

- Candles
- Canned goods
- Powdered milk
- One good, easily readable book about first-aid and emergency procedures. You may not have time to refer to it in an emergency, but if you do, it could make all the difference.

Courses Everyone Should Take

Contact your local Red Cross for information about the following:

- First-aid course
- CPR (cardiopulmonary resuscitation) course
- Infant safety course

For Children

- Almost surely, people other than you and your spouse (a caregiver, grandparent) take your baby or child out of the house occasionally. You can help them be ready for an emergency by preparing an envelope with the following information (print it on the outside of the envelope):
  - Home and work telephone numbers (do not include addresses for security reasons)
  - Telephone number and address of pediatrician
  - Address of nearest emergency room
- If both parents are sometimes difficult to reach, arrange to leave an emergency consent form with your caregiver (place it in the "emergency" envelope). This document, signed by you, gives permission to your caregiver to authorize whatever medical care might be necessary for your child in an emergency. Ask your pediatrician about the correct wording of the document.
- Place twenty dollars in the envelope (usually enough cab fare to get to most places in a city) and at least two quarters for

telephone calls. That way you've provided the information (telephone numbers) and the tools (money) a person needs to best cope with an emergency. The envelope should be kept in the diaper or stroller bag and pointed out to all caregivers.

■ All parents would like a way to guarantee that, if lost, their child would be promptly identified, and they would be immediately notified. Contact your school or local police department for suggestions as to what you can do. Some communities have programs where children can be fingerprinted and photographed for identification purposes.

Teach Your Children

■ As soon as possible (certainly by age three), begin training your child to dial the emergency telephone number in your community (usually 911). Very young children have been credited with saving the lives of others because they knew what to do in an emergency. Help them practice dialing other telephone numbers so they'll be familiar with dialing the phone. Discuss possible scenarios with them in a matter-of-fact way: "If I fell and hit my head on the bathtub and didn't get up, what would you do?" Their response should be that they would make the call.

■ Teach your children their telephone number and address.

26

General Household

Those who say that running a household requires excellent management skills are absolutely right. Family scheduling, performing or delegating tasks, inventory management, purchasing, budgeting, entertaining, and long-term planning (e.g., for a vacation or a household move) are all part of a job that should be described as "household manager." The person responsible for seeing that everything gets done has as challenging a job as any manager in a business or corporation.

Establishing a Notebook

To keep track of the myriad tasks there are to do, I recommend use of a special organizational tool, the Household Notebook. You'll find that having all household-related information neatly collected in one place is a real convenience.

- You're going to need a looseleaf notebook, dividers (you may need as many as ten or twelve of them), and paper. The size of the notebook is up to you. Some people like to use a small, portable notebook so that they can carry it with them; others use a standard large format for home reference. Visit a stationery store and select the notebook that is right for you.

- The notebook is a perfect spot for lists of things, such as items To Buy, To Fix, To Do, and To Call (see Chapter 44).

- Your Notebook is also convenient for keeping track of housekeeping chores (see below), for emergency lists and numbers (see Chapter 25), and for party planning (see Chapter 38). In addition, the Notebook can be as varied as it needs to be. Simply create categories as they become necessary. If you're redecorating, you may want to create a category for decorating ideas; you can even tape swatches of material and paint chips there. If you're house hunting, you can clip and save real estate ads in it. You are sure to find it an invaluable aid in keeping track of a multitude of details.

General Cleaning

Two couples I know once rented a house together for the summer. Both women were fastidious, so it was a perfect match. They tell a story of going on an initial shopping trip together to buy the necessary food and supplies for the house, spending several hours methodically cruising the paper goods, cleaning, and beverage aisles. By the time they got back to the newly rented home, they had spent $100 and had more than enough scouring powder, cleanser, and window polish—but hadn't even thought of purchasing food for lunch!

While people don't usually focus this seriously on cleanliness, most want a tidy home. Here are some suggestions for getting the housework done efficiently.

- Like anything else, housework goes better if there's a plan. Using your Household Notebook, set aside three pages for keeping track of housework. On the first, list jobs that need to be done daily; the second page should have items that need to be done weekly; the third should contain major tasks that can be done less frequently.

- Request help from other family members. (Refer to the chart or dial system in Chapter 55 for additional suggestions on distributing the chores.)

- Hire household help on a regular basis; if you can't afford regular help, consider hiring help for a specific task: cleaning the attic, dusting all the bookshelves, and so forth.

- Keeping up with the day-to-day tasks is vital. Most people find that doing one job each day is ultimately less time-consuming than an occasional full day spent cleaning everything:
  - If it's Monday, I do the laundry.
  - If it's Tuesday, it must be vacuuming day.
  - If it's Wednesday, I need to grocery shop, et cetera.

- Before starting a task, decide how long you're going to spend on it. If you know that you can vacuum the house in thirty minutes, then that's really not so bad.

- If you work outside the home, save low energy tasks for the evening. (One of my students got all her housecleaning done during commercials on television!) Try to do larger tasks on Saturday or before you leave in the morning. One working mother I know prepares the family dinner before leaving for the office.

- Do tasks in bulk. Don't get out the iron to press one or two things. Wait until you have a week's worth to do. Just preparing for a chore like ironing takes long enough that you ought to maximize the "setting up" time.

- Think of how to make chores more convenient. For example, a twelve-foot extension cord on your vacuum can greatly reduce the number of times you have to plug and unplug as you clean.

- Store cleaning supplies (furniture polish, window cleaner, spray cleaner, scouring powder) in a caddy and carry it with you as you clean. That way you're not dashing back to the kitchen to get something you need.

- If you live in a two-level house, keep one set of supplies upstairs and one downstairs.

- When it comes time to select a major chore (clean out attic, etc.), one woman writes various tasks on several slips of paper and draws the "chore for the day" out of the box. Whatever the slip says is what she will do.

- Organize your spring cleaning (the major tasks listed on page three of your Household Notebook housecleaning chores) for set times throughout the year. For instance, once in March and again in September, send rugs and drapes out to be cleaned, have floors waxed, and slipcovers changed. Set a time every other month to buff the floor and wipe out cabinets. Once it becomes a routine, a matter of habit, it will get done automatically without your thinking twice about it.

Reducing Clutter

"My house is more disorganized than ever," said a friend one day. When I asked her why, here's what she told me:

It seems that her mother-in-law used to visit very infrequently, which worked out just fine. According to my friend, the woman is a real neatness nut, and so whenever she is coming, my friend has a "stash day." She empties all the surfaces of desks, tables, and counters into plastic bags (which she neatly labels and stores in the appropriate closets—husband's items in his closet, etc.). "When she arrives, I ask only one thing of her—that she not stand near any closet door while it's being opened," continues my friend.

All went well until there were children. Now the mother-in-law visits four times a year, and my friend (who now uses babysitters to help with the stashing) has quite an accumulation behind all her closed doors.

If your household clutter is building up similarly, please read this section carefully!

- Leave an area as you found it (or better than you found it). If you've been in the den to watch some television and do a few projects, put back the magazines you thumbed through, and return the remote control to the drawer where it belongs. Don't leave anything out.

- Insist that family members help control clutter.

- If doing away with the clutter seems too overwhelming right now, start with just one area, such as the front hall. Make it a point to put everything away as you arrive home and see what it's like to experience a clutter-free front hall. Once you've mastered a system for that area, move on to an area such as the dining room. You'll soon see that tackling just one area at a time will help make housecleaning much simpler.

- Whatever you do, don't tolerate "messy clutter buildup." It will multiply before your eyes! Control it before it gets out of hand.

27

Closets

Closet clutter and chaos! Most people suffer from it. How often have you resolved that "as soon as I have the time, I'll clean out those closets"?

One day when I was visiting my aunt she asked me to help her reorganize her closets. When I said they looked great to me, she said, "Oh well, I thought everything was supposed to be hung by length . . ." I wish everyone was so well organized that "hanging by length" was their greatest problem!

With a little thought—and some imagination—closet organization can greatly simplify your life. The more organized the closet, the more you'll be able to put in it, and the easier the items will be to use. The following tips are designed to help you create your own personal system and to maximize your storage needs.

Getting Started

- Most closets can be reorganized in a day or less; however, in order to do it in that amount of time you need to have all the necessary supplies and organizers on hand. Read through the following information. Then devote a couple of hours to planning for your closet needs. After you've shopped for the necessary items, you can set aside half a day or so for each closet.

- Organization begins with planning. Go to the closet and study its contents. Consider what should and should *not* be stored there. Should your tennis racket really be on the floor of your clothes closet? What about the humidifier? Isn't there somewhere else, a more logical place, for it? Note down your space needs on paper. Often it is not so much a matter of how much space you have as it is how successful you are at dealing with it.

- Get specific measurements of everything (dresses, blouses, jackets, pants, shoes, bags) to allow ample room for them. Measure the longest item in each category of items in determining the length of hanging space needed, and measure how much hanging space (in width) your clothing currently requires so that you'll have provided space for what you have. (Try to allow for "breathing room," too.)

Reorganizing

- Empty the entire closet. Weed out items as you go, throwing out or setting aside to donate what you don't want or haven't used in several years—if you haven't used it in that amount of time, you probably never will.

- Clean the closet thoroughly. Vacuum the floor and baseboards, and wipe down the shelves. If you are repainting, use a high-gloss paint or polyurethane for easier cleanings in the future.

- Measure everything carefully before installing adjustable, multilevel rods.

- In homes with high ceilings, the upper reaches of a closet can often be fitted with a clothes rod, and it's a perfect spot for out-of-season storage.

- Shelves should be adjustable and designed to serve individual requirements. When the shelves are very deep, consider sliding drawers instead.

- Install a light that turns on when the closet door is opened.

Keep Items Visible and Accessible

- Categorize your clothes according to season, type, and color. Items that go together, such as pants and jackets, should stay together.

- Store the clothes and shoes you wear most often within easiest reach.

- Invest in sturdy, well-made hangers. They'll help your clothes keep their shape longer and make it easier to stay organized. (Don't hang knits! Fold them with tissue paper instead.)

- Don't hang up clothes that need mending or cleaning. Establish a place to put them until they can be taken to the cleaners or mended. That way you'll know that all clothes that are hanging are ready to be worn. (Keep a list of what has been sent out; check off the item as it comes back.)

- Never store clothing in plastic bags. Plastic keeps clothes from "breathing" and also can cause discoloration. (Plastic bags are also a safety hazard if there are children in the home.) Instead, store clothes in cotton garment bags, preferably ones that are dark-colored and won't permit light to come through.

- Use boxes for storage, but only if you can readily identify what is in them. The clear plastic boxes available in most home supply stores are ideal, or you can label the box and list its contents.

- Most people store shoes on the floor of the closet, but it is better to keep the floor clutter-free. Otherwise, it becomes a sea of junk and collects dust; items stored there can get ruined. It's also one more area that will soon need cleaning out. Shoes should be stored in labeled (or plastic see-through) shoeboxes, on shoe racks, or on shelves.

- Hang hats and small bags on a pegboard with hooks. You may want to bring the pegboard "out of the closet" and use it as a novel room decoration. Arrange the items in an attractive manner. The pegboard display system will also come in handy when coordinating outfits, accessorizing, or packing for a trip.

- Large purses can be stored on shelves. (Hanging may cause large bags to droop and lose their form.)

- Stuff hats and purses with tissue paper to help them keep their shape.

- Belts and scarves can also be hung, or try rolling and placing them in conveniently located baskets or bins.

The Linen Closet

- In the linen closet, try rolling your towels, especially hand towels and washcloths. You'll find this "jellyroll" method looks neater and saves space.

- When you store linens and tablecloths, put the folded side out so that you take just the item you need. (If the edges are facing out, it's hard to determine how many sheets or towels you are removing.)

- Fold each bed linen set as a unit (flat sheet and pillow cases within fitted sheet) so you pull out a single set each time. This also works well for sets of towels.

- Stack linens by room: Keep all sheets for the master bedroom together, all sheets for the guest room together, and so forth. The same goes for towels.

- If your bathroom lacks adequate storage, the linen closet is a perfect place to keep extra supplies of soap, tissues, toothpaste, and the like.

The Front Hall

- Be sure the floor is clutter-free.

- Buy heavy-duty attractive coat hangers for the closet.

- Divide shelves into sections to organize hats, gloves, and scarves; or use individual bins and baskets that are easy to reach. Large hats can be stored and protected in hatboxes.

- If you have a great deal of storage up above, consider a curtain which draws across the shelf area to hide the clutter from guests.

- Put a mirror on the inside of the closet door for a last-minute peek as you go out the door.

Redesigning

- Decide on the function of a particular closet. Will it be used for clothing? storage? linens?

- If you're building from scratch, decide exactly where the closet should go.
- Will you use doors, shelves, cupboards, pullout drawers?
- Be specific about the amount of space you need and what you're storing.
- Size up your belongings. Measure *everything* to determine rod and shelf placement. Ten sweaters? Six bath towels? You need to allot proper space.
- Leave space for future purchases.
- Consider building compartmentalized drawers and shelves for dividing jewelry, belts, and lingerie. Preplan their arrangement by laying them out and drawing up a blueprint of the space. A carpenter (or you, if you're handy) can take it from there.
- Consider calling in one of the specialty closet companies. They often offer great advice and can arrange to do the design and building for you. Price out a couple of services.

General

- Potpourri and sachets add a pleasing touch by scenting your closets. (If needed, anti-moth sachets are also available.)
- Remember to put things back where they belong. "A place for everything and everything in its place" will put an end to the frustration of hunting for something and not being able to find it when it is most needed. Living by this rule will help simplify your life!

28

The Kitchen

I remember visiting a client who lived on a magnificent estate in upstate New York. Her kitchen was incredible. I had never seen one so large or beautiful. But what struck me most about it was how much walking you had to do in that kitchen—how much time was wasted going from one place to another. To get from the refrigerator to the sink and then to the stove—not to mention the detours along the way for a pot here or utensil there—was like taking a walk around the block.

On the other hand, I remember my first kitchen. It was no larger than a closet, but it was very compact and convenient. I could stretch out my arm and reach anything. Because my space was limited, I really had to plan its usage: pare down, keep my counter clutter-free, use all my wall space and capitalize on the kitchen organizing tricks I knew. But I loved it, and I had many elaborate, smooth-running dinner parties there. The key? Organization, of course.

When it comes to organizing your kitchen, think function, convenience, and space. You need to consider how you most use your kitchen. Are you primarily a baker? If so, creating a baking center where all ingredients and appliances are within easy reach should be a specific goal. If you love to cook Chinese food, you'll want convenient cutting surfaces and clear counter space near the stove.

Many of the suggestions apply to replanning how to use your existing kitchen without major architectural work. However, if you are redesigning, simply use these ideas to help you formulate what your ideal kitchen should be.

Working with Your Plan

- Make a list of your specific needs. Note down the ideal areas you'd like to have (e.g., a good food preparation center, a baking center) as well as your gripes (trash can too far from main work area; pots and pans too far from stove). If nothing comes to mind immediately, over the next few days note what works and what doesn't as you perform your usual tasks.

- If you are working with a designer, he or she should provide you with a plan for the layout as well as information on materials to be used and anticipated costs. While you'll want to give the designer the go-ahead once you are satisfied with the plan, remain flexible. Sometimes better solutions present themselves as the work moves along.

- Plan how you would like to arrange each area of the kitchen, one section at a time. Assemble the items that will need to be stored there. Before installing any of the suggested space-savers or making any structural changes, place the items in the cupboard and be certain the space is workable for what you have in mind. For example, if you put in cup hooks, will the shelf below be too cramped for the plates you planned to store there?

General Rules

- Store items close to where they are used. Potholders should be located near the stove, glasses next to the sink or refrigerator, knives near the cutting board, and so forth.

- Similar items (e.g., baking equipment) should be stored together, except backup grocery items, which belong in the pantry.

- Frequently used items such as spices or coffee filters should be stored in the most accessible spots. Infrequently used items should be stored in the back of cabinets or up high, but not so far out of the way as you forget the item is there.

- Put away canned goods by category. Label shelves for easy restocking. Alphabetize everything, including canned goods and spices. It may seem compulsive, but finding things will become easier!

Cabinet Storage

- The higher your ceiling, the higher you can go. Build cabinets up to the top, and you will get a great deal of extra storage.

- When it comes to deciding where to place an item, consider how often you will need it. In general, remember that floor cabinets should be used for larger, less frequently used items such as pots and pans, while upper cabinets are generally used for glasses and dishes, which you may reach for several times a day.

- Kitchen shelves set at wide intervals are a waste of space when you are storing most things. For storing smaller items, divide the space by building half-shelves in between the larger ones (or you can buy adjustable shelving). If you build, have the shelves made so that they are adjustable. This way, they can be rearranged according to your needs.

- Sliding shelves (or ones that swing out) can be installed easily and can bring forgotten pots and pans out into the open where they are easily accessible. A lid and tray rack will take care of lid storage.

- Have dividers built into a cabinet to store cookie sheets, roasting pans, and trays.

- Store bakeware by stacking in order of usage. If you rarely bake pies, put pie pans on the bottom.

- Make use of wire-coated shelf racks for organizing dishes, cooking bowls, and the like.

- Mount hooks underneath a shelf inside a cabinet to hang cups up out of the way.

- For everyday use, have glasses and dishes that are stackable.

- If your glassware takes up lots of cabinet space, try racks that fasten to cabinet walls or shelves and suspend the glasses from above, leaving enough room for plates, bowls, and so forth, to be stored underneath.

- The back of a door in a cabinet or closet can provide convenient storage space in what would otherwise be wasted space. Several manufacturers make plastic-coated wire storage items, including baskets and grids with hooks and shelves, which can be used in many combinations and which attach to cabinet and door backs.

- You can also buy special organizers, which can be placed on the inside back of a cabinet door, for storing aluminum foil, waxed paper, plastic wrap, and other such items.

- Under the sink, and on the inside of one cabinet door, attach the makings of a storage system for sponges, detergent, scouring powder, rubber gloves, and cleaning brushes.

- Perhaps on the inside of the other door, place a trash can with removable liners, or create a special cabinet with a can for garbage and another for recyclables.

- An awkward corner cabinet can be made accessible by using a spinning caddy (lazy Susan), which can also be used for storing spices or small jars of baby food, for example.

- Customize your kitchen cabinets. Visit your hardware or specialty store or the kitchen area of a department store and ask about the various kits available to extend kitchen space.

Drawers

- For organizing the silverware drawer, use a plastic cutlery tray. It keeps the drawer neat and easily slips out for cleaning.

- To keep a "miscellaneous" (corkscrew, mixing spoons, spatula, etc.) drawer in order, use drawer dividers.

- Drawers are also a good spot for storing spices, aluminum foil, plastic wrap, and food storage bags.

- Convert a drawer into a file cabinet for recipes and warranties. If necessary, cut your file folders to fit.

Counter Space

Your main goal with counters is to keep them clutter-free. The following are some suggestions:

- Canisters and cookbooks are frequently found on many kitchen counters. Find space for them on a handy shelf instead.

- Put away all appliances that aren't used daily. Mixers, blenders, and most food processors should be stored in a cabinet rather than on the counter.

- Some models of toaster ovens and can openers can be mounted beneath the upper cabinet unit, leaving counter space free for food preparation. If you have appliances that need to be out and easily in reach, see if they are available in a top-mount style.

- Microwave ovens also take up counter space. Certain ovens come with a microwave oven above; other styles of microwaves can be mounted under the cabinet.

Creating Extra Work Space

- If there is space available, consider buying or building a work table in the center of the room. It adds more work space, and a shelf underneath can be used for large cookware.

- If you don't have space to add an additional counter permanently, consider building one that flips up (or folds down or slides in) when not in use.

- Build a removable (or sliding) cutting board for the top of a drawer to extend your work area.

- A cutting board that fits across the sink also provides additional work space.

On-the-Wall Storage

- For items used frequently or for those that you simply don't have the storage, consider a grid unit (made of wire on which pans and utensils can be hung from hooks). It's a great decorative item for such cookware as copper pots and very functional as well.

- A collapsible, stainless steel scissoring rack is another type of system for hanging cookware in an attractive way. It is designed with hooks so that pots hang from it and are accessible but out of the way. When the scissoring mechanism is compressed the pots nest within each other, taking up very little space. When the rack is pulled out, the pots can easily be taken down from the rack. To find such a rack, check hardware and specialty stores.

- Attach a wire basket to the wall under the top cabinet but above the counter. It makes a great off-the-counter storage spot for fresh fruit.

- A pegboard with hooks can be a great addition to any kitchen. A large one can be used for storing pots and pans, or a smaller one placed above the counter can be used with an easel attachment to hold a cookbook.

- Consider a wall-mount grip in a closet for the mop and broom.

More Ways to Organize Your Kitchen

- Evaluate your electrical outlets. Are they well placed for kitchen projects that require use of an appliance? If not, outlets can be added at a reasonable cost. Ask friends and neighbors for a referral to a good electrician, or check the Yellow Pages.

- Consider track lighting directed at work areas.

- For serious pastry-making, a piece of marble built into a counter can make all the difference! Because it stays cool, rolling out the dough is much easier.

- Don't forget the ceiling! A rack suspended from it can provide an attractive and functional way to hang pots and pans.

- Certain commercial products, such as a freestanding metal shelving unit to store food, supplies, bowls, dishes, and so forth, are durable and very functional. Visit a commercial supply house to see what would work for your kitchen.

- Plastic stacking-bin units (with or without wheels and usually consisting of three or four bins) can be a terrific spot to store place mats and ripening fruits and vegetables.

- Store cleaning supplies in a carrying caddy, which stores neatly in a cabinet or closet, and can be easily toted around the house.

- Towel racks are sometimes a problem, but adhesive-backed ones are now available that can be put up conveniently near the sink; or if you have an appliance near the sink, you might consider a magnetized one.

- Take advantage of new developments in ironing boards, depending on your space requirements and needs. One type comes as a complete ironing center and the "closet" you buy contains a fold-out ironing board, an electric outlet (that must be wired into the household circuit), a light, and a place for storing the iron. It can be made to fit in flush with cabinets; or if placed against a wall, it protrudes only about five inches. For a person with fewer ironing needs, one that pulls out from a cabinet similar to a drawer may be the answer.

- When loading the dishwasher, group together items such as forks, spoons, knives, salad plates, juice glasses, and so forth, to simplify putting them away.

- Since the kitchen generally serves as the family communication center, establish a message center there. Prepare a chart such as the following:

Mom	Dad	Amanda	Elizabeth	Julia

- Place telephone messages, notes, and reminders here. This is also where you should hang the family calendar so that all family members can jot down where they will be each day.

- Emergency information should also be posted near the telephone and family message center (see Chapter 25).

29

The Refrigerator

In your refrigerator do you have:

- Moldy cheese?
- An unidentified "mystery meat" from who knows when?
- Rotting fruits or vegetables in the crisper?
- Candy left over from the holidays, which ended six months ago?
- Frozen breads and meats of unknown vintage?

Even a refrigerator needs to be managed. By doing so, you'll make meal preparation easier and cut down on wasted foods by using your leftovers efficiently.

Starting Over

- Refrigerators need to be cleaned out and wiped down regularly. The best time to clean your refrigerator is when you are low on food.
- Empty the refrigerator one shelf at a time. Wipe down each shelf as you go.
- Throw out undated items, old cheese, half-used cans of tomato paste, opened jars of spaghetti sauce, jam you'll never use, and all the things that have been in your refrigerator too long or will never be used no matter *how* long they sit there.
- Don't forget to take out and evaluate items stored on the door. Door shelves should also be thoroughly cleaned.
- Empty the meat bin and crisper. These drawers are generally removable so you can clean them more easily.
- Sort through freezer items. Remember that freezing just slows spoilage—it doesn't prevent it.

Storage Tips

- Establish a purpose for each shelf such as one for milk, juice, and other beverages or one for bread, cheese, and cold cuts.

- Group together similar items.

- Put the items used most frequently near the front of the shelves; those used less frequently belong at the back.

- Date and label all home-wrapped items that go in the refrigerator or the freezer. You really won't remember!

- If you store lots of soda in cans, pick up a can dispenser to organize it. Some dispensers attach underneath a shelf, leaving space for storage of something else below.

- A one- or two-tier lazy Susan can aid in making the back of the refrigerator more accessible. Use it to store mustards, pickles, horseradish, and the like.

- Eggs stay freshest if kept in their original carton.

- Milk and other dairy products should be stored on the coldest shelf well inside the refrigerator.

- Store refrigerated meat on the coldest shelf or in the meat bin.

- Cut up carrots and celery sticks as soon as possible after you buy them, and store them with a bit of water in a plastic container for easy snacking.

- Stack loaves of bread (dated and labeled) in the freezer. (Preslice any full loaves you buy for easier thawing.) Then you can even thaw slices as needed.

- Leftovers can be stored in stackable containers, preferable see-through, so you'll know exactly what you've got.

- Keep all lunch-making ingredients together (lettuce, sprouts, meat, etc.) and just pull them out for easy lunch preparation the night before.

30

Supermarket Shopping and Inventory Control

When you're at the supermarket, how many times have you arrived at aisle nine only to realize that you forgot to pick up ketchup in aisle five and cereal in aisle six? While there's nothing particularly serious about this, it's annoying at the very least, and a waste of time if it causes you to forget items, necessitating another trip to the store.

My personal feelings about supermarkets have made me particularly eager to streamline this part of my life. The moment I walk into most of them, I want to walk right out again. The traffic is worse than rush hour, and the shopping carts seem to double as bumper cars. The personnel rarely know where anything is. To top it off, I have developed an uncanny knack for always picking the longest checkout line.

Here's what I do to accomplish my marketing chores more efficiently.

Establishing a System

- Plan all your meals at least one week in advance, and note what foods and ingredients you'll need to buy on your next shopping trip. You don't want to find yourself without tomato sauce if you were planning to feed the family lasagna.

- Make and keep handy a list of ingredients for your most frequently prepared recipes. Then if you want to cook chicken tetrazzini, you have a convenient list of all the items you need.

- Plan to double up on cooking so you can freeze a complete dish for another night. Take this into account as you consider grocery needs. Making extra sauce can add zip to leftovers!

- The key to organized grocery shopping is a good list. Take five to ten minutes to figure out the layout of your supermarket. Or next time you go, take a pencil and paper and note down the general categories in each aisle. Start with the aisle where you generally begin your shopping. This way your list will tell you what you need in the correct sequence: Aisle one has paper goods, and your list will note first that you need napkins and paper towels, and so on. Here is a sample list. This list is alphabetical, which may be more convenient for people who shop at a variety of stores.

GROCERY LIST		
Baked Goods	Frozen Foods	Miscellaneous
Canned Goods	Fruits	Paper Goods
Dairy	Household Cleaning Items	Staples/Seasonings
Drinks	Meats and Fish	Vegetables

- Once this chart is drawn up, make photocopies of it to use on future shopping trips.
- Choose a spot in the kitchen where you can conveniently keep your list and a pen or pencil.
- On the list, record *everything* you need—from the special ingredients for a new recipe to the paper napkins you buy every

week. If you don't write down each item as you think of it, you will eventually forget to pick up something you "always buy."

■ Teach family members to record all of their grocery needs.

■ Watch stores with good kitchen departments or mail-order catalogs for a small coupon billfold. (A very small expandable file would serve the same purpose.) Coupons can be stored by category. Before going to the store, pull out the coupons you know you'll use, but also take the billfold along just in case there's a special on something for which you have a coupon. That way you can take advantage of the special and still get the benefit of your coupon.

■ Your coupon billfold is also the perfect place to store labels or a list of your favorite brands of certain products. (You may forget your favorite type of salad dressing.)

■ Also prepare a list that includes such notations as the different types of lightbulbs you need. Store the list in your coupon billfold. You will find that the list is particularly helpful when taking advantage of specials.

Shopping

■ Shop during periods of least activity, preferably when the store is fully stocked. For example, Monday morning is a poor time for shopping in most stores because the new deliveries are arriving and the aisles are crowded with boxes as the staff tries to restock after the weekend. Wednesday is generally good because supermarkets traditionally run coupon ads in the newspapers that day. Midmorning or midafternoon might be a good time to shop. You can ask the manager when the store is not busy or experiment by going at different times.

■ Buy in bulk or in economy (giant) size. Not only will you save money, but you'll be able to shop less frequently. Sometimes the butcher will give you a discount for buying an entire side of beef and let you take it home as needed.

- Take advantage of specials. If tuna is priced at a discount, buy ten cans instead of one.

- Some people like to minimize the number of trips they make to the store, or they prefer to buy staples at one of the big warehouse stores where they can buy in large quantity. By picking up fresh items such as meats, bakery goods, and fruits and vegetables, you may be able to shop for staples every other week or even once a month. The trick is to buy all your supplies in multiples. For example, you may need to buy three boxes of the family's favorite cereal and a dozen rolls of paper towels if you hope to go a month without having to do major shopping. People with home freezers can reduce the number of times they have to shop for meats by buying in bulk here, too.

At Home

- Establish a pantry area (even if it has to be a closet outside the kitchen) for storing backup items. Both on kitchen and pantry shelves, organize by categories (all canned goods together, all baking supplies together, etc.).

- Once home, rewrap meats in appropriate portions. Wrap some for individual-sized servings in case you're cooking for only one person some night. Label and date them.

- When freezing, always label and date both new purchases and leftovers.

Other Tips

- Whenever possible, order groceries and drug items by phone.

- At smaller shops, such as the butcher or the bakery, you can sometimes phone in your order in advance.

- Buy commercial cleaning supplies from distributors. They are stronger, better, and cheaper.

Inventory Control

- Keep a backup supply of all items. That way when you reach the end of the sugar, for example, you'll open up the extra bag and then add sugar to your next shopping list.
- Teach family members to be diligent about jotting down items when you are low—not out.

Recipes

- Photocopy recipes you clip from the newspaper. They'll last longer that way.
- Buy photo albums with plastic pages that tear back so that recipes can be mounted. Buy different colored books—use one for desserts, one for main courses, and so forth.
- Make notes on recipes such as "use less salt," "serves four people," "cook a little longer."

31

The Laundry

My sister has two sons and recently married a man who has a son of his own. I happened to be there the day they finished doing their first joint laundry. My sister simply looked in horror at a table with piles and piles of undershorts, undershirts, and at least two dozen pairs of dark socks. "Ronni," she said to me, "there has got to be an organized way to do this."

While most of us learn what we need to know about dark loads and light loads and washing towels separately when we first move away from our parents' home, no one gives much thought as to how doing the laundry can be simplified or—in the case of a large family—better organized for speedier sorting.

Before You Wash

Extra care before putting clothes into the washer will save you effort in the long run:

- Reattach loose buttons and do any mending before the item is washed, and remove unwashable items such as belts, shoulder pads, and any ornamentation.
- Turn clothing right-side out.
- Turn pockets inside out and turn down the cuffs. Brush out sand, lint, and dirt.
- Close zippers, fasten hooks, and button up for easier folding.
- To save on hand washing, use a lingerie bag for delicate underwear and stockings.
- Pretreat stains or presoak badly soiled items.

Simplify

- To streamline doing the laundry, you want to do it as seldom as possible but often enough to keep everyone's bureau drawers well stocked with clothing. Some people can wash as seldom as once a week; others must do it two, four, or six times a week.

- If there is really only one reason (say, fresh underwear) that makes frequent washes necessary, consider buying extras.

- Try doing hand laundry in the shower. It makes perfect sense. During the minute or so you would normally luxuriate in the warm spray, you can rinse out a couple of items.

- When putting laundry away, group together items by the room in which they belong: Stack them in the laundry basket in order of which room you will visit first (top) and which you will go to last (bottom).

Organizing for the Larger Family

- As suggested throughout the book, color-coding can be a real aid. Assigning each family member a color can simplify the sorting of some items of clothing (children's pajamas and underwear) as well as bath towels and facecloths. For bedding, have sheets easily identifiable, such as by using different patterns for each bed so there's no confusion about what goes where.

- Have different laundry hampers for different members of the family. When you wash, do an entire load of only one person's clothes or combine the clothes of family members that are easily distinguishable from each other (Mom and oldest son, etc.).

- Use different colored laundry pens for each family member to identify any similar belongings. Make a mark on the tag large enough so that it is noticeable at a glance.

- Purchase an assortment of baskets to keep in the laundry room—one for each family member. Label and use it for that person's laundry. As soon as they are old enough, encourage your children to pick up their own basket and put their laundry away.

32

The Medicine Chest

Let's imagine you have a cold. If you were to go to your medicine chest, how many cold remedies would you have on hand? If you're like most people, you have tablets you purchased when you got sick in Seattle, capsules you bought one day at work, a couple of liquid decongestants from who knows when, and some loose foil-packs of pills (without boxes and therefore without brand names and expiration dates) from some long-forgotten cold.

Now suppose you've cut your finger and need some type of antibiotic ointment to put on it. Do you have any? If so, it's probably in an old crumpled tube from five or six years ago, and most of the cream is probably dried out.

In many of the homes I visit, people seem to "collect" medicines. They suffer a minor illness, buy the latest remedy, take what they need, and store the remainder of the liquid or pills in the medicine chest for use "the next time I'm sick . . . ," but the next time, some other remedy seems more appealing.

Neglecting to organize this part of your life can sometimes be dangerous. I'm sure you've heard stories of people who have gotten up in the middle of the night for an aspirin and have accidentally taken some other type of pill. A woman once told me about a time she had something in her eye; she got out what she thought were the eyedrops—and ended up putting nosedrops in her eye instead. Fortunately, no harm was done.

What people need to do is take stock of their medicines, throw out what isn't needed, organize what is, and make a shopping list for first-aid supplies they really ought to have on hand. That's what we'll do in this chapter.

Taking Stock

- Spread out all items from your medicine chest.

- Old prescription medicines (unless they are for a chronic problem or a recurring ailment such as an allergy) should be thrown out—flush them down the toilet so that a child or pet won't retrieve them from a wastebasket.

- Check expiration dates on all over-the-counter medicines; those that have expired should also be flushed down the toilet.

- Dispose of all over-the-counter medications whose exact use you don't remember and those you don't expect to need again.

- Age and exposure can cause medicines to change, so discard most items over a year old.

- Anything without a label should be thrown away.

- From this time forth, label all medicine you purchase with the date of purchase and what it was for. (How often have you found an old tube of skin cream and can't remember whether it was for a cut or a rash?)

- All prescriptions should be labeled with the type of drug, the date, the person's name, and the instructions. If your pharmacist has not provided that information, add a label of your own.

Organizing Your Medicines and Supplies

- Wipe down the bathroom medicine chest. The items you keep here should be things you use daily—toothpaste, deodorant, comb, brush, razor. Because heat and dampness make medicines age faster, the bathroom is not the best place to store medications.

- Also select and clear out another space where you can store the rest of your medicines and first-aid supplies. Be sure the space is well lighted so you will not mistake one medicine for another. If you have children in the household, select an inaccessible cabinet that can be locked.

- Before you start putting things away, establish categories of items and label shelves in the bathroom and in the place you've chosen to keep medicines accordingly ("Hair Care," "Skin Care," "Daily Medicine"). You'll be able to find things much more quickly and easily—and it will be much more difficult to mistake the nosedrops for eyedrops because you'll have two different spots for them.

- If you have many items to store, buy a lazy Susan for convenient storage of frequently used items.

- Buy a first-aid box so that all emergency supplies can be kept handy in one place.

- Clean out your medicines annually, throwing out anything you haven't used in the past year. Restock on first-aid items you might need.

Safety Tips

- If you have children, buy bottles with childproof caps, but keep in mind that "child resistant" does not mean it's truly tamperproof.

- Keep all medicines in their original containers to avoid having someone mistake one medicine for another.

- Read all labels carefully and administer exactly as directed. At night, turn on a light to make sure you have the right medicine and to see that you are measuring accurately.

- After using a medicine, recap it immediately.

- Always return supplies to storage immediately after use.

- Before purchasing over-the-counter items, ask your doctor for recommendations.

First-Aid Supplies to Have on Hand

- A half-ounce bottle of syrup of ipecac to induce vomiting in case of accidental poisoning as well as a can of activated charcoal to absorb poisons that should not be regurgitated. However, *do not* administer until you have consulted your doctor or the poison control center.

- Antibiotic ointment or spray to prevent infections in cuts
- Antiseptic
- Assorted Band-Aids, butterfly bandages, a sterile roll of gauze with adhesive tape, and scissors to cut tape
- Baking soda for insect stings, heat rash, or itching
- Burn ointment or spray
- Calamine lotion for bites and minor rashes
- Elastic bandage
- Epsom salts
- Eyewash and cup
- Heating pad
- Hydrocortisone cream for skin problems
- Icebag
- Insect repellent
- Oral thermometer; rectal or ear thermometer if you have children
- Petroleum jelly
- Sterile cotton
- Sunscreen
- Tweezers for removing splinters

Basic Over-the-Counter Medicines to Have on Hand

- Antacid
- Antidiarrhea medicine
- Antihistamines for allergic reactions
- Aspirin or acetaminophen
- Laxative or stool softener
- Nasal spray
- Oral decongestant

33

Hiring Household Help

Even if you're an executive at the office, it's often hard to be a boss in your own home. Whether the person you hire is to be a cleaning person or a childcare provider, he or she is likely to arrive some times when you're still in your robe, or be there on days when you're feeling sick or down—not exactly a prime moment to be conveying the image of an employer.

When my baby was about eight months old, I set about hiring a nanny, and I had anything *but* beginner's luck. I set aside an afternoon to be home for interviews, but no one I expected showed up: One woman forgot, another misunderstood, and a third got lost. A fourth did come, but she wasn't the woman I'd expected. The woman who came for the job couldn't speak a word of English; the woman I had interviewed and loved on the telephone was her friend who had agreed to make the introductory phone call for her!

I was so discouraged I gave up for awhile. Then one day, my previous caregiver, who had to leave for medical reasons, called me with a referral. The person she recommended was perfect!

The best way to approach this task is to go about it in a businesslike manner and then do all you can to maintain a good relationship.

Defining the Job

Before you go about looking for the perfect person to solve your problems, you need to make some decisions:

- Think through the job carefully. Decide which hours you will want someone.

- List the duties to be performed.

- Make a list of the qualities and skills you'd like this person to have: Ironing skills? Ability to follow a recipe? Kind and loving with children? Likes pets?

- Will this person travel with you on business or on vacation?
- Talk to friends and relatives about salary, benefits, and vacation, and decide what you want to offer.
- Decide whether you need the person to drive.
- Decide whether you mind if a person smokes.

Starting the Search

- Referrals are the best way to find good household help. Ask friends and family to keep their ears open. You may hear about a friend of a friend who is looking for work.
- Contact agencies.
- Put ads in newspapers. Spend enough money on an ad so you can be very specific about your needs (time availability, non-smoker, driver's license, etc.). That way the majority of calls you get will be from people who meet those criteria.
- Watch for notices on bulletin boards at the pediatrician's office, children's stores, and nursery schools or child care centers, or post a notice yourself.

Prescreening

Especially if you've run an ad, you're going to need a method for deciding which of the callers you want to see in person.

- Make up a questionnaire and photocopy it, leaving copies by each telephone with a pen or pencil. The form should have space for a person's name and telephone number, previous employment, your general feeling about him or her ("sounds cheerful," "English not terrific"), and any point you specifically care about (e.g., nonsmoker, likes pets, willing to travel with you and baby if necessary, will work overtime). Try to clarify by phone whether the person fits your basic needs.
- Look for good language skills (at least good enough to communicate with you), general enthusiasm for the job, and a positive attitude. In the conversation you should:

- Reemphasize the days and hours of the job. Ask about the person's availability during those times.
- Go over job responsibilities and the necessary skills.
- Ask about the person's most recent job. Why is he or she leaving?

■ Describe where you live and ask how the person plans to get there.

■ If you have a positive feeling based on this short conversation, schedule an interview. Or you may prefer to take the person's name and number until you decide on the top three people you want to see. When you set up the appointments, be sure to do the following:

- Emphasize that it's very important they phone if they can't make it.
- Be sure to get their telephone number so you can call and cancel if you need to. Or ask them to call you in advance of the appointment so that you both can confirm.
- Give them explicit directions to your home.

The Interview

Most people are very nervous at interviews, so don't discount them immediately just because they seem ill at ease. Begin by again describing the job so they have time to collect their thoughts. During the course of the interview, you will want to ask:

■ Where did you grow up?

■ Are you currently employed, and if so, what kind of work are you doing? How long have you been employed there?

■ Why are you dissatisfied with your current job?

■ What tasks did you do at your last job?

■ What other responsibilities do you have? (Here you're looking for whether they may have to take their mother to the doctor once a week or anything that might mean they would have difficulty getting to the job regularly.)

- What don't you consider part of the job?

- Are there any special things (bad back, dislike of pets, allergies) I ought to know about you?

- Put together some "What if" questions to get a sense of how he or she would handle certain situations. If you're hiring someone to care for your elderly mother, ask questions like, "What if my mother fell but refused to let you take her to the doctor?" Or for a babysitter: "How would you discipline my child if he ran out into the street before you said it was time to cross?" Or: "What would you do if there were lots of laundry to be done, but the baby cried every time you put her down?"

- Are you willing to follow a checklist of daily tasks? (Show him or her one.)

- If he or she is to live-in, show the person the room where he or she would sleep.

- Check work permits and alien registration cards. Ask for current references.

- If the person is foreign, you might ask if he or she has plans to return home soon. (There's little sense in training someone who won't be around for very long.)

- Be sure to specify days off, pay, vacation, holidays, and benefits.

- If the person is to care for children or the elderly, leave him or her alone with them for a little while. You can wander in and out of the room or eavesdrop to get a sense of how the person handles things. Trust your gut response.

- If the person is to drive, do a driver's license check. You may want to do a criminal-background check as well. If you are working with a placement service, they'll help you with this, or contact your local police department.

Checking References

Do call the references. Ask:

- How long has he/she been with you?

- Why did he/she leave?

- How well did he/she follow instructions?
- Could he/she think quickly in an emergency?
- Was he/she responsible, and did he/she use common sense?
- How well did he/she get along with family members? Was he/she chatty or quiet?
- For child care: How did he/she spend time with your child(ren)? Was he/she particularly good with one age or another? With one type of activity or another? Did your child(ren) like him/her?
- Is there anything important I should know about him/her—positive or negative?
- Was he/she punctual?
- Do you have any advice for us in working with him/her?
- Would you hire this person again?

Working Together

- Once the person has agreed to work for you, review again what the pay, vacation, benefits, system of raises, and sick leave arrangements are.
- Establish exactly what the job is. Discuss any peculiarities of yours, such as "I can't stand to find dishes left in the sink." Or: "Please be sure the baby's room is picked up before you leave."
- Discuss expectations, hours, punctuality, and the use of the phone and television.
- Show the person the appliances and how they operate. (If necessary, compile a How-to-Operate manual.)
- Specify items not to be touched or cleaned.
- Ask him or her about foods he or she likes and any special dietary needs.
- Buy any needed items if the employee is to live in.
- Set up a probationary period.
- Write out instructions and set up tasks to be done daily, weekly, and biweekly.

- Arrange for Social Security and Workmen's Compensation insurance.

- Keep accurate records of sick days and holidays so that you have a tabulation of what has been used and what hasn't.

- Just as you expect your worker to be punctual, you should be as well. If you've said you'll be home at six o'clock, then you should be there by then 99 percent of the time.

- Keep the relationship professional. Mild interest in your employee's personal life is fine; don't try to become his or her best friend.

Additional Tips for Working with a Child Care Provider

- Discuss child-rearing practices.

- Establish a regular time each week when you can discuss how things are going. Perhaps you can come home fifteen minutes early (or leave the house a little later) one day a week.

- Keep in mind that your child's needs will change and what used to be a two-hour nap may now have shrunk to one hour. Realize that the caregiver may need some decrease in his or her other responsibilities because of that.

- Have neighbors keep a watchful eye, and occasionally come home earlier than usual just to see how things are going.

PART V

Main Events

34 Tag Sales

35 Preparing for the
    Painters

36 Moving

37 Job Search

38 Party Planning

39 Travel Planning

40 Travel Packing

34

Tag Sales

One of the most profitable ways to clean house is by having a tag sale. Putting one together is a lot of work, but there are benefits: You clear your household of unwanted clutter and make money at the same time! Friends of mine who had never before had a tag sale made $2,000 on their first try.

My friends say of the experience: "The things we thought would sell—like a set of stoneware dishes—were among the last to go. Things that we almost didn't put out because they seemed like junk were the first things purchased. We never dreamed that we would make so much money!"

What you consider a piece of junk may be another person's idea of a real jewel. You might as well profit from it. Like everything else, the more planning you put into it, the more successful your tag sale will be.

Clean Out Your Home

- Start combing through your house or apartment. Go through each room, closet, and drawer, searching for items you no longer want or need. Also check the attic, basement, and garage—spots that are certain to turn up a treasure trove of junk! If you haven't used something in a few years, put it in the "sell" pile. And if you're thinking of getting something new, like a toaster oven, plan to sell your old one.

- Don't be too selective. Almost anything goes—I've seen typewriters with missing keys, fans with broken blades, and a three-legged chair find new homes. Clothing, tools, appliances, furniture, books, records, plants, toys, and odds and ends all can bring a price.

- Establish a place—shelves, a closet, or part of a room—where you can keep the merchandise until the time of the sale.

Planning the Sale

- If you are daunted at the thought of how much effort a tag sale will require, consider calling in a professional tag sale company. They will estimate what they think the sale will bring (estimates are always low to allow for last-minute price-cutting). On the day of the sale they will be responsible for displaying all items and will come prepared with everything from shopping bags to display tables. Their commission is usually twenty percent.

- Consider holding the sale with another family or two. Multiple-family sales generate more interest because shoppers know that additional merchandise will be on display. It also gives you more people to help with the work.

- Some communities require a permit for having a tag sale. Check with your local police department.

- Good weather is essential for a successful tag sale, so late spring, summer, and early fall are your best bets for having a good turnout.

- Some people prefer to hold two-day sales over the weekend, but this means having to carry the merchandise in and out of your home for two days. It also may mean that Saturday's visitors will be lookers who are hoping prices will drop by Sunday. One-day sales are more efficient, and tag sale veterans usually report that Saturdays are a bit busier than Sundays.

- Select the hours for your sale. Most tag sales begin between 8 and 9 A.M. Figure that early-bird bargain hunters will show up forty-five minutes to an hour earlier than the time you specify.

- Choose the exact location for the sale. In the garage? On the front lawn? The backyard? Ideally, the sale should be held where it is easy to provide shelter in case of rain. Also keep in mind that the cashier's table should be placed in such a way that shoppers will *have to* pass it as they leave.

- Assess what type of display items you're going to need. For example, clothing sells better when hanging (rather than packed in boxes) so you may need to borrow a clothing rack.

- Start saving grocery bags and a few boxes. While you don't need to provide every purchaser with something in which to carry merchandise, plan to have as much as you can on hand.

- The better your merchandise looks, the more you can ask for it, so invest the time to polish silver, shine shoes, mend clothing, and make all items look as good as possible. (If you intend to sell nonworking items, simply mark "as is" on it. A fix-it specialist may be intrigued by the challenge.)

- Consider whether or not you will take checks. Accepting them probably will result in a few sales you might otherwise lose; however, you also run the risk of receiving a bogus check.

Spreading the Word

- A newspaper ad in your daily newspaper or local circular is a must for a serious sale. Look through various local newspapers and see where most tag sales are advertised.

- Also consider running an ad or placing a notice in other local publications such as church bulletins.

- When writing the ad, keep in mind the following:

  - Be sure to include date and time.

  - Include the address. If the location is difficult to find, give exact directions.

  - Don't include your phone number. Callers tend to be phoning in search of specific items. Let them come for themselves—once there, they are likely to buy.

  - Though a longer ad will cost a bit more, tag sale veterans say it is worth it so you can list categories you have to sell like china, children's clothes, antiques, books, and so on.

  - If you are having a sale with other families, state it in the ad, which will signal to shoppers there will be more merchandise: "Two-family sale" explains it.

- "Loss leaders" can also help your ad attract customers. List a few specific items with their prices (low ones, such as Canopy Bed: $25; Croquet Set: $1.50). Those will encourage people to come.

Signs

- Signs can help lead people to your sale even if they haven't seen the ad and will also help those who have seen it to find the exact location. The signs should list the date, time, and address of the sale, and arrows should point potential customers in the right direction.

- Use bright colors for lettering and make letters large enough so that they can be read by passers-by in a moving vehicle.

- Choose busy corners and well-traveled streets for your signs. Hang them high enough (facing toward the traffic) so they can be easily seen.

- Fasten the signs securely by nailing or tying them to a pole which can be used as a stake.

- Other signs you'll need include:
  - Tag Sale Today (to identify your home as the sale site)
  - No Parking in Driveway (By saving the driveway for people who want to drive closer to pick up a large item, you also reduce the chance of one driver blocking another.)
  - No Returns, No Guarantees
  - Cash Only (if applicable)
  - Sold Out (to notify customers that the sale is over)

Fliers

- One-page fliers can also attract attention. The wording of your ad will often suffice, but in a flier you can include additional categories and be even more specific. Post the fliers on the neighborhood bulletin boards or distribute them at the local supermarket. Be sure the date, address, and time are included!

Pricing Your Merchandise

Pricing merchandise is time-consuming, so begin well in advance of the sale. If possible, work with a group. Other adults can offer you level-headed advice as to what certain items are worth.

- Buy sticker labels (in white and in colors) at a stationery store.

- For many items, the easiest system will be to price by category. Group items according to price, and use color-coded labels to identify them. Then create a chart to give you the prices for each color code.

- The most difficult part of pricing items is remaining unemotional—yes, your husband's old football jersey may bring back great memories, but realistically, how many people have heard of Mumford High?

- Price fairly. High prices are a turnoff to veteran shoppers who will leave if they think a sale is overpriced. Try to visit other tag sales and secondhand stores to get a feel for the going rate.

- If you have potential antiques (coin collection, china doll, silver, glass, et cetera), refer to books on the topic, talk to dealers, and visit antique shows.

- You may even want to get an item appraised. One family priced at $2 a lamp which a savvy shopper bought, cleaned up, and discovered to be a very valuable Lalique lamp. Don't let that happen to you!

- Keep prices simple. Where $2.95 may have a nice ring to it, remember that your cashier will have his or her hands full trying to total prices and make change. Think in simple terms.

- If you're holding a joint sale, put the price and the initials of the family who owns the item on the price tag. That way the cashier can check the price, take off the sticker, and put it on a tally sheet that will be totaled up at the end of the day.

- Create boxes that contain miscellaneous items, priced at 25¢, 50¢, or $1.00, that might otherwise be too small to sell. People love poking through such boxes for "hidden treasures." Clearly label the boxes with the price of the items in it.

■ Expect some haggling. For many buyers, part of the fun of a tag sale is the feeling that they got a deal. Don't take it as an insult, but expect that people will offer you less for an item than the price marked.

Final Preparations

■ Do as much as possible in advance. Have the 25¢, 50¢, and $1.00 boxes organized and ready to go the day before; have as many displays set up as you can; do everything possible to reduce setup time.

■ Have one person be responsible for knowing where the cash box is at all times. Have $10 in quarters, nickels, and dimes, and have $20 in $5 and $1 bills to get started.

■ Make certain that two people will be available at all times throughout the day.

■ Plan to place valuable items on a display table near the cashier where they can be watched closely.

■ Have on hand:

• Cash box

• Pencil, paper, and calculator for tabulating costs

• Tally sheet (pad of paper) where you can collect price stickers from each item sold

• Yardstick or measuring tape just in case shoppers want to check dimensions of items

• Shopping bags/boxes

• Twine for packaging bulky items

• Plastic tarps for covering items in case of rain

■ Set your alarm for early enough the next day so that you'll have plenty of time to arrange an attractive display.

The Big Day

- Be ready early.

- Confine customers to the selling area.

- Secure your home so that no one can wander through it.

- Friendliness and good salesmanship, bolstered by knowledge of what you're selling, are key elements of a good tag sale. Make people feel welcome. If they show interest in an item, you may want to be available for any questions, or you can volunteer information that might be helpful (how something works, age of quilt, etc.).

- Have the cashier take away the money periodically.

- Be firm about no parking in the driveway.

- Expect to mark down prices at some point.

If Everything Does Not Sell

- Consider donating items to a local charity.

- If any large items are left, try placing an ad just for them. Give a telephone number but no address so that you can set up appointments.

- If you were visited by any secondhand store dealers, see if they will make a bid on the remaining merchandise. They won't give you the price you would have gotten selling the items individually, but something is better than nothing!

- Pack items away for the next sale!

35

Preparing for the Painters

If you think getting ready for the painters is going to be bad, consider the plight of my neighbor: One evening about five years ago, she rang our doorbell. She was exhausted and in a real dither about getting ready for this "monumental" task, which was taking place the next day. When we went next door, the only thing that had been moved in preparation was an extensive collection of beautiful, delicate glass bottles! It had taken her so long just to do this that she hadn't even begun to prepare the rest of her home!

Some people say that having your home painted is worse then moving, and they may be right. Certainly having to pack up all your belongings and stash them in the center of a room is a time-consuming process. However, if you can keep in mind how beautiful a new color scheme and a freshly painted room will look, the nuisance of having to prepare for it won't seem as bad.

Choosing a Painter

- Get referrals from friends. Ask to see the person's work, if at all possible.
- Get bids from at least three painters.
- Ask prospective painters:
  - Who will actually be doing the work? The painter? An assistant? Will he or she be there throughout the job?
  - How will the walls be prepared?
  - Who will order and pick up the paint?
  - Is paint included in the price?

- Show the painter the space that is to be painted, asking if he or she envisions any problems.

- Make sure the person has the proper insurance.

- Check with previous clients as to whether or not the person stayed on schedule, stuck to the stated price, and was pleasant to have around.

- Once you've selected a painter, go over everything step by step. Make sure the person cleans up each night so you can still live in your home.

- Prepare a room-by-room checklist before the job begins. (How will the painter protect items such as doorknobs and switch plates? Should you remove them? Or will the painter?)

- If carpeting will be installed afterward, make an agreement for the painter to come back to do touch-ups.

- Work out a pay schedule consisting of a deposit and payment of the balance. Some workers request a midpoint payment, but specifying what is "halfway" can pose a problem.

- Draw up a written agreement that is very specific.

Choosing a Color

- Collect swatches of wallpaper, pillows, and upholstery fabric to take to the paint store.

- Initially, shop for a general color without worrying about the exact shade. At the paint store, you can pick up a wide variety of paint chip samples to avoid lots of trips to the store.

- Once you've selected the basic color, buy a small quantity of that shade and two others—the immediate lighter and darker shades. When you get home, paint test patches in the room on different walls in order to see the different colors in various lights.

- For high-traffic areas (particularly if you have children) consider a finish that is easy to wipe clean, such as a gloss.

- If you're responsible for buying the paint, ask the painter how much you will need.

- If the painter picks up the paint, be sure he or she does a test patch for color.

- Label paint cans according to room.

- Keep a record of the paint used for each room. Note the color, formula, brand, and finish. File this information in your filing cabinet or in your Household Notebook (see Chapter 26).

Preparing for the Painters

- Buy lots of plastic dropcloths to cover the furniture. You'll need tape, too.

- If closets are to be painted, clean them out. Borrow coatracks (ask friends and neighbors), and gather boxes (from grocery and liquor stores) for temporary storage. If the closets needn't be painted, take a plastic tarp and cover all the clothing within. Even when the door is closed, dust from preliminary sanding will get in.

- As you go through your closets, pull out items you no longer want. Give them to charity or have a tag sale.

- Send out rugs, window draperies, and curtains to be cleaned.

- Protect hardware. If the painter is not going to remove it, you should put each unit (e.g., one switch plate and accompanying screws) in a plastic bag and label it. Keep all hardware and decorative switch plates together in a box to avoid hunting for them later.

- Put the furniture in the middle of the room, cover fully with dropcloths, and tape down to the floor.

- If the paint job is complicated, draw a plan and code it. Put numbers on the wall and label each paint can accordingly. This lessens the chance of error.

- Have the living room done first. It's usually the largest room in the home and when it's finished, you can store things from other rooms there while they are being painted. However, be careful not to nick the walls!

- Plan projects to do at home during the time you'll have to be there to supervise.

- Keep available all the things you'll need (appointment calendar, outfit for the next day) so you won't have to dig for them.

- Make alternative meal plans for the period when the kitchen is being painted. The family can have cold cereal for breakfast for a few days; a toaster oven, a hot plate, and an electric kettle will allow you to prepare simple meals without disturbing the "kitchen prep." You can request that you still have access to the refrigerator.

Afterward

- Return clothes to closet.
- Move back furniture.
- Reinstall doorknobs, fixtures, switch plates, shelves, brackets, etcetera, and hang pictures.
- Clean windows.
- Get rugs back from cleaners.
- Get draperies back from the cleaners and hang them.
- Clean your home once the job is over, but don't do an extensive job until you're *sure* the painters are finished!

36

Moving

Whether it is across the country or just next door, moving is a major undertaking that requires a great deal of planning and hard work.

People suffer from various moving miseries: Some are still knee-deep in boxes months after a move is over; others never do unpack some of the things they moved with; still others *intend* to unpack efficiently, but become overwhelmed when faced with a new living room full of boxes marked "Miscellaneous." I've never heard anyone say, "I loved moving and can't wait to do it again!"

Moving should not be thought of as one major task—but many small tasks instead. Use this list and check off each task as you accomplish it; you'll soon see that by breaking down the move into parts, it *can* be managed and it *will* happen.

Sharing the News with Your Family

- Tell your children about the move early enough to let them adjust to the idea. As a general guide, children ages eight and over should be told early—probably as soon as *you* know. With children ages four to eight, give two to three months notice; children under four should hear the news about a month ahead of time.

- On each child's level, explain *why* you're moving: "Daddy's new job is in this town," or "We'll be closer to Grandma," et cetera.

- Tell children what moving will mean to them: "We're moving to a new house, but you'll still go to the same school . . ." "When we move to Des Moines, we'll take all your toys, your furniture, and *you*, and in our new house, you'll have a room all your own." Bring the subject up regularly so that it can be reexplained. Preschool children may wonder exactly what gets packed, and some fear they will be forgotten in the shuffle, so always address how he or she will make the move, too.

- Young children don't understand time references such as "next month," so give them a reference such as "When school is out."

- Find one or two features of the community that you know each child will love. For a toddler it may be a terrific playground; for your eleven-year-old son, it may be the hockey team for which he'll be eligible. If you can stress what will be new and special, it will help the kids anticipate the move positively.

- Ask your librarian to recommend age-appropriate books on moving.

- If you're showing the old house to prospective buyers, it's ideal if the kids can be out of the house during appointments. The house will show better without chaos, but more important, the kids won't have to focus on the fact that soon *their* house will belong to someone else.

- When to move? Mid or late August is good (and if the move is totally at your discretion, between schools—nursery and grammar; grammar and middle school, etc.—is optimum). The summer provides a natural break in the year, and it is generally easier for children to adjust when they can get absorbed by the school schedule, meet new friends, and begin to learn the ropes along with other new kids. If you have to move earlier in the summer, enroll your children in a local camp or some type of regular activity (swim team? tennis class? dance lessons?) so that they can begin to meet other children right away. Neighborhoods can be very quiet in the summer with kids at day camps or at the beach or pool.

Things to Do as Far in Advance as Possible

- Get referrals about movers or check the Yellow Pages. Have two or three come to your home for an estimate. Before they arrive, you'll want to have a general idea of what goes and what stays. If an entire bedroom set is to be given away, you won't want the cost of moving it figured into the overall estimate. Local moves are generally charged on an hourly basis; long-distance moves are usually based on the weight of the shipment, the miles it will be moved, and the size and number of packing cartons and services you'll need.

■ When the mover arrives, you'll want to learn the following:
   • Estimated moving costs
   • How movers will pack fragile items
   • Provisions of the contract
   • Insurance coverage (which you may need to supplement)
   • Who will handle the move on the other end if you're moving to a city where the movers don't have an office.

■ Ask the movers if they will help you disconnect the washer and dryer, stove, refrigerator, freezer, television set, and air-conditioners. You'll want to know now if you need to make other arrangements.

■ Carefully read the bill of lading (the contract that outlines the terms of your move).

■ If the mover was not referred to you by someone you know, check with the Better Business Bureau to see if there have been any complaints about the company. While prices may not vary that much from one company to another, the way they handle your belongings will. Make certain that your belongings will be in safe hands.

■ Consider what work might be done in your new home prior to your arrival. You can probably arrange with the owners for a designer or an architect to make a visit there. If the home will be vacant for a few days or weeks before you arrive, you may be able to get some construction out of the way. Consider, too, whether an exterminator, cleaning team, or window washer should come in before you arrive.

- You don't want to move what you don't want, so start taking stock of all your belongings. Sort everything into four groups:

  - Items to throw out. (Don't insist that your children throw things out—this will only make the move more difficult.)
  - Items to give to charity
  - Items to give to friends or relatives
  - Items to go with you

- Start collecting packing materials. The local liquor store may be a good source of boxes. (Grocery boxes usually aren't strong enough, and most stores now take the tops off.) Better yet, buy collapsible boxes from the moving company. They are strong, have tops, and can be used for storage (or collapsed and stored) after the move. You'll also need tape. Newspaper makes the best packing material but can soil your belongings. Try to get unprinted newspaper stock. (Call your local newspaper, printer, or paper company.)

If You Are Moving to a New Community

- Write to the local Chamber of Commerce for information on the new community. School-age children may want to write the letters themselves.

- Subscribe to the local newspaper to get a sense of the local news and the events for children.

- Research nursery schools and activities for older children prior to moving; you may need to preregister. Nursery schools start sending out applications the autumn prior to a child's entry, so you'll want to put down a deposit at your favorite as soon as possible. Some dance schools fill fall classes by late spring, and you'll want to know that. How to research? Realtors can put you in contact with other families who have moved to the area recently. Ask about local scout troops, soccer teams, extracurricular activities, etc. Also inquire about sitters. There may be a service everyone uses; they may know of someone who is looking for a job. Find out what the general system is so that you'll be able to find someone when you're ready.

- Take the kids to visit the new house and community as often as possible. Test out the pizza places, try some ice cream, visit the park, and find the video store. You may even want to see if you can arrange a play date or two before the move.

- If the kids can't come with you to visit the new location, bring back brochures, and take lots of pictures of things that will interest them.

- Assemble a photo essay of where your family is moving, using pictures you've taken of what you imagine will be their favorite spots: the park, the swings at school, the ice rink, the community pool, your new backyard, et cetera. Younger kids will love taking it in to share with classmates, and it will help them realize how terrific it will be to have a playroom or to live in a community with a roller rink.

Things to Do Four Weeks in Advance

- Begin sorting through your mail to make a list of places you'll need to notify regarding your change of address. Note magazines to which you subscribe, credit card companies, department stores where you have charge accounts, and so forth. Most can be notified by filling out the change-of-address section of a regular bill or statement. Notify all other companies and agencies by letter (photocopies of a form letter you draw up will be fine), or use the post office's standard change-of-address cards. On your list, note the date you notified each person or place. (At a later date, you will notify the post office about forwarding your mail.)

- Check and clear tax assessments.

- Have your W-2s and other tax forms forwarded.

- Confirm packing and moving dates.

- Begin to use up food from the refrigerator and freezer, and only restock what you'll need during the next month.

Things to Do Four Weeks in Advance of a Move to Another City

- Make whatever travel plans are necessary. Do you need plane reservations? Will you need to stay in a hotel the night after your old house is packed? Will you need hotel reservations in the new community?

- Make travel arrangements for pets. Ask your veterinarian about tranquilizers, and be sure all vaccination papers are in order.

- Notify schools to forward transcripts.

- Gather medical and dental records for all members of the family. Be sure to collect all information on allergies and special prescriptions, and request recent X-rays (both dental and medical) as well. Contact doctors and dentists personally to ask them for referrals in the new community.

- Collect birth, baptism, or any other records from the church or synagogue, and request a recommendation to a place of worship in the new community.

- Close out local charge accounts.

- Check with local creditors to make arrangements for transfer of cars or any other possessions not fully paid for. You will likely need written permission to take mortgaged property out of state.

- Return all you've borrowed (including library books), and collect what you've loaned out.

Four Weeks in Advance: Packing Tips

- Start packing items you're not using regularly such as good china, out-of-season clothing, and the contents of your attic, basement, or storage shed.

- Clean items before packing to save time when unpacking.

- If possible, send carpets, drapes, and quilts to be cleaned and have them delivered to the new address. Keep a list of all that is sent out so you can be certain everything comes back.

- Keep things that belong together in the same carton: pans with their lids, stationery with envelopes, coffee pot cord with coffee pot, remote control with VCR or television.
- Fill all boxes to the top so that items won't bounce around.
- Try to distribute the weight within a carton evenly.
- Use sheets, towels, and blankets to cushion the contents of some of the boxes.
- Arrange to take houseplants with you, as movers will generally not be responsible for them. If you can't, you'll need to give them away. Also be aware that some states don't allow plants to be brought in.
- Pack books flat so their spines don't break, and put them in smaller cartons so they won't be too heavy. Add additional packing material to empty corners so the books won't slide around. Books that will be shelved together should be packed in the same box.
- When packing lamps, remove bulbs before wrapping the base in a towel or blanket. Shades can be nested inside one another and packed in a separate box. Use packing material (not newspaper) to fill in extra space.
- Don't add heavy linens to drawers in furniture. Leave bureaus and desks as they would be normally.
- Consider having movers pack kitchen and fragile items. (Some movers will not take responsibility for items they have not packed.) Otherwise, fragile items and all dishes should be individually wrapped using newsprint or paper towels. Cushion them well.
- Leave rugs, pictures, and mirrors in place. The movers are best prepared to pack and wrap these.
- Hanging clothes are best moved in the moving company's wardrobe cartons. If you buy no other boxes from the mover, indulge in these so that you don't have to pack your clothes.
- Fold curtains and linens so they can be draped over a hanger. Then they, too, can be moved in a wardrobe carton.

- Provide each child with a moving box for special treasures. If driving to your new home, consider taking these with you. If that is impossible, label it LOAD LAST, UNLOAD FIRST.

- Establish a box for those items you will need throughout the move: plane tickets, driving itinerary, important papers, keys to the new house, jewelry, and so forth. Keep the box handy so you can add to it as needed.

- In another box labeled LOAD LAST, UNLOAD FIRST, put clean bed linens and towels so they will be accessible as quickly as possible once the truck arrives at your new home.

- Also put together a survival kit with a hammer and screwdriver, tape, scissors, lightbulbs, a first-aid kit (including children's and adult pain reliever, Band-Aids, antiseptic, tweezers, clean needle, cold tablets, and medicine for an upset stomach), paper plates, cups and napkins, plastic tableware, a small saucepan, instant coffee or tea bags, snack food, a can opener, paper towels, toilet paper, detergent, sponges, plastic trash bags, and washcloths.

- Number each box, and then label it as to its contents and the room where it will go. Also note the information on a separate sheet of paper; if you discover that box thirty-three is missing, you'll automatically know it had living room lamps in it.

- Dispose of all flammables, such as cleaning fluid, paint, and aerosol cans. Drain gasoline-powered equipment. The movers will not take these things.

Things to Do Two to Three Weeks in Advance

- If you're driving to a new community, have the car tuned up for the trip. Check the oil, water, battery, and tires.
- Call charity for pick up.
- Deliver or have picked up the items you plan to give to friends.
- Arrange to have all utilities disconnected at your old home *after departure* (plan the disconnection date for later than your

moving date so you won't be without utilities), and instruct the companies as to where the final bill should be sent. Disconnect:

- Gas/electric
- Water
- Telephone
- Cable TV

▪ Notify the above utilities of the date you'd like service to start in the new location. (Have the telephone in service at least one day prior to the moving truck's arrival.)

▪ Contact the following to let them know of your departure:

- Diaper service
- Dry cleaning delivery service
- Garbage collection
- Laundry
- Newspaper

▪ Similarly, notify the appropriate places when to start service in your new home.

▪ Call your insurance agent for policy changes. Also discuss any special coverage that might be necessary during the move.

▪ Arrange for the plumber or the appropriate service repair person to install your appliances.

Things to Do One Week in Advance

▪ Pick up any items you might still have at the cleaners, laundry, or repair shop.

▪ If you're moving to a new community, go to the bank to take care of the following:

- Have the bank transfer accounts or arrange for a letter of credit to facilitate establishing an account in your new community.

- Have the bank transfer the contents of your safe-deposit box, or withdraw the contents of the box yourself and have the box released.
- Purchase sufficient traveler's checks to cover your expenses until you reach your destination.

■ Arrange for the forwarding of mail by the post office (what you've done earlier is to notify regular subscriptions and correspondents; now you need to arrange for the post office to send on whatever mail still comes to your old address) by filling out the standard change-of-address form. Turn it in.

■ Send address change to your friends. Include your new telephone number.

■ Arrange for child care. While it's a good idea for children to be at home on moving day, make someone else responsible for their well-being.

■ Confirm appointments with the exterminator, the cleaning team, or the window washer.

■ Give away or dispose of all alcoholic beverages. Movers will not transport liquor.

■ For a long-distance move, pack suitcases with the clothing and items you'll need during the move.

■ Mark DO NOT MOVE on all items you plan to take with you.

Two Days Before

■ Tape shut the tops of bottles and spillable items.

■ Remove window coverings (drapes, shades, rods) and take down special light fixtures not included in the sale of the house that you plan to take with you. Movers do not routinely perform such tasks.

■ Don't pack perishables.

■ Type out directions to your new home for the movers.

Day Before (Packing Day)

- When the movers arrive to pack any items you've requested, point out fragile items as well as items not to be moved.

- As they pack, work with movers by quickly checking the contents of each packed box. Label it according to its new location (master bedroom, kitchen, basement) and contents. Number each box and add it to your list of boxes and their contents. This will make unloading easier.

- Finish packing personal items.

- Make a final inspection of the house to check for details that need to be taken care of before the next day.

- Plan a simple breakfast for the next morning that can be eaten on paper plates.

Moving Day

- Strip the beds, but leave the bottom fitted sheets on mattresses and the bed assembled.

- Have the vacuum handy to clean behind the refrigerator, stove, and elsewhere to leave the place in good condition for the new owner.

- Include your children in the day's activities. Let them see that all their treasures are being packed with the rest of the household belongings. Movers will generally let children visit the back of the van to see that, indeed, *everything* is going.

- To avoid disputes later, accompany the van operator during the compiling of the inventory of goods to be moved.

- As the movers are finishing, make a final tour of the house to be sure you have everything. Don't forget the vacuum!

- Check, sign, and save a copy of the bill of lading. Verify the address of your new home and the phone number of the person to be called if there are problems on the way.

- Give the driver directions to the new address.

- Confirm delivery date and time.
- In summer, turn the air-conditioning system off before leaving. In winter, turn the furnace down but not off.
- Leave keys with real-estate agent, new occupant, or neighbor.
- Make sure all the windows and doors are closed and locked. Turn out all the lights.
- Check with the mover regarding final cost (determined on long-distance moves after van is weighed). Make sure you'll have the needed cash, money order, or certified check before the van is unloaded at your destination, as payment is generally required before unloading.

Delivery Day

- Be on hand to show the movers where things go.
- Do not sign delivery papers until you've checked the inventory and inspected for damage. If any loss or damage is noted, have the driver make specific notations of loss or damage on the inventory list.
- If it's necessary to file a claim for damaged or missing items, notify the moving company as soon as possible. They will send you claim forms.

After Arrival: Getting Settled in the New Community

- Shortly after arrival, take the family on a walk around the neighborhood. You should also take them on a drive to familiarize yourself with the community at large.
- Stop by and introduce yourself to your neighbors.
- Find out about local transportation such as bus, subway, or train schedules. Get appropriate maps.
- Contact the local Department of Motor Vehicles to obtain a new driver's license. If you've moved within the same state, you'll simply need to arrange for a change of address.

- Research the emergency numbers you'll need in the new area. Get the location of the nearest hospital, and find out where the police station and fire boxes are.

- Enroll your children in school, and if they are starting right away, visit the school to get your child settled. If it suits the circumstances, you might suggest to the school that your child be assigned a "buddy" to help him or her through the first days.

- Discuss with your children good "opening lines" for getting to know people. Don't minimize the difficulty of making new friends; talk about how you yourself are going to go about meeting new people.

- Arrange for check-cashing privileges at a neighborhood grocery or pharmacy that is open on the weekends.

- Arrange for a friend or neighbor to keep an extra set of house and car keys.

- Check on voter registration. Sometimes a certain period of residency is required, so you'll want to be in touch with the Board of Elections right away.

- Arrange for change of address on any other official papers such as your passport.

- For the entire family, choose and sign up for some activities (to do separately or together) that would allow you to meet some local people.

- Visit the library and apply for a library card.

37

Job Search

It's often been said that getting a new job is a job in itself, which is why organization is so important. If you're still working, you need a very organized method for pursuing leads and following up during the time you can spare for the job hunt. If you're currently unemployed, setting up a system for your job hunt will keep you from becoming depressed by treating it like the nine-to-five job it should be.

Organizing Your Job Search

- Buy a three-ring looseleaf notebook, dividers with pockets, and paper. (You could keep records of your search on the computer, but the notebook provides total portability.) You will need to divide it into the following sections:

  - *Career Goal.* This section is for recording your thoughts (and final decision) regarding what type of job you are currently looking for (or could do). Long-term career planning ideas should also be a part of this section.

  - *Contacts.* In this section, you will list all the people whom you should contact to help you with your search. Also note down names of helpful organizations and target companies (those likely to have the type of job you are seeking).

  - *Letters Sent.* File copies of all the letters you send out here. On the back of the letters, you can keep notes regarding subsequent conversations and meetings.

  - *Interview Preparations.* This section will include a list of general questions for which you will want to be prepared, as well as notes, brochures, annual reports, and other information regarding specific companies.

- *Follow Up.* Keep a thank-you note list and check off after you've written to someone. Once you have been interviewed at a company, letters and related material should be moved here. This will provide an organized method for following up.

▪ Buy high-quality paper for cover letters.

▪ Get an answering machine and record a pleasant, businesslike message on it.

Identifying Your Goal

Be as specific as possible in setting a job goal. Use your notebook to record your thoughts. Take a long weekend or even a full week to consider exactly what type of job you're looking for (or could do). You may even want to visit a career counselor for help in this area. Are you looking for the exact same position you've had only in a different or larger environment? Are you looking for a specific job in a field related to yours? Are you seeking a career change?

▪ Now identify your target companies. You may already have some in mind, or your local library will have directories of firms in various industries. Ask the librarian for help.

▪ Consider salary expectations. This will probably involve some personal research. Find out what the going rate is in the field. If you're very experienced, you can probably ask for more. If you're a novice, you should expect less.

▪ Set goals regarding the number of letters to be sent and contacts to be made each week. The number you establish will depend on whether this is a full- or a part-time effort.

Preparing Your Résumé

▪ Prepare your résumé on a computer. This will make it easy to edit the résumé frequently, and you'll also be able to provide pristine copies as needed.

- Tailor your résumé to the type of job you are seeking. You may need to write more than one. For example, a person with writing or public relations experience in the health field might prepare résumés for the following types of jobs:

  - Public relations representative for a pharmaceutical company—résumé should emphasize P.R. background.
  - Editor of a health publication—résumé should emphasize editorial work experience.
  - Speech writer for nonprofit health organization—résumé should emphasize speech writing experience.
  - Newspaper health reporter—résumé should emphasize writing and reporting experience.

- Your résumé should be no longer than one page. Remember, it's the places where you've worked and your education that get you the interview, so sacrifice other information.

- Describe your jobs with active verbs, emphasizing responsibilities and accomplishments: "increased profits . . ." "planned and executed program . . ." "supervised staff of thirty . . ."

- Go over your résumé's layout and content with someone whose business judgment you trust.

- Proofread your résumé carefully. There's nothing worse than a prospective employer finding a typographical error.

- If you provide the names of references on your résumé, notify them that they may be contacted.

Preparing Your Cover Letter

- Your cover letter is the gift wrapping for your résumé. It should help make your résumé stand out.

- Prepare a good basic letter. This will ensure against writer's block each time you send out your résumé. Keep in mind that you will revise your letter each time, making it specific to the job and to the person to whom you are writing.

- Make the letter brief and to the point. Its content should focus on how you can help the company, not on how the company can help you.

Starting Your Search

- Turn to the Contacts section of your notebook and begin to note down all the people who might help you find a job: family members, friends, business associates, acquaintances. Because seventy percent of all jobs are found through personal contacts, such people are very important.

- Also note down executive recruiters, placement officers (such as your college placement officer or even your employer, who may be offering help if many jobs are being phased out). Clip newspaper and trade magazine job ads that sound interesting.

- Also keep up with trade journals and the business section of your local newspaper. Clip articles about people or companies that interest you. A savvy person who is smart enough to follow up on an article may well get a job interview!

- You can also obtain new contacts by attending industry programs, meetings, lectures, and seminars.

- Once you have a list of names, begin looking up addresses and telephone numbers. You may need to call for the person's exact title, the correct spelling of his or her name, telephone extension, and suite number.

- Be sure to list target companies at which you would like to work. If you don't have an inside contact there, call and get the name of the person responsible for hiring in the division that interests you.

- Since your basic cover letter and résumé are now prepared, you can immediately begin to approach the people you've listed on your Contacts page. In many cases, your goal is simply to be referred to someone who might have a job opening, so your cover letter should state that and note that you will follow up with a call.

- Photocopy each letter you send out, and file it in the Letters Sent section.

- Once the letters have been sent, use your calendar to note the days on which you need to follow up.

- When you phone the person (as you must do with every letter you send), keep notes regarding your conversation on the back of the cover letter. Note down the date of conversation and referrals, and be sure to get the name of the secretary/assistant. That person is the key to your getting through again if you need to.

- Any referrals you are given should be added to your Contacts list. Be sure to note by whom you were referred.

Prepare Yourself Before Each Interview

- Research the company. If possible, talk to people who work there or who know others who do; try to locate and read any printed material about the company.

- Acquaint yourself with the company's product(s), if applicable.

- Think through the position for which you're applying, and note down any questions you'll want to ask. For example, you'll want to learn how the position works, what the responsibilities are, how much travel must be done, and where you would fit into the hierarchy. These questions should be filed in the Interview Preparations section of your notebook for handy reference.

- With the specific company and job in mind, consider any special questions the interviewer may ask.

- Ask someone to help you rehearse. If you were eased out because of a company merger, you should have a positive explanation concerning what happened. If you've taken a couple of years off to go to graduate school, you ought to speak of the way that experience will benefit you in future jobs.

- Prepare an answer to the standard line: "Tell me about yourself." Don't be afraid to sell yourself. I once went on an interview where the opening statement was: "Okay. You're on."

■ For artists, writers, and advertising and public relations executives, showing samples of work can be important on a job interview. If this applies to you, consider what samples you'll want to include and how you will package them.

■ Go through your closet and choose two outfits you can wear on interviews (or shop for them, if necessary). That way one will be ready at all times. The outfits should look as expensive as the salary you aspire to make, and they should suit the style of the industry to which you're applying. For example, conservative attire is appropriate for an accounting firm, while a bit more flair is suitable in the advertising field.

■ Choose outfits that make you feel comfortable. You don't want to be fussing with a stiff collar or a wrap skirt that won't stay closed during the interview.

The Interview

Be on time. Take a minute to make sure you're still looking neat before you enter the building.

■ Choose a chair that places you comfortably near the interviewer.

■ Try to assess how much time has been allotted for the interview. If the interviewer seems rushed, don't launch into any long stories.

■ If you're not sure what the interviewer is looking for, try to encourage him or her to speak first. Respond accordingly, emphasizing your skills and experience.

■ Stick to the business at hand.

■ Work at keeping good eye contact.

■ Be positive about yourself and your attributes, and be enthusiastic about the job.

■ Ask questions about the company to show that you've done some homework.

■ Ask about their time frame for hiring. As you leave, you should have a good idea of how much longer they expect to be interviewing for the position.

After the Interview

- As soon as you get home, make notes regarding the job, points discussed, and your impressions of the people and the company. This information should be filed in the Follow Up section of your notebook. On a separate sheet of paper (to be filed in the Interview Preparations section), note down any points of the conversation that went badly so you can review them before your next interview and thereby benefit from your mistakes.

- Promptly send any additional material the interviewer may have requested.

- Send a thank-you note right away, emphasizing any points you'd like the interviewer to remember (e.g., your experience at fundraising, your willingness to relocate).

- Do not wait to hear from the company. Based on the information you gained at the interview, choose an appropriate time to follow up, mark it on your calendar, and call on that date to see what is happening.

- If you don't get through, don't be disheartened. Keep trying. Sometimes people are genuinely so busy they don't have time to return all their calls. Befriend the secretary/assistant, and perhaps he or she will tell you the best times to call.

- If you don't get a definite no, keep following up until the job is filled. If you do get a no, ask for a referral. If you were a serious contender, the interviewer may well have some good suggestions and be pleased to help out.

It may never be a "perfect" time to look for a job, but remember, you only need one job for the search to be a success! I've always believed that if you work steadily and persistently, you'll get what you want. Just keep trying!

38

Party Planning

While we all know people who can pull a party together at the last minute and have it be a smash, for most of us planning a party requires foresight, thought, coordination, and a dash of good luck. To be able to have a gathering that both you and your guests can enjoy is an ideal celebration.

General Planning: Six to Eight Weeks in Advance

- Set a budget.
- Decide on what type of party you will have—a big cocktail party, a sit-down dinner, Sunday brunch, an open house.
- Set the day, time, and place.
- If you're going to need a caterer, select the one you want to use and make certain the caterer is free on that date.
- Buy invitations. You'll need additional time if ordering them.
- Prepare a guest list (use your Household Notebook), and include on it guests' phone numbers in case you need to call them. After the invitations have been mailed, retain the list and use it to keep track of RSVPs.

To Do: Three to Four Weeks in Advance

- Arrange for extra help if necessary. Will you need a bartender? Cook? Server? Babysitter?
- Arrange for entertainment, such as a pianist.
- If the party will be held in cool weather, or if rain is a possibility, think about what you will do with the guests' coats. You may need to rent or borrow a coatrack.

- Consider your other needs. If you must rent/borrow chairs, dishes, glasses, serving pieces, or anything else, make the necessary arrangements.

- Think about what you want to wear. If you need to shop for something new, do so at least four weeks in advance to allow time for any alterations. If you've chosen something you already own, make sure it is clean and in good repair.

- Order flowers. If ordering a floral centerpiece for a sit-down affair, be certain to specify a low one. You don't want the arrangement to block the vision of any of the guests at the dinner table.

- Address and mail invitations.

To Shop for: Three to Four Weeks in Advance

- Plan your menu. Whether you're serving dinner for eight or just hors d'oeuvres, write down each dish you plan to have. If working with a caterer, consult with him or her.

- If you're doing the party on your own, try to select some dishes you can cook ahead and freeze.

- Assemble all the recipes for the dishes that need to be prepared.

- Go through the recipes and make a complete list of all ingredients. Even make note of the items you're "sure" you have. There's nothing worse than discovering you're out of a necessary ingredient the day of the party!

- Check the list against the items you have on hand.

- Divide the list into categories for easier grocery shopping, or simply transfer the needed items onto one of the form grocery lists described in Chapter 30.

- Go back through the recipes and separate out those dishes that can be made in advance. Also group the recipes that will need to be made at the last minute. (Although I don't recommend last-minute dishes!)

- Consider your liquor needs. A well-stocked bar would contain a good representation of the following:

  - Beer
  - Bourbon
  - Brandy
  - Champagne
  - Gin
  - Rum

  - Scotch
  - Vermouth
  - Vodka
  - Whisky
  - Wine, red and white

- Ask at the liquor store about how much you should get based on the number of guests who are coming.

- You'll also want to have on hand:

  - Club soda
  - Cola and diet soda
  - Lemons
  - Limes

  - Mineral water
  - Olives
  - Tomato and orange juice
  - Tonic water

If you know the drinking habits of your friends, you may be able to narrow the above lists somewhat.

- Here are some miscellaneous items you may need to shop for:

  - Candies
  - Cocktail napkins
  - Decorations

  - Paper plates, napkins, and cups
  - Placecards
  - Plastic glasses

- In addition, you will want to have the following on hand:

  - Bottle opener
  - Can opener
  - Coasters
  - Corkscrew
  - Dish towels
  - Guest towels
  - Hand soaps

  - Ice
  - Ice bucket
  - Matches for candles
  - Napkins
  - Paper towels
  - Place mats
  - Tablecloth

■ If shopping will be done by two people, decide in advance who will purchase what.

To Do: One Week in Advance

■ Call to confirm all orders and arrangements, including any help you have coming (bartender, cook, server, babysitter, musician), and tell them to arrive earlier than they are really needed. That way traffic problems or some type of delay won't cause you to panic. They should still arrive well before the guests do.

■ Unless you have a "smoke-free" house, have plenty of ashtrays on hand.

■ Be sure you have enough hangers.

Food Preparation: One Week in Advance

■ Prepare and freeze any of the dishes that can be made in advance.

To Do: One to Two Days in Advance

■ Get out the serving pieces and linens.

■ Get down the china and crystal, and check to see if they need to be washed.

■ Get out the silver and see if it needs polishing.

■ Clean your home or apartment.

■ Think about your space needs for the event. Should the furniture be arranged differently?

■ Be sure you have a good supply of dish towels and paper towels on hand.

■ Unless you're paying the help by check, arrange to have cash.

■ Create a time chart to help guide you on the day of the party. Plan at what time you need to set the table (early), when the oven needs to be turned on, and so forth. This type of chart is also helpful for anyone who is going to help you. Create a list of their tasks and the time at which each should be done so that everything will go like clockwork.

Food Preparation: One to Two Days in Advance

▪ Organize the dishes that need to be made the day of the party—especially those (such as stir-frying) that have to be done just prior to or at the time of the meal. Premeasure as many ingredients as you can and keep them in small dishes or measuring cups, covered and wrapped in plastic wrap. Group them by recipe in your refrigerator.

To Do: The Day of the Event

▪ Set the table as early as possible.

▪ If you live in an apartment building with a doorman, give the guest list to him.

▪ Clear off the kitchen counters.

▪ Run the dishwasher before the guests come so that it is empty and ready for party dishes.

▪ Do a last-minute straightening of the house, and wipe down the bathrooms to clean off water spots and fingerprints.

▪ Put out hand towels.

Food Preparation: The Day of the Event

▪ Get out any of the utensils and dishes you will need for cooking.

▪ Use a tray to organize the ingredients needed to prepare dishes that must be made just prior to or during the party.

▪ Use the kitchen timer as a reminder for various things, such as to start preparing a certain dish or to take something out of the refrigerator.

▪ Cheese should be removed from the refrigerator one hour before being served so that it will reach room temperature.

- Red wine should be opened an hour in advance so that it can "breathe." White wine should be chilled in advance, and can even be opened and recorked before refrigerating to save you time once your guests arrive.
- Prepare breadbaskets in advance.
- Fill ice bucket.

For the Future

- Keep a record in the back of your Household Notebook (see Chapter 26), or create an Entertaining category in your file cabinet, which should include a guest list of those who attended as well as those who were unable to come. Note the date, time, and food served, and keep an itemized list of costs. Make notes regarding things that could have gone better, comments on the food, and ideas for the future. This will be helpful in planning another party.

39

Travel Planning

For some people, travel problems begin the moment a trip is being planned—so many unfamiliar things to do, so many details to take care of. What flights will be best? Where shall we stay? What arrangements must be worked out at home? The questions go on and on.

For others, problems don't arise until it's almost time for them to leave: They didn't get as much office work done as they'd intended; they're worried about leaving the children behind; they're exhausted from burning the midnight oil by packing at the last minute; and there's always the nagging feeling that something has been forgotten.

Yet whether you're traveling for business or pleasure, being away provides you with a change of scene that can be interesting, fun, and often relaxing. An unsettling departure detracts from some of these benefits since the disorganized traveler must often contend with more than his or her share of unforeseen problems. The following travelers would have benefited from better planning.

After reading only an ad in their newspaper's travel section, one couple departed for what they naively assumed would be a lovely Labor Day weekend at a luxury dude ranch, only to discover that facilities were extremely modest and service almost nonexistent. For instance, the driver of the bus that was to pick them up at the train station simply forgot to meet the train! And after they telephoned the resort, the couple still had to wait several hours before they were picked up.

Another family forgot to book their airline seats at the time they bought their tickets. They arrived at the airport to discover that the only seats available for the parents and two toddlers were four separate seats in different parts of the plane. Only after several discussions with airline personnel were they able to get their seats changed.

Another woman grew up in a family in which they often went on long car trips. Invariably, their first stop was pulling into a gas station so that they could phone a neighbor (who had a house key) to stop in and make sure the morning tea kettle had been turned off.

Traveling is hard work in terms of detail management, and of course, the above examples are very human stories. However, think how much more pleasant your trip would be if you had a useful checklist (for such things as turning off the tea kettle), and had thought through your trip plans and made certain standing arrangements in order to minimize the disruptions of travel.

Here are some suggestions that should improve your frame of mind at departure, make your time away more enjoyable, and help better prepare you for a smooth return.

Advance Planning

- Use a good travel agent, one whose knowledge about plane routes and airfares can save you both time and money. Make sure your agent knows your seating preference (aisle or window), so that he or she can book a seat and get a boarding pass for you ahead of time.

- Call ahead regarding meals if you don't want the traditional airline fare. Most airlines offer low-calorie, low- or no-salt, low-cholesterol, vegetarian, kosher, fish, and children's meals. You should let your travel agent know your preferences.

- If you're traveling abroad, purchase enough of the appropriate currency before you leave to pay for getting to your hotel, making phone calls, and the like.

- Make a photocopy of your passport and take it with you if you're traveling overseas. If the original is lost or stolen, the nearest U.S. embassy can use the photocopy to issue a new one immediately.

- Write an itinerary of your trip. Include phone numbers and addresses of the places you'll be staying each night as well as airline and flight details. Make four copies. Give one copy to someone at work; another copy to the person looking after your home or apartment, and take one with you. Pack another copy in your suitcase, so that if your luggage gets lost, it can be sent to you at any stage of your trip.

- At the office, delegate as much as possible. Leave clear instructions as to how certain issues should be handled so that you won't have to do it when you return.

- Look over your calendar. Reschedule any appointments that fall during the time you'll be away.

- Plan for a free day when you return. If you're going on a trip of any length, try to schedule it so that you can stay home your first day back. This will give you the time to take care of the laundry and cleaning, to pick up the dog, et cetera.

- Arrange for a friend or neighbor to bring in mail and newspapers so that they don't accumulate. Does someone need to take care of your plants or pet? Leave him or her written instructions as to what to do. You can streamline this process by writing the instructions once. Then make photocopies of the information and file it for future trips. That way you'll never need to write those instructions again.

- If you have household help, tell them you'll be away and discuss any special tasks to be undertaken. If there is no ironing because you are gone, would you like to have the cupboards cleaned instead?

- If no one will be at home while you're gone, go through the refrigerator to throw out food that will spoil. Stock up on items you can freeze and use after your return.

- Arrange for a grocery order upon your return.

- Pack (see Chapter 40). Start this two days prior to departure.

- Confirm your plane reservation and double-check your overnight arrangements.

- Be sure you have photo identification with you. For security reasons, airlines are now requesting that all ticketed passengers show ID at the time they check in for the flight.

- Get a copy of a current pocket flight guide. If your plane is canceled or you miss a flight, you can map out a new flight plan for yourself.

- Purchase a telephone calling card, or carry six or eight quarters for pay telephones and a good supply of one dollar bills for tipping.
- Take any phone numbers or travel directions you may need.
- As a welcome home gift, put fresh linens on the bed for your return.

For the Children

If children will be staying behind with a grandparent or caregiver, refer to Chapter 57 for additional advice.

Before You Walk Out the Door

- Check to see that you have keys, directions, money, tickets, and an itinerary.
- If you live alone or if other family members will be away too, you'll also want to do the following:
  - Run the dishwasher early enough that it will have finished before you depart.
  - Shut and lock windows.
  - Unplug appliances.
  - Adjust thermostat.
  - Be sure the stove is off.
  - Take out the trash.
  - Leave on a light and/or radio with a timer.
  - Lock all doors.

The Trip

- Travel in comfortable clothes such as no-wrinkle knit or wool jersey slacks. Wear a sweater (in the summer you can wear a light cotton one) in case it's chilly on the train, plane, or bus. A pair of travel slippers is handy for long airplane flights.

- If you are traveling from cold to warmer weather, consider wearing layered clothing. Upon reaching your destination, you can remove the outer layers and you'll be all set for the new climate!

- If this is a business trip, take along a special file or envelope to keep track of the information and papers you will be collecting (business cards, reports, fliers, receipts, and so on). If your work is going to generate a lot of paperwork, try to handle as much as possible while you're away.

- Plan to arrive at the airport one hour early to check in and check your bags before departure.

At the Hotel

- When you are first shown to your hotel room, check the bathroom, bed, and pillows. Test the air conditioner or heater and try out the television. If you're not satisfied, now is the time to discuss the possibility of a room change.

- Once in a satisfactory room, check for the fire exit. Read the hotel literature regarding escape methods.

- Request a hair dryer, ironing board, or iron, if needed. Most housekeeping departments now supply these at little or no charge.

- If you'll be in a rush the next morning, place your breakfast order with room service the might before.

Your Return

While it always feels good to come home, the part that is often the least pleasant is coping with the accumulation of mail and messages that have come in while you were away. Here are some tips to help you manage:

- Both at home and at the office, set aside a couple of hours to sort through mail and paperwork. Try to do this as soon as possible after your arrival.

- Set priorities on the items you will handle first.
- Try to return all telephone calls at one sitting.
- At the office, check with coworkers about any events that may have occurred while you were away.
- Check your calendar so that you're prepared for upcoming events.
- Select reading material or simple work projects you might be able to fit into odd moments of the day, such as while you're waiting at the bank. Carry those items with you and pull them out when you have time.

40

Travel Packing

What happened to my best friend should never happen to anyone. When her husband was asked to argue a case in front of the U.S. Supreme Court in Washington, D.C., she wanted to go along. Upon arriving at the hotel, she opened her suitcases and realized that in her excitement she had packed all the right blouses and jackets but had totally forgotten to pack her skirts. She literally had nothing to wear!

Had my friend been using an orderly system for packing, she would have arrived with all her outfits intact. However, many people are nearly paralyzed by the decision-making process involved in taking a trip, so they tend to prepare in a haphazard manner—usually at the last minute. (My sister's honeymoon was delayed because instead of going directly to the airport after the reception, they had to go back to her new husband's apartment so he could pack!)

One client of mine starts early enough; however, to me, her system seems equally fraught with potential disasters. She calls her method the "lazy woman's" way of packing. About a week before her trip she opens her suitcase and just keeps throwing into it things she knows she'll want. In addition to the inconvenience of having certain items out of circulation for a week, this approach offers no method for verifying that she has what she needs. Apparently it works for her, but there are better ways to pack.

Developing a system that works for you will make packing a simple procedure, and will allow you to leave for any type of trip feeling comfortable and well prepared.

Let's begin by checking to be sure you have the right travel equipment and accessories:

- Check your luggage to make sure it is roomy and sturdy enough to accommodate what you plan to take. If you're buying new items, look for lightweight bags. Larger pieces should have wheels built into the bottom to make them easier to transport.

▪ Invest in a good piece of light, carry-on luggage. Companies today are offering roomy styles with wheels that can be quite handy. Whenever possible, you should limit your luggage to carry-on to avoid having to wait while the baggage is sorted after the flight.

▪ Be sure you have luggage tags for your bags (inside and out). Some airlines insist that all suitcases have external labels, so you'll save yourself time at the airport if your bags are already tagged. (If you have a suitcase that looks like everyone else's, tie a fabric ribbon around the handle for easy identification at the bag carrousel.)

▪ Visit a store that carries travelers' aids such as small alarm clocks, shower caps, portable wash lines, collapsible plastic hangers, sewing kits, travel irons, electric voltage adapters, and small plastic bottles. But don't buy anything you won't really use.

Planning

Planning is the next step, and several weeks before (when possible) is not too early to begin thinking about what you'll need for the trip. You may need extra time to get shoes repaired or to shop for items you don't already have (bathing suit coverup, etc.).

As soon as you know you are going out of town, begin to prepare a checklist of everything you think you'll need for your trip. You can probably use the checklist on pages 212-213 as a starting point.

▪ Using the checklist, consider every aspect of your trip and note down clothing, accessories, medications, reading material, and emergency supplies. Try to anticipate everything you might need for the locale you'll be in and the kinds of things you'll be doing.

▪ When planning what clothes to take, prepare for all weather possibilities. When Indian summer turns to crisp fall overnight,

TRAVEL CHECKLIST

Clothing

_____	Belts	_____	Jeans	_____	Slippers
_____	Blouses	_____	Raincoat	_____	Slips
_____	Boots	_____	Robe	_____	Socks
_____	Bras	_____	Scarves	_____	Stockings
_____	Coat	_____	Shirts	_____	Suits
_____	Dresses	_____	Shoes	_____	Sweaters
_____	Gloves	_____	Skirts	_____	Swimsuit
_____	Gowns	_____	Slacks	_____	Ties
_____	Hats	_____	Sleepwear	_____	Underwear
_____	Jackets				

Grooming Items

_____	Aftershave	_____	Moist towelettes
_____	Brush, comb	_____	Mouthwash
_____	Cottonballs	_____	Perfume
_____	Cotton swabs	_____	Razor blades
_____	Creams, lotions		or shaver
_____	Dental floss	_____	Shampoo,
_____	Deodorant		conditioner
_____	Feminine needs	_____	Shaving kit
_____	Hairclips, pins,	_____	Showercap
	ornaments	_____	Soap
_____	Hair curlers,	_____	Sunblock lotion
	curling iron	_____	Talc
_____	Hair dryer	_____	Toothbrush
_____	Hair spray	_____	Toothpaste
_____	Makeup	_____	Tweezers
_____	Manicure items		

Medical Items

_____	Adhesive bandages	_____	Prescription and
_____	Backup pair of		necessary
	glasses or pre-		nonprescription
	scription for		medications
	glasses	_____	Thermometer
_____	First-aid ointment	_____	Vitamins
_____	Insect repellent		

Additional Items

_____	Address book	_____	Jewelry
_____	Alarm clock	_____	Pen
_____	Camera and film	_____	Playing cards
_____	Cash, traveler's	_____	Radio
	checks	_____	Reading material
_____	Checkbook	_____	Safety pins
_____	Converter,	_____	Scissors
	electric (for	_____	Sewing kit
	foreign travel)	_____	Stamps
_____	Credit cards	_____	Sunglasses
_____	Cufflinks,	_____	Travel tickets
	collar stays	_____	Umbrella
_____	Flashlight		

you could be left shivering if you didn't pack a sweater or wrap of some kind. But be realistic. Overdoing "just-in-case" items can weigh you down. One person I know took snow hats on a trip to Acapulco just in case the plane had to make an emergency landing in the middle of a snowstorm en route. That's what I mean by overdoing it!

- If you're hesitant to leave one or two "just-in-case" items behind, try to determine whether or not you *could* purchase the item at your destination if you needed to. A friend felt it was worth traveling with a one-week supply of disposable diapers for her one-year-old when she learned that they were not yet available for purchase where she was visiting overseas. To help you make such decisions, talk to people who have recently visited the places you are going.

- Avoid excess bulk. Select clothes that coordinate, and keep your choices to a minimum. Most of us take too much.

- Buy a small folding coatrack where you can display all items of clothing before you pack them. Seeing your clothes together often helps you eliminate the excess or discover a problem (missing button, stain on shirt, etc.). Many clients have reported night-before-departure panic when they realize that a favorite suit needed cleaning and there was no time to get it done. It's important to pack your clothes in first-class condition—clean, unwrinkled, and ready to wear.

The "Ever-Ready" Toiletry Kit

When it comes to packing, a permanently prepared toiletry kit is a must. Why pack and repack the same items every trip?

- For the kit, choose a small case (preferably a transparent, soft-sided, waterproof bag). The number of toiletries to be packed should be the determining factor as to bag size.

- Invest in an extra toothbrush, shaver, and hairbrush to keep permanently packed in your kit.

- Buy travel-sized toothpaste, shampoo, lotion, and aspirin, reserved for travel use.

- Transfer items such as your facial cleanser into small plastic bottles (available at travel and drugstores). Any liquids you must take should be in tightly sealed plastic containers, filled only three-fourths of the way, and put in secured plastic bags. At the end of each trip, refill any that are getting low.

- Compartmentalize your toiletry bag for easy retrieval. Divide essentials into categories: body care (lotion, deodorant), makeup (foundation, lipstick), hair care (shampoo, conditioner), and dental items (toothpaste, toothbrush, and floss).
- Try to travel with as few spillables as possible. But if you feel you absolutely must take your own bottle of Pepto-Bismol, wrap and pack it *very* carefully, preferably in your toiletry bag. My cousin learned that lesson the hard way when he opened his suitcase and discovered his bottle of Pepto-Bismol coating everything but his stomach. To ensure against this, carry doubtful items on the plane with you.
- Use scented lotion instead of perfume. It saves space and avoids the chance of costly spills.
- Call ahead regarding hair dryers. Many hotels now provide them, and this will mean you'll have one less thing to bring.

Your Carry-On Bag

For trips during which you'll check some luggage, you'll still want a good carry-on bag. Items that are too important to be without and that will make plane travel more pleasant are those you'll pack in your carry-on bag.

- Buy a lightweight, compartmentalized bag (smaller than the carry-on bag you would use for clothes for a short trip).
- Plan to carry tickets, jewelry, toiletries, important papers, a pocket flight guide, maps, money, your address book, and passport (for foreign travel).
- To pass the time, have on hand your laptop, business material you haven't had time to study, a novel you've been longing to read, or personal stationery with which to catch up on correspondence.
- For additional comfort: Pressurization on planes dries out the air, so a small tube of moisturizer or hand lotion can keep you feeling refreshed. Men might carry a disposable razor for a quick shave before reaching their destination. Other items to consider carrying on board might include moist towelettes, toothbrush

and toothpaste, tissues, a small container of freshening facial cleanser, and a pen and pocket-sized notebook for jotting down thoughts, questions, and ideas.

Packing

You should actually begin putting items in your bags about two days before your departure. It's too tiring to pack the night before when you'll have other details to take care of such as last-minute instructions to co-workers or to the person who will be watching the house, and so forth. (I shudder when I think of one friend who is always up until 3 A.M. the night before her trip doing laundry and ironing.)

- Begin by hanging or laying out your garments.

- When departing with more than one piece of luggage, divide your clothes among the suitcases. This avoids being left with only a suitcase full of your shoes and underwear while your bag filled with suits and dresses is lost.

- Just as department stores use tissue paper to transport your purchases wrinkle-free, you can do the same by saving the paper acquired in gifts and purchases to fold within your clothing when packing. Some people like to roll their clothing rather than laying it flat. With some items it takes up less room and can prevent wrinkling.

- Put heavier, most wrinkle-resistant items (sweaters, robe, jeans) on the bottom. To minimize wasted space, alternate the layers of remaining clothes: first, a layer from left to right, then one from front to back.

- Store underwear and hosiery in separate, transparent plastic bags, and tuck them into the corners of your suitcase.

- Pack items inside one another. For example, socks and shoehorn should go inside shoes, hosiery inside a folded sweater.

- Put your shoes, paired, in plastic bags or cloth shoebags and place them along the sides of the suitcase as you are packing. Since these will probably be the heaviest items in your luggage, keep them to a minimum.

- The nooks and crannies that remain should be filled with rolled-up belts, socks, and scarves. These items will cushion and hold the other items when the suitcase is closed and standing upright.

- If you can anticipate your needs ahead of time, make sure that the last layer of clothing you pack will be the articles you will need first upon your arrival.

- Plastic bags are useful for laundry and to hold clothes that may be damp.

- Some people like to pack clothes right along with their hangers. Women may want to take along extra skirt hangers.

- Pack a lightweight tote bag. It will surely come in handy while you are away and you can use it coming home if you need to.

- Add a sachet to keep your clothes smelling fresh.

- When packing to come home, you may fear you'll never be able to fit in the extras you bought. Roll your clothing instead of laying it flat.

- Keep your checklist! While there will always be variations in clothing, it will serve as a helpful guide in packing the next time. You need never forget your address book or sunglasses again!

PART VI

Personal Agenda

41 Beauty Routine

42 Dates to Remember

43 Doctors: Organizing a Selective Search

44 Errands

45 Gift Shopping

46 Handbag

47 Briefcase

48 How to Stop Losing Things

49 Organizing Your Spouse

50 Wardrobe Shopping for Women

51 Wardrobe Shopping for Men

41

Beauty Routine

I once needed to attend a meeting with a beauty/fashion consultant and since we both lived in the same neighborhood, we decided to share a cab to midtown. I was very surprised when she came downstairs and got into the cab fully dressed but with no makeup. She then proceeded to pull out a small pouch and spent ten of the fifteen minutes we were in the cab applying foundation, eye makeup, blusher, and lipstick. When we arrived, she looked terrific!

Since most of us can't count on having a hands-free cab ride for doing our makeup (let alone having the ability to apply makeup in a bump-filled excursion), it's important to establish a simple beauty regimen that becomes an easy and natural part of the day.

The key to an efficient beauty routine lies partly in organizing your supplies so they are accessible and convenient, but it also has to do with making the routine a matter of habit.

Here's how to get started:

Simplifying Your Morning Routine

- Consider your haircut. With today's easy styles, there is no reason to wear one that requires much effort. Choose a cut that is easy to care for, and then get it trimmed regularly so that you benefit fully from the easy styling.

- Consider your skin care system. Are you mixing and matching various soaps and moisturizers depending on what's handy that day? Instead, choose one basic skin care treatment, perhaps one where all the products are designed to go together. It will be easier to follow, and you'll have two or three products to store instead of many.

■ Consider your makeup routine. Try to establish one or two simple "looks," using minimal amounts of products. Visit a makeup consultant at one of your local department stores to help you select complementary products and make a fresh start.

Organizing Your Makeup

■ Evaluate the area where you put on your makeup. Is this the best place to do it? Is the lighting good? Is there a convenient spot for storing your makeup? If you use a vanity, devote a drawer to it. If you apply your makeup in the bathroom, select a convenient place to store it.

■ Go through your makeup and toss what you no longer use. Also throw out those items that are more than a year old or that you think you might not use again—you probably won't, and makeup doesn't age well. Some products gather bacteria and can even be dangerous to use if allowed to sit for a long period of time.

■ Buy a compartmentalized plastic caddy for your makeup with separate slots for lipstick and brushes, and places for foundation and blusher.

■ Within the caddy, organize the items by type. For example, store all brushes in one spot, all lipsticks in another, and all eye shadows in another. Items used first (or most frequently) should be most accessible.

■ Consider an all-purpose makeup kit (available at most department stores), complete with coordinated eye, cheek, and lip colors.

■ When your makeup needs to be altered with the changing of the seasons (more moisturizing products for winter; lighter products for summer), pack away the cosmetics you don't use during the current season.

■ When you find a product that works, stick with it.

■ Keep lotion and handcream in all the rooms where you use it— in the bathroom, the kitchen, and the bedroom. A pump-style lotion dispenser saves times, and for double duty, rub cream or lotion into your cuticles while you're applying it to your hands.

- Use clear nail polish. It's easier to touch up if it gets chipped, and it doesn't need to be applied as frequently as colored polish.

- Pick up travel-sized makeup items and extras of lipstick, mascara, and blusher to store in a makeup pouch at the office or to carry with you in your purse.

- For travel, keep a lightweight makeup bag stocked and ready to go with all your essentials. Stock up on travel-sized quantities of skin care and makeup items, and buy sample sizes of items such as lotion and shampoo. When you get home, replace your travel supplies so you'll automatically be ready for the next trip.

Establishing Your Routine

Next time you take a trip, note how much more you must concentrate on applying your makeup simply because your products aren't where your hands are trained to find them. If you've not yet developed a system that your hands seem to perform automatically, you've not simplified your routine as much as possible. Here's how to do so:

- Choose a specific time of day (after your morning shower or before breakfast) when you apply your makeup, and do it at that same time every day—including weekends. The more automatically the routine is performed, the more quickly you can do it.

- Establish a set routine for putting on your makeup (concealer followed by foundation, followed by powder, etc.).

- In the morning, stay in one room until you've finished everything you need to do there. For example, after your shower, stay in the bathroom and do your makeup while you're waiting for your hair to dry.

- Establish a set time for appointments such as weekly manicures so they become an expected part of your schedule.

- "Double up" on time. Time spent commuting can be perfect for muscle-firming exercises. If you're not driving, you can also touch up your makeup. Time spent watching the news or your favorite television program is a perfect opportunity to give yourself a manicure. And before sitting down at your desk, give yourself a facial that can work while you pay your bills.

42

Dates to Remember

My husband is often late with cards and gifts. After he'd forgotten to buy anything for our ninth wedding anniversary, I put him on "notice" and said he had one year to plan for our tenth. So there would be no excuses, I kept reminding him as the date grew nearer. On the morning of our anniversary, he did present me with a wonderful gift—but much to his chagrin, he'd still forgotten the card!

If you've cornered the market on belated birthday cards (or even if you've only missed one or two special dates this year), you're causing yourself needless frustration by having forgotten to send good wishes to someone you care about.

When it comes to special occasions, late is better than never, but nothing beats being on time. All that's required for remembering important dates is a simple system that works for you. Here are several from which to choose:

The Birthday Book

Stationery, gift, and specialty stores usually carry special datebooks (actually called birthday books) that are designed for keeping track of special occasions. Museum gift shops frequently sell ones that are especially beautiful. One advantage of the birthday book is that it can be used year after year, so you need to record only once the dates you want to remember.

- Buy a birthday book you find appealing. (You may want to buy two or three—they make great gifts!)
- Enter all the special occasions of which you want to be reminded.

▪ As you make each entry, also note the year of the birth or, for anniversaries, the year of the marriage. That way you can always figure out how old Mary's son is, and fortieth birthdays and silver wedding anniversaries won't slip by without appropriate fanfare.

▪ Consult your birthday book at the end of each month to note the special dates for the weeks ahead.

▪ The only way the birthday book can fail you is if you forget to use it. If you're just starting out with this system, make a note in your calendar or Tickler File (see below) for the next few months to remind yourself to consult your book.

Calendar Reminders

If you don't think you can adjust to referring to a special book regularly, a calendar reminder method whereby you note a person's birthday or a special occasion on the upcoming year's calendar may work better for you. (If you're working with a calendar on computer or one of the hand-held electronic calendars, this information will transfer from year to year, saving you the time of rewriting it.)

▪ Go through your calendar today and note all special occasions you intend to remember.

▪ Use a special color of ink, perhaps red or turquoise, to distinguish these notations from other information.

▪ In late December, sit down and transfer all the dates from the old calendar to the new one. Because you've used a special color, the notations should pop out at you, thus minimizing the chance of error when making the annual date transfer.

Tickler Files

Your Tickler Files (see Chapter 12) offer another simple way to be reminded of special occasions. With this system, you'll pull out your reminder at the beginning of each month.

- Using a separate card for each month, record special occasions on index cards, which can then be filed in the appropriate file folders.

- In order to plan and buy in advance, put the February card in the January file (so that in January you'll be thinking of the February dates you need to shop for) and the March card in the February file, and so on. This gives you enough warning to plan for occasions falling early in the following month.

Use a Service

In some parts of the country, department and specialty stores are responding to customers' lack of time and are developing a new type of service. For an annual fee, they will do your shopping for you—hunting for something you suggest (or they recommend)—and sending out a wrapped gift on time.

Following Through

Regardless of the system you choose, nothing works unless you follow through.

- Establish a regular time each month to review upcoming dates and shop for all the cards or gifts you will need in the coming weeks.

- Purchase a selection of blank cards that will serve a variety of purposes (get well, congratulations, thank you, happy birthday) for those times when something unexpected comes up.

- Upon arriving home with your newly purchased cards, address and sign each one. Write the date they are to be mailed in the corner where the stamp should go. Store the cards in a mail or "out" basket near your front door and put a stamp on them the day they are to be sent. (Keep a small supply of stamps in the out basket.)

By choosing and using one of these systems, you can say good-bye to those last-minute dashes to the store to get a card or gift. (For tips on gift shopping for holidays and special occasions, see Chapter 45.)

43

Doctors: Organizing a Selective Search

Searching for the right doctor is an important investment in time. Whether you've just moved to a new community or are simply dissatisfied with your current professional, devote the time now. When you need an opinion on your own health or the health of a family member, you'll have access to someone whose opinion you value and trust.

If you've recently switched to some type of managed care health program, you may still have some choice in the matter. Some programs permit you to select your own doctor from those who are members of the plan; others will pay for certain specialists if your regular doctor has referred you elsewhere.

In order to make your search an effective one, it pays to plan carefully.

Getting Referrals

- Ask other doctors. Your internist might recommend a good dermatologist, for example. (If you are working from a managed care list, see which of those doctors come most highly recommended by the doctor with whom you're consulting.)

- Ask friends whose opinions you value. Find out what their experience has been with the doctor, and try to get a sense of the doctor's style from what they describe.

- Call the office of the chief of staff of a hospital (preferably a teaching hospital) or medical center, or the head of a medical school. Ask: "Could you give me the name of your best _____ specialist?"

- Call the office of the hospital's chief resident of the department in which you're interested and ask for a referral.

- Ask nurses. If you know one, he or she may be able to refer you to a hospital nurse who works in the field in which you're interested (obstetrics, orthopedics, etc.), who can then give a referral. If you don't know a nurse to ask, perhaps one of your friends does.

- Add to your list any doctors whose comments impressed you either in print or on radio or television.

Narrowing the Search

Once you have half a dozen names, you'll want to narrow the list by calling the appropriate offices to get some information from the nurse or receptionist. Ask:

- What is the doctor's hospital affiliation?

- How many associates are in the office?

- What provisions are made for night, weekend, and vacation coverage?

- What are the doctor's office hours?

- Are there specific "telephone hours?"

- What is the typical waiting time at an appointment?

- What is the fee structure?

- Where do patients park? (This is an especially helpful question for the elderly or the ill.)

- If you are satisfied with the answers you receive, you can arrange an appointment with the doctor. Policies vary as to whether or not the doctor will schedule a free exploratory chat with you. If not, it is probably worth the money to invest in scheduling office visits with two or three different doctors before making a decision. Some people spread their search out over a year's time and visit the doctors over that period rather than doing it all at one time.

- Once you meet with the doctor, you will want to get answers to some additional questions.

  - What is your experience with (or your opinion on)_____?
  - Do you have a specialty?
  - What do I do if I need to reach you at some time other than office hours?
  - Who covers for you when you aren't available?

- Check the walls in the doctor's office for information regarding what medical school he or she attended.

- While you are waiting to see the doctor, or as you leave, try to talk to other patients who are there. Be sure to ask how long they typically wait to be seen. Pay attention to other information they are willing to share.

Keep in Mind

- *Style.* Do you want someone who is friendly and reassuring, or do you simply want someone with the best medical expertise? Be sure the doctor you select has a style with which you feel comfortable.

- *Age.* Do you feel more at ease with an older, more experienced doctor, or do you feel comfortable with someone about your own age?

- *Gender.* Do you feel more comfortable with a man or a woman?

Making a Decision

- At the end of the visit, were you satisfied? What is your gut reaction?

- Take time to think through the answers to your questions. Were your questions answered carefully?

- Was the doctor caring or condescending?

- Were you rushed, or did the doctor take time with you?

■ If you have any remaining questions (about education, residency, training, age, status in department, etc.) that you don't want to ask the doctor about, phone the hospital or the state's physicians licensing authority.

■ If no one seems right, remember that it may be impossible to find a terrific dermatologist with a "fun" personality. Set priorities, and decide what quality (Brilliant diagnostician? Good bedside manner? Reasonable fee?) is the most important to you in this particular instance.

It's Time to Change When the Doctor Consistently . . .

■ Doesn't remember your name

■ Forgets or confuses your problem (e.g., mixes up your problem of spontaneous abortion—miscarriage—for inability to conceive)

■ Misdiagnoses your problem

■ Doesn't brief you about a procedure

■ Doesn't give a complete explanation about a medication and how to take it

■ Doesn't give proper postoperative instructions

■ Doesn't listen to your instincts about something

■ Is unwilling or unpleasant about reexplaining something you don't understand

44

Errands

How many times have you arrived home from doing errands, only to remember that there was something you forgot? As you venture back out, it may seem like the errands are running you rather than the other way around! The main difficulty people encounter with running errands is they forget to plan ahead. One day I dropped by my neighbor's to see if she needed any help with arrangements for a party she was having that night. She commented about how tired she was from going to the store. Well, it turned out she wasn't tired from *one* trip to the store; she was tired from three. Each time she had come back home, she remembered something else she needed and had to go back out again!

With a little creative planning, you can avoid these last-minute dashes and streamline the chores that fill your free time.

Establishing a System

- An ongoing list is the first step in getting errands done more efficiently. I recommend using your looseleaf Household Notebook (see Chapter 26). Establish a section for items "To Buy" (chandelier lightbulbs, gloves, a new couch), "To Fix" (the suit that needs to go to the tailor or the doll that needs to be taken in for repair), and "To Do" (donate blood, stop by the library, check new hotel for possible place for Mom and Dad to stay). Then you can transfer the items you plan to do each day onto your To Do list in your calendar. Or if you plan a full day of errands, simply take the notebook with you.

- Teach family members to tell you about general errands (shoes that need reheeling, shirts for the laundry, the blender isn't working, etc.) that must be entered into your notebook. Also make it clear that family members should let you know when the supply of items to be purchased (such as shaving cream, shampoo, transparent tape, index cards) is *low,* not out.

■ Anticipate upcoming needs. Buy a season's supply of hosiery, several rolls of stamps, and five or six tubes of toothpaste (especially if you catch a sale!) at the same time.

■ Establish a table, desk, or chair near the front door where you can lay out all you need for upcoming errands (suits for the cleaners; an item to be returned to the store). Your keys, pocketbook, and briefcase should also be located here for an easy exit.

Consolidating Your Errands

■ Always plan your errands around your schedule, not the other way around.

■ On Sunday evening, sit down with your Household Notebook and your calendar, which should also have space for each day's To Do list. Are any of your upcoming appointments in a neighborhood where you can accomplish another chore? If so, write a reminder in your calendar for that day.

■ For regular errands to be done during the week, select one or two blocks of time (after work on Tuesday? during lunch time on Thursday?) when you can conveniently get some errands done. Then list on your calendar what you plan to accomplish.

■ Organize your errands by location. For example, before going out to do errands around your neighborhood, map out a route so that each stop takes you part of the way to the next one. Once you're finished, you can go directly on to your next activity or plan a circle route that brings you back home again.

■ Try to shop during periods of least activity—midmorning rather than noon, for example.

Carryall Convenience

■ Buy an unstructured nylon bag to use for errands. These carryalls are light, completely collapsible (use as a pocketbook/tote or fold up and keep on reserve in your briefcase or car), and easy to wipe out in case of spills. Many feature long straps for shoulder-carrying.

■ Also buy a rain poncho that folds into a small pouch. The poncho is of lighter weight and more compact than a portable umbrella when not in use, and when needed, it keeps your hands free. Also tuck into your carryall an extra plastic shopping bag or two to cover or to carry packages in the rain.

On-the-Go

It's your turn to pay the cashier, you're balancing several parcels, the man behind you is in a rush, and you can't find the right credit card . . . Sound familiar? A few tips may help out:

■ In your wallet, categorize your money by denomination. Don't run the risk of giving a merchant a twenty-dollar bill when you intended to give him one dollar.

■ Alphabetize your credit cards so you'll quickly be able to find the ones you want.

■ Organize your purse for convenient shopping (see Chapter 46). Items you may need on your errands—shopping list, pen, calculator—should be kept in an outer flap or some other easily accessible spot.

■ Since you will need your shopping receipts when you get home (to verify charges, in case of possible returns, and for tax purposes), always ask that the receipts be handed to you rather than dropped in the bag. Then store them in one part of your wallet, handbag, or briefcase where you can sort through them later. To separate business and home receipts when shopping, simply carry two different colored envelopes and do part of the sorting right there in the store.

■ Always carry some change and/or tokens in your pocket so you'll have change for a phone call or a token for the bus. Phone cards are terrific to have along, too.

The Homecoming

"What do you do when you get home with all the packages?" asked one of my clients who told a story about how she had been putting things away for half an hour one night when she realized she hadn't even taken off her coat.

Other people tend to arrive home, dump their packages, and let days go by before putting everything away.

Remember the chair or table near the door? Well, that's your home base for arrival too. Here's how to proceed from there:

- Unload all parcels as you come in.

- As soon as you've put away your coat and hat, return and start putting things away.

- Begin by putting away perishables.

- Categorize items by room to avoid unnecessary trips.

- Unwrap items as you go and clip tags before putting away. You may be in a rush the day you need them.

Tips to Save Wear and Tear

- Get to know merchants in the neighborhood who can help smooth the errand process. The owner of the local pharmacy might cash a check over the weekend, for example.

- Take advantage of any merchant who will pick up and deliver. (If your cleaner is one of them, keep a checklist of items left there in your Household Notebook to verify that everything is returned.)

- Anytime you can find a professional—manicurist, haircutter, exercise instructor—who will come to your home or office, take advantage of it.

- If you have extra time before or after an appointment, pull out your Notebook and see what you can get done.

- If you happen to pass by a specialty shop and remember something you need, stop in and buy it right away.

- Prepare for possible waiting time during the errand-running process. Write down a menu, plan a party list in your Notebook, or read while waiting in line.

- Ask family members to help out with errands.

What to Do When You Dread Doing an Errand

We all have certain things we just hate doing, like returning an item or dropping things off at a tailor who is clear across town. Here's how to overcome your own resistance:

- Ask, "What will happen if I don't do this task?" If there are no dire consequences, forget it.

- Cooperate. Team up with another parent for buying supplies for a school picnic, for example.

- Trade. If your neighbor will shop for something you need near his office, offer to do something special for him.

- Nervous about returning merchandise? Enlist a friend for moral support.

- Pay someone to do it for you. It might be worth it!

45

Gift Shopping

How often have you received one of the following as a gift:

- A shirt or blouse two sizes too big—or too small?
- A sweater in a shade you detest and would *never* wear?
- An outfit that would have been perfect for you—five years ago?
- An absolutely useless knickknack?

While there is no way to prevent others from giving you the unwanted and the unusable, you can avoid contributing to the white elephant collection of others by organizing your gift-buying system.

By making gift-buying a year-round process you will save time (no rushing around at the last minute) and money (how often have you said, "I don't care what it costs, I need a gift for tonight!"). You'll also find that your gifts are more appreciated because they'll show the thought and planning that went into them.

Buying gifts for others is a two-step process. First, you need to *remember* that a birthday or anniversary is drawing near (see Chapter 42); then you need to have a system for choosing an appropriate gift.

Establishing a System

- Establish a Gifts file in your file cabinet (as suggested in Chapter 12) where you can store gift lists as well as clippings and articles about perfect gifts for family and friends.
- Buy 5" × 8" index cards.
- On the front of each card, write the name of a friend, family member, or business associate with whom you exchange gifts. (This could also be done on your computer, but make a printout for your file.) Note the date of birth (and other important occasions). Make notes about the person's likes and dislikes.

Note sizes, favorite colors, hobbies, and special interests. The
front of the card will also be used for noting gift ideas. Whenever
you think of a terrific gift idea, write it down immediately! The
front of a card for a friend might look like this:

TRACEY ROLANDS

Birthday: March 11, 1960   Blouse size: 10

Favorite colors: pink and blue   Sweater: medium

Collects antique clothing and loves floppy hats
Hobbies include photography and home restoration
Gift ideas: handmade photo albums (at J.J. and Co.); also try
country auction for other ideas

▪ On the back of the card, keep a running record of what you give
each year. That way you'll avoid giving the same gift twice. A
sample card for your father might look like this:

DAD

Birthday 1996	book on coin collecting
Christmas 1996	shirt and tie
Birthday 1997	engraved shoe horn
Christmas 1997	V-neck sweater

▪ How to use the system? At the beginning of each month, when you
consult your birthday book (see Chapter 42) or Tickler File and
note down whose birthday is coming up, simply go to your Gifts
file and pull the appropriate index cards. You've automatically got
all the information you need to buy a thoughtful, personal gift!

▪ If a gift is business-related, it may be tax deductible. Keep a
record of these gifts in the Taxes section of your Household
Affairs Folder, or note it in your computer software if you use a
program for your personal finances. You can check on the
deductibility with your tax preparer at the end of the year.

Getting It Done

- See Chapter 44 for tips on faster, easier shopping.

- Scout out small boutiques and specialty stores where you can shop for unusual items without having to fight long lines. When you do need to shop in department stores, be sure to go as soon as the stores open, when they're likely to be less crowded.

- "Buy it when you see it" is a good rule of thumb. Make all types of gift-buying (even Christmas) a year-round project. If you wait, you may have difficulty finding the item that seemed so perfect when you saw it a few months ago.

- Shopping by mail or phone is a time-saver. That item you saw while flipping through a catalog may solve the dilemma of what to give your dad for Father's Day. And if the gift must be mailed elsewhere, have the store or mail-order house do it for you.

- When you get home, wrap it up! Almost as bad as not having a gift on hand is discovering at the last minute that the one you have isn't wrapped. Note its contents on a detachable label. Or if you know who will receive it, put on the appropriate gift tag.

- Keep extra gifts on hand for unexpected needs. Stock up on exotic mustards, spices, jams, and vinegars, which can be attractively packed in a basket or box for a handy, last-minute gift.

- Consider gifts that don't require shopping: a magazine subscription (roll up a current issue and put a bow around it); tickets to the theater, a concert, or sports event; membership in a local museum; a handwritten card informing the person of something you've set up for them—a massage, a class, a visit to a palm reader or psychic; an IOU such as offering to clean a closet, babysit, or run an errand.

If you implement these suggestions, what happened to my cousin won't happen to you. At the last minute, she realized that she hadn't purchased a gift for her friend's birthday. Then she remembered an unopened bottle of fine wine she had received as a gift a few months before. How embarrassed she was when the present was opened and her friend commented that it was the exact same gift that she had given my cousin for her last birthday!

46

Handbag

When I give speeches about getting organized to groups of women, I often begin my talk by requesting that they take out their handbags and see how quickly they can locate a quarter for a telephone call. You'd be surprised at how few women can produce one quickly! What would happen if I put that test to you?

You *should* have an organized handbag. It's a nuisance to have to take several moments to fish for a pen, and it's nothing short of dangerous not to be able to put your hands on your car or house keys quickly at night.

First, you'll need a well-made, functional bag. Choose one with pockets and zippered compartments for categorizing your belongings. (Ideally, look for a pocketbook that will double as a briefcase.) Stay away from a formless bag, as its contents will scatter everywhere within it and you'll constantly be hunting for what you need.

You may want to select a nylon or vinyl bag for wet weather. The contents will stay dry and it can be wiped off easily once you're at home or in the office.

What to carry? Keep it simple. Here are the necessities and some tips for each:

- *Wallet.* Categorize your money by denomination, small bills first. Then you won't mistakenly give a merchant twenty dollars when you intended to give him one dollar. If you have a wallet with two sections for change, put coins in one side and quarters for telephone calls in the other.

- *Credit Card Case.* Alphabetize your cards within the case. Don't forget to make a list of cards and their numbers. Keep one copy of the list at home and one at work or with your spouse, in case you should ever have to cancel them in a hurry. (Now that so many stores accept the major bank cards in addition to their store charge cards, you might consider simplifying your life by reducing the number of cards you carry.)

You can double up on the above by shopping for a wallet/card case combination. It's easier to manage; however, you do run the risk of losing everything if it's stolen.

- *Keys.* Keep them in a pocket or compartment within your bag so they are easily accessible. Identify them by number or use different colors of nail polish to code them, but *don't* put your name and address on the chain.

- *Day Planner.* Use only one appointment calendar, and carry this with you at all times (see Chapter 9).

- *Small Telephone Directory.* Carry frequently called telephone numbers here.

- *Business Card Case.* Keep the case in a special part of your purse where it can be easily located. At a business gathering, slip it in your pocket for greater convenience.

- *Pen and Paper* (or small spiral notebook). Handy for jotting down notes and things to do.

- *Reading Material.* Always have something with you in case you encounter an unexpected delay.

- *Small Pouch.* This can serve one of three purposes:

  • Use it as a bag within a bag. At lunch, transfer valuables, money, keys, and your calendar to the pouch and leave your big bag at the office.

  • Keep all of your cosmetics here.

  • Use it to hold receipts, business cards, and other items given to you during the day.

Take Along for the Unexpected

- *On-the-Go Survival Kit.* In your cosmetic bag or in another small pouch, pack a safety pin or two, Band-Aids, packaged moist towelettes, lip balm, tissues, aspirin, and needle and thread.

- *Stockings.* An extra pair comes in handy when the ones you're wearing run on the way to an important function. Roll them into a small ball and store in a small plastic bag to keep from snagging in your purse.
- *Paper Towels.* On a day when rain is predicted, slip in a few extra paper towels or a hand towel to help dry off rain or snow from your face and hands if you get soaked. (If you're wearing boots that day, carry your shoes in a plastic bag with a drawstring, available at some shoe stores.)

Make a habit of sorting through your pocketbook daily. Take out notes, receipts, and information gathered while out; process them; and make sure your pocketbook is resupplied for the next day.

Though it may be difficult to believe, there are a number of smart, well-groomed women who *never* carry a handbag. They trim down what they want to have with them and carry all their valuables in a few select pockets or in the tiniest pouch. It's something to consider, anyway!

47

Briefcase

When you travel the streets of a big city, where people walk or take public transportation, you begin to realize that men and women use their briefcases to carry *everything:* I've seen people carrying their lunches, their laundry, and even their pets. Some people pack their cases so full that they lean to one side as they carry it.

The most important thing to remember about a briefcase is that its primary purpose is to transport items (usually papers) from one place to another. It is not a suitcase; it is not a storeroom; it is not a place to pack everything you were afraid to leave behind. It is your briefcase. Pack it carefully and it will serve you well.

Shopping for a Briefcase

- Basically, briefcases come in two styles: a hard-sided suitcase type and an expandable type. Personal preference (or the style carried by people in your industry) should dictate which style you choose. However, remember that the expandable type tends to be lighter, though it doesn't always preserve papers as well as the hard-sided style since there's a tendency to overstuff it.

- Look for a briefcase that totally seals so that papers don't get wet in rain or snow.

- A good briefcase has pockets and at least one zippered inside compartment where you can put your belongings. Some brief-cases have sections specifically designed to hold items such as pens, calculators, notebook-size computers, and the like.

- If a style you like doesn't have inner pockets or compartments, you can buy a small zippered travel bag or transparent pencil case to serve this purpose.

- Many people like a pocket on the outside where they can slip their newspaper or magazine for reading in transit.

- Expandable briefcases sometimes come with removable shoulder straps. This can be a real plus for easy hands-free carrying. If that style doesn't work well for you during the business week, consider looking for an inexpensive one with a shoulder strap for travel. Being able to toss the briefcase on your shoulder makes it easier to handle your carry-on luggage.

- Many women find that having a briefcase that doubles as a purse is an additional convenience.

What to Carry

Here are some suggested items to have along. For convenience, they are broken down into categories:

- *Must Have:*

  - Business cards
  - Pad of paper
  - Pen or pencil with eraser
  - Reading material
  - Calendar and address book (to have with you at all times) or your electronic organizer/palmtop computer

- *Would Like to Have:*

  - Calculator
  - Envelopes
  - Extra file folders
  - Highlighter
  - Paper clips
  - Stamps
  - Sticky-backed notepads

■ *Might Come in Handy:*
- Extra set of keys
- Moist towelettes
- Nail file and clipper
- Pain relievers and Band-Aids
- Small tape recorder
- Small sewing kit, such as the ones provided by some hotels
- Stockings (roll and store in a small plastic bag)

■ All small items (pen, stamps, aspirin, sewing kit) should be kept in the compartments of your briefcase (or in small travel bags) for accessibility. Keep personal items in one compartment, desk supplies in another.

■ Be certain that all papers you carry are put in their own file folder and labeled appropriately. (Some people prefer to use manila envelopes.) Within the briefcase, folders can be in chronological order according to the stops you'll be making or in alphabetical order.

Other Tips

■ If you have a business meeting, make a list of what you'll need. Pack your briefcase according to the list. If your list is handy, you'll have an easy way to do a last-minute cross-check to see that you're ready for the meeting.

■ Your briefcase should be thoroughly reorganized at least once a week. Resupply as needed and be certain that items such as your calculator are in good working order. Don't forget to clean out old papers.

48

How to Stop Losing Things

Though everyone has left an umbrella in a taxicab, misplaced a favorite pen, or dropped a glove somewhere, far more often we are frustrated at losing something because we *know* it's right there in front of us—if only we could find it!

One client was fairly efficient about most things, but he didn't have a system for items he used occasionally. Every trip to the library was preceded by a frustrating search of the house for the place where he had last put his library card.

Another person I know simply had no system for anything. She was constantly losing things, but the magnitude of her problem didn't really strike me until the time she went to the store to buy something and lost the purchase on the way home!

The old saying "A place for everything and everything in its place" takes the misery out of losing things. Here are some simple ways to make it work for you.

Don't Scatter—Categorize

- Items used frequently should be placed within easy reach.
- Infrequently used items should be stored away so they don't clutter up the storage areas for more frequently needed things.
- Items that are alike should be kept together. (All stamps, paper, envelopes, and pens or pencils should be stored in or near your desk; barrettes and hair clips and combs should have a special box or drawer in your bureau.)
- Items used together should be stored together. For example, establish a bag where you keep all items for a trip to the beach.

- Items should be stored near where they are used. (Exercise equipment should be kept in the room where you use it; extra tote bags should be near the front door.)
- How to make it work? When you're finished with something, put it back in its place right away.

Establish a Permanent Home for Frequently Used One and Only Items

Here are two examples:

- *Keys.* A special hook, drawer, or bowl on a counter near the door is a good place for them. Always put them there!
- *Glasses.* If you mainly wear them for desk work, keep them in your briefcase or in your desk drawer. If you wear them for driving, keep them in your purse or near the front door.

Storage Tips

- Use color-coding or written labels on boxes for items stored on deep or high shelves. Label everything!
- Egg cartons, film tubes, lazy Susans, Lucite trays (for makeup, etc.), or even homemade drawer partitions fashioned from cardboard can be a great help in categorizing small things. Be imaginative!
- Establish a shelf or box for giveaway items. Add to it as you find things you're tempted to toss.
- Create a gift drawer or shelf so you have a designated spot for presents you purchase ahead of time.
- Junk drawers are a real trap. Don't even consider having one.

49

Organizing Your Spouse

"**I**t's time my husband started making my life easier—I'm tired of picking up after him." Or: "My wife is so disorganized she even forgets to put the milk back in the refrigerator—we need help!" These are common sentiments I hear over and over in the seminars I conduct across the country.

What's more, I can identify with what it's like to live with someone who has a completely different approach to organization. My husband enjoys making lists, and occasionally makes lists of lists. There are many times, though, when he forgets or loses them—leaving him at a loss for the day!

When it comes to organizing your spouse, tolerance will have to be the order of the day. You won't survive as a couple if you try to totally reform him or her. Helpful resolves are the following:

- I respect his or her right to live the way he or she is most comfortable.

- I reserve the right to request certain changes so that his or her sloppiness or disorganization no longer affects me or impedes the overall functioning of the household.

For example, I am more efficient than my husband at getting ready for things, so when we travel, I'm responsible for all the packing; he's responsible for bringing the keys and loading and unloading the car. Rather than argue that I am doing most of the work, I simply accept what he *can* do in this situation. Then in other parts of our life, such as with our tax preparation, he does the lion's share of the work.

So after you've tried yelling, pleading, and other desperate tactics, think "compromise," and improve what you can by using the following tips:

Establishing a System

- Coordinate schedules. Establish at least two nights (such as Wednesday and Sunday) when you sit down together and compare calendars. Make certain that each of you records the plans that affect you both.

- Provide him or her with a specific space so that his or her habits have less effect on you. Separate desks, shelves, closets, and suitcases are a good investment.

- A color-coding system will help identify towels, toothbrushes, and cups.

- When it comes to household chores, ask for his or her input and you'll get more cooperation. A discussion may reveal that he hates to vacuum but doesn't mind doing the dishes. If you don't mind vacuuming, you can each do what you feel is a tolerable chore and thus avoid an argument.

- Divide tasks fairly. Each of you can take certain chores or parts of chores. For example, for a dinner party, let her do the shopping and you do the cooking. A task chart of what must be done each week or day by day will sort out responsibilities.

Hoping for Modest Reform

- Set a good example. You can't force organization, but you can encourage it.

- Inspire your spouse. If your desk is constantly clear, he or she may be interested in learning from you.

- Communicate. Show him/her exactly where things belong. How do you want the health records filed so that you can find them again? Where do the out-of-season clothes belong? How should the medicine chest be arranged?

- Don't become a personal butler. If you always do the picking up, your spouse has no reason to do it. It may be as simple as a lesson. Your husband simply may not know how to fold a sweater. Or your wife might not understand the importance of setting up a Personal Property Inventory.

■ Give positive reinforcement. It can help!

I remember a skit by Carol Burnett in which she played the part of a real "neatness freak." Her husband came home from work and she just couldn't stop cleaning. If he got up from his chair, she would clean the seat; she dusted the floor where he walked; the ashtray he used; and so forth. One night he couldn't stand it anymore, so he took out a gun to shoot her. The end of the scene showed her dusting off the gun and the floor before she fell. So inspire, but don't seek total reform!

50

Wardrobe Shopping for Women

Have you ever made a shopping excursion where you walked into a store and became so confused and overwhelmed you turned around and walked out again?

Or have you ever gone shopping, intending to buy one red sweater and walked out with two instead—one green and one blue?

Have you ever come home with a terrific skirt only to have it hang in your closet, never worn, because you didn't make time to shop for the "perfect" blouse to go with it?

Everyone has mistakes hanging in their closets—the dress you bought to wear "when I lose some weight," or the outfit that "really isn't me after all. . . ."

But when the mistakes in the closet outnumber the rest of your clothes, you know you're doing something wrong. It's time to rethink your shopping methods.

With thought and planning, you can build a coordinated wardrobe that will give you more outfits, with fewer purchases, than what you have now. Here's how:

Planning Your New Wardrobe

- Consider your budget. This will help you keep your shopping goals in perspective and force you to focus on what you really need. For example, in order to build a good wardrobe for work, you may not be able to add new casual clothes this spring, but those can be the first thing you buy in the fall.

- Coordination is the key to a successful wardrobe. To achieve this, you will need to build your wardrobe around a color scheme.

Begin by choosing two major colors in which you look good. The two colors (e.g., black and ivory) should work well together so that the items you buy will easily coordinate. That way you'll have twice as many outfits from the same number of pieces.

▪ Weed through your current wardrobe. Take everything out of your closet, drawers, and shelves (see Chapter 27). Discard items you haven't worn in the past two years. (Honestly, if you haven't worn it after several years, you probably never will.) With the other items, ask: "Is this still fashionable? Do I look good in it?" (Don't guess. Try it on.) "Do I still *like it?*"

▪ Of the remaining items, decide which ones you want to use as a base for your new wardrobe. Select the clothing that makes you look terrific and feel comfortable. You may have a wonderful jacket and blouse, or one good suit you'd like to use as your base item. Keep your work and lifestyle requirements in mind.

▪ Make a list of what you need to fill in with your basic wardrobe items and put this list in your Household Notebook (see Chapter 26) under To Buy. The list will give you an action plan for your shopping trip and should help you avoid impulse buying. (Remember, that's how you gained most of the mismatches you have now!)

▪ Organize your list into categories (shoes, accessories, etc.).

▪ Look through magazines and tear out pictures of fashions you like. Paste these in your Notebook as a reminder.

Planning the Shopping Trip

▪ Plan to devote the better part of a day to your first shopping trip. A couple of hours just isn't enough time. (But don't shop so long that you get overtired. It will affect your decision making.)

▪ Think ahead about where you'd like to shop. Where are your favorite stores? Plan to restrict each trip to a single geographical area so you can focus on accomplishing the task at hand.

▪ Of course, you'll need to take a list with you. Some people have chosen a portable size for their Household Notebook because they like to carry it with them; thus they have their list close at hand. I usually recommend you carry just the appropriate pages with you. Or you can go through the Household Notebook list and transfer pertinent information (what you plan to shop for on this expedition) to your calendar To Do list, which you should have with you at all times.

Getting Ready

- Wear an outfit (such as separates) that will simplify trying clothes on in the store. That way you won't have to take a dress off if you're only trying on a blouse. If you're shopping for a new item to coordinate with something you already have, try to wear part of your basic wardrobe (the skirt? the blouse and jacket?) to save carrying it.

- If you're choosing a skirt to go with a blouse and jacket you already have and you decide not to wear them, you'll need to take the blouse and jacket with you. It can be difficult to remember the lines of clothing well enough to know if the "look" will be right once you have on all three pieces.

- Avoid wearing anything that has lots of buttons; don't wear a turtleneck pullover that can be hard to pull on over your head, high boots (especially a boots-and-pants combination), or lots of jewelry, which can get tangled.

- Wear a hairstyle that keeps the hair out of your face but can be neatened easily once you've finished in the dressing room.

- Wear (or take) the bra you'll be wearing with the type of outfit for which you're shopping. If you're trying on evening wear, be sure to take the appropriate lingerie.

- Choose comfortable shoes that are easy to slip on and off.

- If you will be having a dress or skirt hem adjusted, take (or wear) the shoes you intend to wear with the outfit. (If you need just a rough idea of how the heel height will affect the dress, carry along only one of the shoes.)

- Take a lightweight shoulder bag. A bag tends to get in the way when you're combing through racks and carrying clothing into the dressing room. A heavy one also makes you tire faster simply because you're carrying the added weight.

When Shopping

- Think coordination. Aim to create a variety of outfits from three or four pieces.

- Consider the seasonality of clothes. Some fabrics such as knits can be worn all year round. They are easy to fold, don't wrinkle, and look smart all day. It also simplifies shopping because there will be less need for seasonal shopping.

- Go for the classics. If you want to be stylish, try to adapt a classic outfit to the fashions of the season. Or add this year's accessories to a more conservative outfit you already own. Steer clear of hard-to-wear accessories, however. If you're not comfortable when you try it on, it won't improve with time.

- Try on everything! Just because a sweater is marked medium doesn't mean it will fit you properly. I know several women who buy without trying on, but if I dared to do that, I'd spend the rest of my life on the return lines!

- If you find a pair of slacks, shoes, or a blouse you look great in, consider buying two. If it's perfect for you and you can use more than one color of the same style, it's a good investment.

- Judge each article of clothing based on how you *feel* in it. Even if it's a beautiful outfit, you've got to look well in it and feel good about yourself.

- Check the garment care label. Is the item going to be more trouble than it's worth to take care of?

- Avoid impulse purchases. Stick to your list.

- Don't buy what you don't need or won't wear again.

Other Tips

- Consider using a personal shopper. With more and more working women having less and less time to shop, shopping services are available in department stores nationwide. (Sometimes a small fee is charged.) When you shop, a personal shopper accompanies you throughout the store. Then all garments are taken back to one dressing room so that you only have to undress once. (Sometimes your shopper will even pull some appropriate outfits in advance.) If sizes are wrong or if another blouse is needed, your shopper will run to the appropriate department to fetch the needed item so that you needn't get dressed again. It's a great one-stop shopping system. You save time and because you buy much of your wardrobe at once, you have a better chance of it all working well together. Though it seems like an expensive luxury, some women report that they actually *save* money because they no longer waste time or money on impulse purchases that aren't right.

- Shop by mail. This is especially helpful for items where fit is not important such as when shopping for a scarf, tote, or beach coverup.

- Shop alone. While everyone likes support, too many second opinions may encourage you to make purchases you'd never dream of making on your own. It's also a real time-waster when you have your mind set on getting things done.

51

Wardrobe Shopping for Men

Most men would prefer to do anything other than shop for clothing. That's probably why the men's department of most stores is right at street level. Merchants must assume that they're doing well if a fellow has stepped in the door—why push their luck by expecting him to go much farther!

While I can't promise that this chapter will make you love shopping, what I can promise is that there is a way to simplify the system and make it as efficient as possible. And remember, the more efficient you are, the less time you'll have to spend at it and the fewer trips you'll have to make!

Planning Your Wardrobe Shopping

- Assess your clothing needs. Most executives find that the following basics meet their needs:

  - Three suits—one gray, one blue, and one conservatively striped in gray or blue
  - One navy blue blazer
  - Trousers in gray wool, brown wool, khaki, and white (all go with the blue blazer)
  - Seven dress shirts. Because the suits and blazer are in basic colors, shop for shirts that coordinate with everything. A supply of at least seven shirts allows for one for each day of the business week with a couple left over for travel or for delays at the laundry.
  - An assortment of ties that coordinate with the above. (You can vary the look of your outfits by mixing and matching shirts and ties.)

- Seven pairs of dress socks in gray, black, navy, and brown
- Shoes—one black pair, one brown, and one cordovan or burgundy

■ For summer, repeat the basic colors you've chosen for your winter suits (instead of a blue wool suit, you'll now have a wool blend in blue), so that all your shirts and ties will coordinate with both your summer and winter wardrobes.

■ As you take stock of your current wardrobe, give away anything that is frayed or beginning to look worn, and *discard anything you haven't worn in the last two years.*

■ Also note if you are low on underwear or casual clothing, and add those items to your shopping list.

■ Organize your list into categories (casual clothing, dress shirts, accessories) to simplify your time in the store.

■ Set a budget.

Simplifying the Shopping Trip

■ To avoid confusion about your correct sizes, record your suit size, collar measurement, shoe and hat size, as well as waist and trouser length measurements on a 3" × 5" index card to be carried in your wallet. (Give a copy to your wife, mother, or girlfriend to guarantee that, from now on, you'll receive gifts that fit!)

■ Decide where you would like to shop. Some men prefer to go to one department store and get their shopping done all at one time. Others feel overwhelmed by large stores and prefer to shop at smaller specialty stores.

■ If you want to visit more than one store to comparison shop, limit the number to three. Going to more won't necessarily bring you better prices or merchandise, and it *will* wear you out. If possible, choose stores that are in close proximity to each other to make the excursion as easy as possible.

■ Select stores that fit your image.

- Shop at a store where the sales help is reliable and professional. Try to develop a relationship with a salesperson, as it can save you time and money. Have the person call you when a specific raincoat in your size comes in or when the annual sale begins. If you become a loyal customer, you may even be able to phone ahead and have some items pulled for you. Or you may simply want to call to be certain that your favorite salesperson is in.

- In order to shop efficiently, it is best to go to the stores at a time when they are least likely to be crowded. The fewer the people, the faster you can be in and out. Listed below, in order of preference, are some possible shopping times:
  - A business day right after the store opens
  - Just after a store opens on Saturday morning
  - Evenings
  - Middle of the business day

What to Wear

- Wear clothing appropriate to what you want to buy. If you're buying a blazer, suit, or raincoat, be sure to wear a dress shirt, tie, and a blazer or suit jacket so you can get a feel for how the outfit will look.

- Proper shoes are important for making certain that the pants' length is correct. Proper socks are important if you're buying shoes.

- Go over your list and be sure to take it with you.

What to Buy

- Don't buy on impulse. Stick to your list.

- Plan to coordinate your entire ensemble on the day you shop for a suit. Buy the tie, the pocket handkerchief, and the shirt that goes with it. It's hard to coordinate by trying to remember what you bought, and it's inconvenient to take a suit with you on a future shopping trip.

- Buy classic American designs. The clothing lasts, and it won't go out of style as quickly. If you want to look trendy, do it by adding a stylish shirt or tie.

- Don't depend on designer labels. They don't always mean quality.

- Look for quality in make and fabric.

- Try on anything of which you're unsure of the fit. It will save you the tedium of having to return it.

- With items such as underwear or sport shirts, buy in bulk if it's a good fit or if the items are on sale.

Closet Tips

- If you anticipate having trouble remembering which items can be worn together, set up a coded system showing how your wardrobe can be coordinated. Place into groups all garments that go together and assign a letter (A,B,C) to each group. Then mark or sew that letter on the inside label of each garment. (A salesperson might be interested in helping you by listing which items coordinate if you buy from him regularly or if you've just bought several coordinated purchases.) This system will automatically simplify dressing in the morning.

- Men's closets can benefit by a double row of rods (one high, one lower). One can be for trousers and shirts; the other can hold suits and blazers.

- Use shoe trees to help shoes keep their shape.

- Purchase a tie rack to hang on the back of your closet door. There are many good styles available, so base your decision on what will work well for you. Having your ties conveniently displayed will make neckwear selection easier in the morning.

- Roll underwear, socks, and belts for easy storage. (Don't ball socks one inside the other; it stretches out the elastic.)

- A light that goes on as the closet door opens is a handy luxury.

- At the end of the season, check all your clothing for mending or possible discarding. (Old shirts make terrific rags.) Have everything laundered or cleaned before putting it in storage until next season.

Clothing Care

- Each night, inspect your suit, shirt, and tie for stains, tears, pulls, and lost buttons. If repairs are needed, get them done before returning the items to your closet.

- Frequent dry cleaning takes the life out of clothing, so clean only as needed.

- Buy a steamer to take creases and wrinkles out of suits and slacks. It's ideal for home use and perfect for travel.

- Laundries seem to thrive on breaking buttons, so be sure to check your shirt the night before to avoid early morning panic over a broken button. Keep a supply of extra buttons on hand so that they can be repaired as needed.

PART VII

Children

52 Pregnancy Checklist

53 Post-Pregnancy: Organization After the Baby Is Born

54 Children's Rooms

55 Teaching Children About Organization

56 Traveling with Children

57 When Travel Means Leaving the Kids Behind

Pregnancy Checklist

The pregnant woman who expects to spend fifty hours a week on the job, entertain friends, volunteer for committee work, and still bake home-made bread is making a big mistake. You can do anything, but not everything!

Some women are very fortunate and report having excess energy throughout pregnancy; however, more women find that sometimes they just can't quite keep up with their regular schedule. For some, it comes at the beginning of the pregnancy when nausea and an increased need for sleep are common. In my own case (and that of many others), it was the end of pregnancy when I had to slow down. I had made a big effort to get everything done well in advance, and I was so glad I did. Toward the end of my pregnancy, I was confined to bed for a brief period, and I would have been frantic if there had been many things left to take care of. (I will also warn you of what all mothers learn firsthand: With a newborn, it seems you are busy all day, but if you had to describe what occupied all your time, it would either sound silly or it would not sound very time-consuming. But believe me, it is!)

At any rate, you need to start preparing as soon as your pregnancy is confirmed. Your main goal is to be ready when your baby arrives, and that means taking a systematic approach to pregnancy by setting your priorities now—what you want to do; what you need to do.

Here are some ways to handle the many responsibilities ahead.

First Trimester

To Do

- Make the following decisions about medical care, keeping in mind that each decision will affect the other:

- Select doctor and hospital or birthing center.
- Select method of childbirth.
- Discuss any testing your doctor recommends.

■ Start thinking about how to rearrange your home for the baby. Will you need to move or can you remodel? Consider your options so you'll have time to act before the baby arrives.

■ Begin a Household Projects page in your Household Notebook (see Chapter 26). List anything you want to do to get the house in order before the baby is born: reorganize closets, clean rugs, wax floors, buy washing machine, and so forth.

■ Revise the budget to accommodate the new family member.

■ Organize family files and records and start a Pregnancy File, which includes articles and information on pregnancy, childbirth, and parenting.

To Buy

■ Select new bras with good support. (You'll want them!)
■ Buy books on pregnancy, childbirth, breastfeeding, and infant care.

To Call

■ Call the personnel department of your company and inquire about their benefits and leave-of-absence policy. Some firms require that you work until two to four weeks before your delivery date to qualify for benefits.

■ Call your insurance agent or the company insurance representative to ask exactly what is covered. (Doctor's fee? Hospital bill? Any limitations?) Also inquire about what type of coverage you will have for your new family member.

To Enjoy

■ Take advantage of leisurely weekend mornings and sleep late!

Second Trimester

To Do

- Many women find this the ideal time to share the good news with family and friends. (Most miscarriages occur in the first trimester, so you're less likely to have problems now.)
- Discuss your preferred leave-of-absence schedule with your boss.
- Have amniocentesis, if you plan to do so.
- If you plan to move or remodel, try to complete as much of the project as possible now.
- If you intend to breastfeed, start to prepare your nipples now. Check with your doctor or consult a book on breastfeeding for instructions.
- Most new parents like to have extra assistance when the baby comes. With whom would you feel most comfortable—your mother? Sister? A baby nurse? A doula (a woman who comes in to help out with the household and the things the mother needs so that the mother can focus on the baby or her other children)? If you decide on a relative, discuss it now.
- If you plan to use a nurse or a doula, ask friends to recommend one or ask them for referrals to good agencies. If you find a real gem, reserve her now. (Most agencies will take bookings on a few days notice, so you still have plenty of time.)
- If you have other children at home, plan for their care while you'll be in the hospital.
- Borrow any baby clothes you can. Make a list of each item you've borrowed and to whom it belongs. The list will also help you in a few months when you go shopping because you'll know what you don't need to buy. Wash the clothing and put it away.
- Start a Gifts-We'd-Love-to-Receive list and tell people exactly what you want when asked.
- Start your list of potential names for the baby.

To Buy

- Shop for (or borrow) maternity clothing. Don't forget about a coat or jacket.

To Call

- Register for childbirth classes, which will start in your seventh or eighth month.
- Get information on first-aid classes at the Red Cross. Knowing emergency procedures is very important in parenting.

To Enjoy

- Sneak off for a wonderful vacation with your husband!

Third Trimester

To Do

- Visit your dentist (no X-rays).
- If you plan to leave work early, make the necessary preparations for a smooth departure.
- Attend childbirth classes with your husband.
- Begin to decorate the baby's room (paint walls, put down carpet, hang curtains, etc.).
- Take a tour of the hospital or birthing center and learn about the check-in system. (You may also want to ask if you'll be allowed to take photographs in the delivery room.)
- Prepare a list of tasks that will need to be done while you're in the hospital, such as calls to spread the good news and to arrange for deliveries. (Be sure to list all phone numbers!) Also include information your husband may need to function at home without you.
- Consider changes to be made in your insurance policies and wills, and choose a guardian for your child. Discuss any changes

with your insurance representative and your attorney, and arrange for them to take effect after the baby's birth.

To Buy

- Shop for baby furniture.
- Shop for baby's layette (clothes, receiving blankets, accessories) and arrange for delivery.
- Find a pharmacy that will deliver and establish credit there. On your initial visit, pick up the baby's drug and medical needs (vaporizer, rectal thermometer, baby oil, cottonballs, lotion, diaper ointment, etc.).
- Select birth announcements and arrange to call the printer when the baby is born. You can get a head start by addressing the envelopes now.

To Call

- Check with the hospital or local Y about childcare classes and enroll.
- Book a doula or baby nurse if you haven't already. Give the agency your due date. They'll provide you with someone whether you're early or late.
- Call pediatricians for interviews. Get recommendations from friends or your obstetrician. Consultations in person or by phone between doctor and parents-to-be are expected. There may be a nominal charge for in-person interviews so ask when you call.
- Arrange for diaper service if you plan to use one.
- Call friends for names of potential babysitters.

To Enjoy

- Pamper yourself! Get a haircut, enjoy a manicure or facial, or read a good book.

Last Month

To Do

- Cook ahead and freeze meals for your homecoming.
- Prepare a suitcase for the hospital.
- Prepare a childbirth bag.
- Start interviewing now if you'll need full-time household help when you come home.

To Buy

- Buy nursing bras if you plan to breastfeed.

To Call

- Confirm furniture and/or layette deliveries.
- Confirm childcare arrangements for children at home.

To Enjoy

- Celebrate the fact that you are prepared.

At the Hospital

To Call

- Contact stores for delivery.
- Tell diaper service their starting date.
- Notify nurse or nursing agency.
- Give the printer details for birth announcement.

53

Post-Pregnancy: Organization After the Baby Is Born

There is no time that is more disorganized or confusing than after coming home with a new baby. There are generally extra people around, no one is following their normal schedule, and everyone is simply basing their actions on what they anticipate the baby's schedule will be—and of course, the little character usually does his or her best to surprise everyone!

Now that I've had twins, I realize how much "free" time I had when my firstborn, Julia, came along. However, you couldn't have convinced me of that at the time! My first little half-pint had me going in circles! To cope, I had to develop a way to do all my regular activities—only faster (now I shower more quickly, have a simpler haircut, and do an easier makeup routine). And I had to figure out how to do all the childcare chores while still saving time just to be with my baby. It's not easy, but it's possible—eventually.

The art of getting through the early days lies largely in simply remaining flexible enough to cope with what comes; however, there are some measures you can take to help things along.

If You Have Not Done So Already

Ideally, you will have taken care of many of the following points prior to your baby's birth:

- Buy one or two good books on baby care. (Get recommendations from friends.) You won't have time to read many, but having a voice of authority illuminate what the pediatrician told you about early feedings, putting an infant to sleep, or coping with first sniffles can be enormously reassuring.

- If planning to breastfeed, set up a support network. Get the number of your local La Leche League and talk to friends who have breastfed successfully.
- Stock the freezer with breads and precooked dinners for the first days at home.
- Find stores that deliver.
- With your husband's help, prepare a list—complete with phone numbers—of all people who should be called as soon as the baby is born.
- Preaddress announcement envelopes.
- At the office, stay on top of your work, and establish systems so that the staff can run things in your absence.
- Change your will (or have one drawn up) and your insurance policy.

After the Birth

- Notify close friends and relatives. To make it simpler, have some of the first people you call phone other people.
- Arrange for a circumcision or bris, if appropriate.
- Arrange for a christening or naming ceremony.
- Select godparents, guardians.
- Send announcements.

The Early Days at Home

- Don't even attempt to get organized right away. Just do nothing for awhile and give yourself time to get back on track. (Babies don't know about organization and they really don't care—they just want you to be available when they need you.)
- There's nothing wrong with asking people not to come over right away. Give yourself time to adjust and rest.
- Accept help from anyone who offers. Don't be afraid to ask for help. This is one time when people are only too glad to lend a hand.

- Relax whenever you can, during the baby's nap or while someone else is with him or her. Only if you are well-rested and calm will you be able to enjoy your baby!

- Keep your list of announcements and use it to note down gifts as they arrive. Then check off each as the thank-you note is sent.

- Write several thank-you notes each day so that doing so doesn't become overwhelming.

- Plan to cook dinners in the morning or arrange to have someone else cook.

- Use a store that delivers, or have someone stock up on diapers (buy a case), formula, and food for you.

- Start thinking about what type of household help you will need, but wait to hire until after you've evaluated what your needs will be.

- Arrange an appointment with the pediatrician for a one-month checkup.

- Schedule your own doctor's appointment for a postpartum checkup (usually at six weeks, but ask your doctor just to be sure).

- Start a photo album and a journal.

- Make an audiotape of your baby's first sounds including crying, laughing, babbling, and cooing. And of course, you've likely been videotaping throughout.

- Check out support groups for mothers and fathers through your local Y, church, or temple, and hospitals. Having the opportunity to speak with other parents and share information during this transitional time is very helpful.

- Arrange time for yourself whenever possible. Take the nap time for yourself, and book a temporary babysitter (or call upon a relative or friend) when you need more than an hour or so off.

Starting the Day

One of the most common pitfalls new mothers face is finding time to get dressed. I constantly hear, "And there it was noon, and I was still in my nightgown!" Here's what to do:

- If your baby takes an early nap (many go right back to sleep after their first feeding), get up and use that time for showering, getting dressed, and having breakfast. If you're dressed and feeling somewhat organized, it is easier to face the day. You can use other naps for getting the additional rest you need.

- Not all babies are so cooperative about taking that early nap. Try putting the infant in a baby seat placed on the bathroom floor to watch you shower, dry your hair, and the like. If your baby becomes conditioned to the fact that this is one ten-minute period when you have something else to do, he or she will generally make the most of that time looking around—and plotting how to keep you busy for the rest of the day!

Organizing Food-Related Supplies

- If your baby is formula-fed, prepare all the bottles at one time so that you're prepared for the day.

- Always clean the bottles after use so that rotation is easy.

- Store nipples and caps in a closed jar or can so you'll always have presterilized equipment handy. Put used items in another spot (a bowl or another jar) so that you'll know what is ready for sterilizing.

- Have one shelf or cupboard for all of baby's things (bottles, warming dish, spoon, cups).

- A three-tier lazy Susan is terrific for storage jars of food or juice.

- In the refrigerator, have one section for baby food so that it's easy to find what's open and available.

Laundry and Bath-Time Tips

- Always keep up with the baby's wash so that you don't run out of stretchies, T-shirts, burp cloths, and bibs.

- Have at least three sets of crib sheets: one on the bed, one in the laundry, and a fresh one in the drawer.

- Soak clothing immediately after a stain. It's easier to keep it white and fresh that way. (Have a bucket on hand in which to throw soiled items.)

- Select easy-to-wear clothes with snaps in all the important places (for diaper changes and for extending the neck opening). Once you've tried to dress a screaming baby, you'll be especially glad. Also, always buy big. They grow so quickly!

- Save trips at bath time by using a caddy to store baby soap, shampoo, lotion, powder, and toys.

- Buy canisters meant for storing flour, sugar, and tea to hold baby items (cotton, ribbons, nail scissors, thermometer, etc.).

- For after bath, put the bottle of baby lotion in hot water. The lotion will be warm when you rub it on the baby's skin.

- Put towels in a warm dryer for a few minutes. Remove just before the bath. It's a wonderful way to get baby dry!

Getting Out of the House

At no time is a parent's organizational skill more sorely tested than when trying to get out of the house with a baby (or a child of any age for that matter!) in tow.

- Always have a prepacked diaper bag ready to go. Choose one that is soft and featherweight. Velcro fastenings make for easy opening and closing. Outside pockets help you find what you need (baby wipes, tissues, money, or keys) quickly. A vinyl inside makes for easy cleaning. Always repack it as soon as you get home. What goes inside? Carry a change of clothing, a blanket, extra formula, a package of nipples and caps, plastic bags with ties for soiled diapers, several sheets of paper towels, moist towelettes and ointment for diaper changes, small bottles of lotion and powder, and at least two extra diapers. Also carry a puppet or some attention-getting toy to get you through a rough time. It sounds like a trunk full, but it's really not so bad—once you're used to it.

■ If you have an appointment to go to the pediatrician or to meet a friend, leave an extra thirty minutes for last-minute "surprises" (and babies will always provide them!), such as an unexpected diaper change, a longer-than-usual feeding, or a spitup—or all of the above and more.

■ If possible, borrow an extra snowsuit for a winter baby. That way if one gets dirty and you're going out again, you've got something else for the baby to wear.

How to Get Non-Baby Work Done

If you're trying to accomplish something during the early days of motherhood (job search, work-related project, or even finishing thank you notes), you really can't count on getting much done during the baby's nap. Sleep patterns often change from day to day, and often what you need during that period is a good rest yourself. Here are some suggestions:

■ Get backup help. Consider your needs. Perhaps a babysitter one day a week will be enough, or you may need help three days a week. Establish a set routine with the sitter so that you have one person coming to you regularly. Then the baby will become accustomed to one person, you won't have to reinstruct every time, and you'll know that you will definitely have a specific time to accomplish what needs to be done. Schedule that time, for example:

Monday:	Stay home to work.
Wednesday:	Errands, food shopping, dentist appointment.
Friday:	Stay home to work.

Be consistent or the time will slip away from you.

- Choose an area of the house in which to work where you aren't in sight of the baby, and close the door. Try not to listen. If you've chosen well, your sitter should be given the authority to handle whatever comes up. If you teach your child that you'll come in at an especially loud wail, the baby will work very hard to wring out those mother-producing wails that bring you.

- Teach your sitter to schedule and organize. You may need to explain such management techniques as starting the washer before going out for a walk with the baby so that the laundry will be finished when she comes back in.

- When you've been out, plan to come home at least fifteen minutes before the sitter has to leave to have time to hang up your coat, wash, change clothes, and put away your packages, so your home won't be in chaos for the rest of the day.

Additional Suggestions

- For night feedings, set up a system with your mate so that each of you takes full duty every other night—doing all feedings during that time. That way you each have one full night on—but one full night off for badly needed sleep.

- If you must leave immediately after a nursing, get completely ready with makeup, stockings, and shoes, but put on a robe rather than your clothes. Then you can feed the baby without having to worry about milk getting on the outfit. As soon as you're finished with the feeding, you can slip into your outfit and leave.

- Consider putting a telephone extension in the baby's room. It can be turned off during naps, and it's certainly handy when the phone rings during a diaper change.

54

Children's Rooms

When it comes to household organization, one of the most difficult areas to keep well organized is a child's room. Offspring of all ages are experts at creating chaos.

Obviously, picking up after the kids or nagging them is no solution. The first step is to create an environment that is conducive to organization. This involves letting your children's interests dictate the basic plan for the environment (so that the most interesting items are the most available) and then creating a system that allows your child to help maintain order.

General Planning

- The first thing to do is to rethink the use of the child's space and, if necessary, rearrange it so that his or her interests are taken into consideration. If he loves to build with blocks but they are difficult to get out and put away, you've automatically created a difficult activity to keep organized. Consider the use of play areas and set up the room accordingly. For your block builder, create a clear space in a corner of his room and store the blocks nearby. If your child is an avid reader, establish a seat near the bookcase and make sure there is good lighting. For a young artist, choose a place where you can put a child's table with art supplies nearby. If a three year old can take out (and put away) paper and crayons for herself, you've created an effective system.

- Though I have stressed the importance of color-coding throughout the book, nowhere is it more important than in a child's room. There are two practical uses for it:

- *In keeping belongings separate.* Amanda knows her tooth-brush is red, so she always knows which toothbrush/towel/bathroom glass is hers.
- *In putting things away.* By using different colored bins or painting shelves in different colors, you can create a system for your toddler to put toys away. No reading necessary! The dinosaur figures go on the green shelf, the blocks go on the red, and so on.

■ Establish a spot where clutter is allowed on a temporary basis. No child should have to put away everything all the time. If your daughter wants to spread out all her dollhouse toys in a preestab-lished corner of the room, that should be all right for several days. (Set up a system such as Monday and Thursday for cleaning up most projects.) Allow the spot to move occasionally. If the kids want to build a card table house in the living room for a night or two and the family won't be inconvenienced, they ought to be able to trade that mess for those in their rooms.

■ For toddlers and preschoolers who mainly play with a variety of big toys, establish baskets or bins in each room in which they can keep a few toys they like to play with. It makes cleanup in the room much easier, and the bins can be moved easily if company is to arrive. In addition, by moving the kitchen bin into the living room occasionally, the kids get a whole new perspective on the toys!

■ If you live in a home where the children have their own bed-room as well as playroom, reserve their rooms for special or new toys. Use the playroom as the main storage area. This simplifies pickup time because everyone knows that all toys go to the playroom; You needn't determine what goes to Todd's room and what goes to Adam's.

■ Some families like to establish one room (such as the parents' bedroom) as "off-limits." While this shouldn't be overdone, it may be workable for some areas. Certainly, most parents should stipulate that because of potential hazards, the bathrooms and areas of the kitchen (such as around the stove) are off-limits for unsupervised play. Another possibility for preserving a room's neatness while still allowing your children some freedom might be to stipulate that certain rooms must be used as intended. Being in the living room is fine if a child wants to sit on the couch with his or her feet on a stool or the floor, but romping and climbing are not allowed.

Storage Tips

- Lower closet hanging poles and hooks so that your children can reach them. This will make dressing and putting things away much easier.

- Keep toys where they are used. Bath toys should be in a plastic basket in the bathroom; toys for the den might be in a bin or stored in a cupboard; outdoor toys should go on the back porch.

- Group together similar toys. All puzzles should be together, likewise all games and all stuffed animals.

- Transparent plastic shoe boxes or bins are terrific for storage since the children can see what's in them.

- If you use shelves for storage, be sure they are fastened securely. Bookcases should be anchored as well. Active toddlers are prone to scaling any type of shelving.

- Mesh laundry bags that tie or zip closed make terrific toy sacks for large, awkward items. They're see-through so there is no problem with identification, and it's a good way to keep all parts of a toy together.

- Use sketches or a catalog photograph taped to a box to identify certain items. Children too young to read can easily identify the "beads" box if it has a picture of beads on the outside.

- Plastic dishpans and coffee cans are also good for storage. Make sure there are no sharp edges!

- Are puzzle pieces constantly getting mixed up? When a puzzle arrives, assign it a number and write that number on the back of each piece. Also note the number on the box. When a piece is found, you'll know exactly in which box it goes.

- Try a toy sheet for an infant's toys or for a toy that has a lot of pieces. Collect the toys (or pieces) on a sheet on which the child can play. When the child is done, simply fold up the sheet—toys and all—and put it away for the next time.

- Encourage children to pull out only a few toys at a time. If they want to do puzzles, encourage them to put away the game first.

Weeding Out

- Automatically throw away any toy that becomes hazardous. If a part snaps off and there's a sharp edge, or if eyes on a stuffed animal cannot be secured and might come off and cause a child to choke, throw it away.

- Until your child is old enough to take care of his or her own room and keep it somewhat neat, you have the right to weed things out periodically. After all, the clay sculpture her best friend gave her six months ago and the Barbie shoe whose mate is missing really can't be saved forever.

- Give your child the chance to make the decision to part with a toy. If you've noticed one that hasn't been used in awhile, you might ask if it's okay to give it away (to a hospital or a thrift shop). Sometimes a child will surprise you with a "yes!" (However, if your child is a pack rat and is going to make it impossible for you to *ever* give or throw anything away, wait a few months or a year before asking permission again. For the time being, you'd better make the decisions yourself.)

- If a part is lost (and it's not such a favorite toy that you are met with a flood of tears until you promise to replace the part), use that as a reason to throw a toy out.

- Favorite toys can often be fixed. Some cities have doll "hospitals." For other types of toys, contact your local toy store or the manufacturer.

- Suggest that your child give away one toy when he or she receives a new one.

- Let your child help pack toys in a box for charity; talk about how happy another child will be to receive them.

- Rotate toys. If your child just can't part with some toys but you need to clear space, establish a "surprise" bin and cycle some of the toys out for awhile. Then if your child is home sick or you feel trapped inside on a rainy day, you can put down the bin. Chances are, you'll both be in for a surprise at how much fun your child will have playing with the old toys. (If any toy doesn't catch the child's interest after being taken out of circulation for awhile, toss it out.)

- Exchange toys. Perhaps your child and his friend would like to trade games (or puzzles or books) for a time. Specify a date when the toys should be returned (trading for "keeps" is hard at almost any age).

55

Teaching Children About Organization

Parents who teach their children an organizational system and the value of it will have given their young ones a head start in life. The toddler will begin to learn responsibility and be better prepared to cope with the "putting away" rules of nursery school. And as the child matures, he or she will be learning some basic organizational skills that will help him build lifelong work habits.

As a youngster, it never dawned on me that people could be disorganized. I thought everyone knew where their shoes, socks, toys, and books were; what time school began; when their homework was due; and so on. By the time I was ten I had determined that to save time in the morning, I could put my packed bookbag by the front door the night before so that when it was time to leave in the morning, all I had to do was "grab and run." I guess I was just better organized than anyone else, and it has helped me throughout my life.

Organization is a skill that *can* be learned. The earlier you start instilling in your children these habits and the benefits, the easier it will be for them.

With toddlers, the place to start is by having them help with the day-to-day toy cleanup. As they grow older, you'll want to teach them how to be responsible for their own room and have them help with specific tasks around the house. This will help promote a feeling of self-reliance and give them more control over their lives. Another important benefit of good organizational habits is when it comes to schoolwork.

Cleaning Up, Toddler-Style

Toddlers should learn that what comes out must go back. There are fun ways to encourage your child to help and still allow you to get the job done efficiently.

- Encourage your child to help with cleanup, but don't overwhelm him or her. Request help with just one thing at a time. "You pick up the doll clothes; I'll do the books."

- Sing while you work together.

- Ask, "How quickly can we get this done?" Set the kitchen timer for five or ten minutes and see if you can get everything done before the bell rings.

- Make a game of it. Ask, "Can you pick up all the stuffed animals and put them back before I finish with the blocks?"

As They Grow—Taking Responsibility for Their Own Rooms

- Simplify a task according to age level. Teach a preschooler how to make a bed by standing at the head of the bed and pulling up the covers.

- Establish a standard so that your child knows what is expected. For example, you may care only that your eight year old pull the comforter over the bed—not that the sheets underneath be wrinkle-free. Tell your child exactly what is expected.

- Involve your children in your efforts by taking them shopping with you for organizers. Let them help choose the colors and styles.

- Label where everything goes (via color-coding or written labels) so that your child knows what goes where.

- Assign a special drawer or shelf in the bathroom for their belongings.

- Suggest ways to get the job done pleasantly by putting on a favorite CD, telling yourself a story, pretending to be Cinderella, or the like.

- Have a laundry basket in the child's room, and make him or her responsible for putting dirty clothes there. At a later date, you can teach children to be responsible for putting away as well. Show them how you want the clothes placed and in what drawers—but don't expect perfection!

■ Help children build personal pride in their room. Let them have a hand in decorating it and praise them for the times when they are showing an interest in beautifying it (despite the fact that the two of you may have a different definition of "beauty!").

■ Children usually get attention for *not* cleaning their room. Be sure to pay attention when they do.

Taking On Other Responsibilities

■ Set an example of planning and priorities by talking in those terms about everyday household events. For example, the child who can read can help plan a trip to the grocery store by reviewing the chocolate chip cookie recipe and listing those ingredients that must be purchased before cookies can be made.

■ Getting an older child to do household chores usually involves constant reminding. You can establish a chart or create a "dial" system that can help your child determine what he or she is supposed to do on a given day. A chart should list each family member's name, followed by the tasks for which he or she is currently responsible, and the day on which each is to be done. (Note that each person gets a free day occasionally.)

	Mon.	Tues.	Wed.	Thurs.	Fri.	Sat.	Sun.
Mom	dishes	FREE	trash	dust	set table	dishes	FREE
Dad	set table	dishes	FREE	trash	FREE	set table	dishes
Amanda	FREE	set table	dishes	pick up main rooms	trash	FREE	set table
Elizabeth	trash	FREE	set table	dishes	wipe counters	trash	FREE
Julia	dust	trash	FREE	set table	dishes	dust	FREE

- A job dial can be made by cutting out two cardboard circles, one larger than the other. The large circle records the tasks to be done (take responsibility for the dishes, set the table, take out the trash); the smaller circle notes each family member's name.

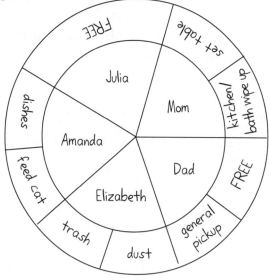

Using a brad (available at stationery stores), the two are put together, circle upon circle. (The larger circle is stationary, the smaller one turns.) Every day the smaller dial is moved one position to the right. Then each family member is responsible for the tasks that appear adjacent to his or her name.

- As your children mature, let them take charge of marking their own dates on the family calendar. You're the best judge of when each is ready for that responsibility.

- Check with your child about upcoming events at school so that no one misses a date because a note was lost. (The child is responsible, but you offer a system of cross-checking.)

Teaching Self-Reliance

I once met a friend's daughter, Jamie, who was very self-sufficient even at age six. I visited her family one day when my daughter Julia was five months old, and Jamie was always one step ahead of me—getting out a fresh diaper, feeding Julia her cereal, and pushing the stroller. Young children *can* do a lot!

- Both mother and father should play active roles in the picking up and organizational work of the home. The best way to teach is by example.

- Help children become more independent by teaching them how to tie their shoes, button their sweater, get their own snack, or operate the VCR. The more they can do, the better they'll feel about themselves, and the more organized you can be.

Schoolwork and Organization

As a child begins to assume responsibility for schoolwork, organization becomes more important than ever. The children who learn how to arrange their books, desks, lockers, and notebooks will likely become more organized adults.

- For schoolwork, provide your child with a well-lighted, comfortable work area.

- Suggest that your child establish a color-coding system for homework folders by subject. Most children enjoy a trip to the stationery store to buy the necessary supplies, and the system will help them throughout the year.

- Teach your child how to label notebooks and arrange desk supplies.

- When you first see your child after school, ask about homework and discuss what the assignments are and about how long they should take. You can help them set up a time management system. If necessary, you can establish a reward such as "After you finish you can watch a half hour of television."

- If your child seems stuck, stop and help him or her plan steps to complete something (break a large task down into parts, etc.).
- Praise your child for work well done. Talk about what great progress he or she is making in developing positive work habits for later in life.

56

Traveling with Children

While the hours you spend on a plane or in a car with your child may not be the highlight of your life, remember what someone once said: All places should be seen through a child's eyes. After all, it is the children who stop to notice the small details, and it is they who take the time to sit by a fountain rather than rushing from one museum to another.

If you're brave enough to pack your youngsters and go, chances are you'll have a wonderful time.

General Planning

- If possible, plan to travel during the child's nap time.
- Think through your child's day and make a checklist so you won't forget certain "must have's" (blanket, washcloths, etc.). One woman I know had made a great list of clothing and bedding needs but had neglected to note the everyday items such as diapers, pacifiers, and bottles. Sure enough, she forgot the bottles—they were in the dishwasher!
- Let one person do the packing. One mother assumed her husband packed the baby food and the bottles, and they were both distressed to discover that he hadn't.
- Take at least one full change of clothes in case of spills or motion sickness. (The younger the child, the more clothes you are likely to need. For an infant, take along two or three changes—the second set of backup clothes can be lightweight so they are easy to pack, and you can add a sweater if it's chilly.) Pack separates when possible. That way if the shirt gets juice all over it, at least you don't have to change the pants.

- Expect the unexpected. If you'll be in the car or on the plane for five hours, take enough diapers for ten to fifteen hours. (In your suitcase, be sure to pack diapers for your arrival so you don't immediately have to head for the store.)

- Take an adequate supply of plastic bags for diapers and trash. A nervous child can develop diarrhea, and you don't want to be caught short without a way to dispose of the diapers!

- Take any and all medications your child might need. Colds are a particular worry when traveling, so take along the remedies your doctor recommends. And if your child has a tendency to any illness, such as ear infections, also take any medication the doctor may have prescribed. There's nothing worse than being in a strange city and not having the necessary medicine in the middle of the night. Remember, anticipate the unexpected.

- For very young children, pack familiar toys and books so there will be something to give them the feeling of home. Ideally, pack these toys (all but the true favorites) about a week in advance so that they seem new but familiar at the same time. A few new toys are nice, but there's no need to overdo. For entertainment at your destination, blow-up toys are wonderful because they pack so easily.

- If you're comfortable with your baby in a frontpack (or back-pack) baby carrier or a sling, be sure to plan on traveling with it. It makes you far more mobile than having to totally rely on using a stroller.

- If your child is under three, invest in a toddler seat that attaches to the table (a collapsible model is now available). Not all restaurants have highchairs, so having one along will make meals much more manageable. If you're traveling by plane, pack the seat in the bottom of your suitcase; if traveling by car, put it in an accessible spot in the trunk in case you need it en route.

- Buy a travel clothesline so that you can wash light clothing by hand and hang to dry.

- If you are going away on business, bring a relative or babysitter to help out or arrange for one at your destination.

- Select a family-oriented hotel. If you're traveling to a foreign country, make certain that you'll have your own bath, and try to clarify what they mean by certain words such as "suite." One family expected a separate bedroom for the children and discovered that the bedroom was an alcove that couldn't be darkened unless everyone in the family went to bed at the same time.

- When you reserve your room, ask for a crib, if needed, and inquire about a babysitting service. If a hotel regularly serves families, you can have some degree of confidence in the service, as the hotel wouldn't recommend it if they received complaints. If you have any concerns, ask for and check references.

- If you're traveling to a foreign country, tell your pediatrician where you're going. His or her advice will make your trip a smoother one. Also check regarding immunizations.

Planning for a Plane Trip

- When possible, book seats in advance so that all family members will be together. Tell them if a nonpaying infant will be sharing one of the seats. They will generally try to save a seat next to you unless the plane is 100 percent full. When you get to the airport, remind the ticket agent that you are traveling with an infant and would like a seat held if possible.

- If your child will need any medication during the trip or right after, be sure to carry it on board with you in case your bags are lost.

- Select a carry-on bag made of lightweight material, and choose one with lots of outside pockets for greater accessibility. You will want to pack as much as you need without overdoing. Heavy carry-on luggage is a real nuisance. Keep in mind that you may be carrying:

  - Diapers, plastic bags, wipes, diaper ointment
  - Food
  - Medicine

- Extra clothes, blankets, sweaters
- Toys, games, books

▪ Expect that there may be variations in cabin temperature so all family members should dress in layers they can add and take off as needed.

▪ If grandparents will be waiting at your destination, you may want to pack one special outfit in your carry-on bag so that you can change the child just before arrival.

Travel and Food

▪ With plane travel, phone ahead to find out what the special child's meal is, and if it's something he or she likes, reserve it for your youngster.

▪ Be overprepared when it comes to food. One mother spent an additional five hours on a plane with her infant, but fortunately she was carrying enough formula to get through.

▪ Don't expect that the airplane meal will really be your child's regular meal. If the plane is delayed, "lunch" may be served at 4 P.M., so pack enough substantial food that your child can use the plane meal as entertainment, not nourishment.

▪ If your child is particular, take along lots of whatever you think might not be available where you are going (e.g., juices in Europe are different, so you may want to take your own). A friend who took her infant to Japan sent a box of supplies ahead of her, and she was glad she did.

▪ For any type of travel, food is a real help. Raisins and Cheerios are easy and fun. Pack in plastic food-storage bags so you can throw them away when you're done.

On Board

▪ Try to avoid checking your collapsible stroller. Carrying an infant or child in addition to your carry-on luggage is just too much—especially if there are delays and you are stranded at an airport for several hours.

- Having something to suck on during take-off and landing will help your child's ears adjust to the changes in air pressure. Nursing or a bottle (dip the nipple in a little cane sugar for a very fussy child) or lollipops for an older child can help get them through this time.

- Some families like the bulkhead seats because those rows offer more leg room; however, there are disadvantages. You generally must give up your carry-on luggage during take-off and landing since there is no nearby storage available for it. In addition, you sometimes must rely on the flight attendant to set up tray tables. Thus, many families prefer to be part of a regular row where the children can control their own tray table to eat or do artwork when they like.

- If traveling alone with a baby, avoid getting a center seat. If you are booked for one on a full flight, a flight attendant can generally work out a trade for you. People do have sympathy!

- Ask the flight attendant for any items the children might enjoy, perhaps a deck of cards or flight wings.

At the Hotel

- If you are in a foreign country, have bottled water sent to your room.

- Check the hotel crib for sturdiness. Be certain that the sides lock firmly into a raised position.

- Ask for four to six large towels to roll up and use as crib bumpers.

- Babyproof the hotel room. Go over it on your hands and knees to evaluate what your child might get into. Travel with outlet plugs (in foreign countries, you'll need to use tape) and bring tape for sharp corners and edges. Ask that any glass tables be removed.

Traveling with Older Children

- Older children love the new and unexpected. Visit a toy store and pick up activity books, games, and crossword puzzles for the trip.

- If you travel frequently, create a travel art-and-activity bag. Keep it permanently packed with paper, crayons, scissors, stickers, stars, an activity book, and mazes. It's easier than packing fresh every time, and it gives a child something specific to look forward to.

- Make tapes of CDs (or record your own stories). If traveling by car, you can play them in the tape deck. If traveling by plane, bring a tape player with ear phones.

- Let your child pack his or her own small bag of special belongings, perhaps in an easy-to-carry backpack. A child as young as three will enjoy the importance of being able to pack for him- or herself. Check it out once it's packed; your child may have created a bag that weighs a ton, and you'll want to help him or her be a little more realistic about what should go with you. However, remember that you can't rely on those items to keep your youngster busy for the trip. You'll need to pack special items for entertainment.

- When you get to the place you're visiting, try to locate a playmate for your child. Many children are rejuvenated by seeing other youngsters.

- Ask about local playgrounds. An hour at one can often wear off enough of a child's excess energy that the family can devote the rest of the day to sightseeing.

When I look back on my childhood, the warmest memories I have are the family trips we made. Even ten-hour car rides (and I got carsick!) were happy times for me. I loved traveling with my parents and enjoyed those special times of being with them. So while you pack an unending supply of diapers and toys and games, just remember that it will almost certainly pay off for your family in the long run!

57

When Travel Means Leaving the Kids Behind

When one or both parents must be away, it's difficult for the entire family. Parents are under stress to make all the family arrangements, and children are concerned about missing their parents for a time. Even if only one parent is gone, family dynamics change, and kids keenly feel a parent's absence.

I learned firsthand the importance of preparing the family for our absence. A year ago my husband and I were just returning home from our first trip in ten years without the children, and as we pulled into the driveway at 10 P.M., we were alarmed to see our neighbor standing in our doorway. Upon entering the house, we learned that one of our three-year-old twins, who had just started sleeping in a "big bed," had fallen out of the bed and had gotten a deep cut above his eye. Per my written "in case of emergency" instructions, my child care person had called the neighbor to come care for the girls while she took Harrison to the emergency room. Of course, our return meant that we handled the situation, but all my neighbor could say to me was, "I couldn't believe it. Your nanny was so *prepared*. She had your list and emergency envelope in her hand when I arrived, and she knew just what to do."

While you will rarely return to find that the family has encountered a true emergency, there are many measures to take that will lessen your worries and keep the house running smoothly while you're away.

Making Special Preparations

- Children should be told ahead of time. For a business trip, little ones need just a few days' notice; children seven and older can be told a week or two in advance. Tell them where you're going, why, and when you'll be back. Even a toddler should get a clear explanation.

■ You can share your trip with your children by pointing out on a map where you're going and talking a bit about what you expect (or know) it will be like: "Denver is surrounded by mountains. If I look out the window during my meeting, I'll see some of the biggest mountains you can imagine. Maybe one day we can go there together to ski."

■ With small children, create a visual way of explaining how long you'll be gone. Using an ordinary notebook, make your own page-a-day calendar system that a sitter or your spouse can review with them each morning. For each day that you'll be gone, write or sketch what they'll be doing (school? special play date? visit from Grandma?); on the bottom of the page, draw what you'll be doing (driving to your destination? riding in an airplane?). Continue this on each page representing a day you'll be gone. Perhaps the "day-after-I-return" page could feature a picture of all of you doing something special together.

■ Leave a special sticker or a small piece of candy for each day you're away. By seeing how many treats they have left until you return, they'll have a method for measuring time. You can combine this with your page-a-day trip calendar by attaching the special treat to each page.

■ For children seven and older, mark the family calendar with the days of your absence. In addition, you can create a child-oriented itinerary for older children to read. Although they usually don't want to know about your daily meetings, they might like to note that on Wednesday night you're attending a banquet where a popular entertainer they admire will perform. We put a "happy face" on our wall calendar, marking the day of our return, and the twins like to take turns putting a big red "X" on each day as it passes.

■ Plan special activities for the children while you're away. Arrange play dates with favorite friends; ask Grandma to take them to McDonald's.

- Leave special messages, some to be packed in the lunchbox. At bedside, place a photograph of yourself.

- Record stories, messages, or songs for your children to listen to each night while you're gone. (Stories or songs recorded on tape can be put away for use during the next trip.)

- If the stay is somewhat indefinite (helping a family member through an illness, for example), overestimate the time you'll be gone.

- Explain to the children relevant instructions that you've left with the sitter: "I've told Aunt Mary you can watch an extra half-hour of television Friday night, but otherwise, I expect you to follow family rules."

- If car-pooling systems change because of your absence, tell the children what to expect.

- Will you miss a significant event such as a play or a recital? Ask the teacher if you may come to a dress rehearsal instead.

- If you travel regularly, establish a going-away ritual. With a preschooler it might be going for ice cream the night before you leave; older children might prefer playing a game. Even teens look forward to something special like a dinner out.

- If your child is going through a rough time, you might try to postpone the trip, shorten it by a day or two, or even bring the child with you. If none of these solutions is workable, tell your child that you really must go, and then promise a special treat for the two of you when you return. This always takes the sting out of being left behind at our house!

Household Organization

Step #1: Assembling Important Information

- The person in charge of your children while you are away should have:

  - Complete medical information on each child: History of ear infections? Allergies? Special diet? Any medication? Any other concerns?

- List of important telephone numbers such as the doctor, the drugstore, the veterinarian, a relative, the school, etc.
- Medical insurance information.
- Medical treatment consent form, authorizing your caregiver to make emergency medical care decisions in your absence. (Check with your doctor for correct wording.)
- A detailed day-to-day schedule of where you'll be, complete with phone numbers (hotel? business office?) and dates and times. Also leave flight information, with phone numbers of the airlines. If the weather is bad or there is a reason for a delay, your sitter or children can check your flight progress throughout the day.

ITINERARY

Monday, September 28

7:00 A.M.—Dexter Airlines #22 to Miami
(Dexter: 1-(800)-555-3478.)

10:23 A.M.—Arrive Miami. Going straight to hotel: Palm Tree
Hotel: 1-(305)-555-1234.

12:00 P.M.—Lunch at Smith & Stone Advertising.
1-(305)-555-4321. In emergency, leave message with
Sarah Jones.

2:30 P.M.—To convention hall. Paging Number:
1-(305)-555-6543.

5:00-6:30 P.M.—At hotel.

6:30 P.M.—Banquet dinner. Hotel Ballroom.

Step #2: Assembling Detailed Lists

- Your sitter or spouse should be left with a complete list of what is to be done each day. If it's a regular sitter who knows the general routine, write the extra activities or chores on sticky-backed notes that can be attached to the calendar on the appropriate day. As the task gets done, the note gets tossed.

- If the person doesn't know the household well, you'll need two lists. One will be the basics of household management and should be general enough to last for a year or two of absences. The other list provides your children's schedules, including specifics about meals, homework, and play dates.

- To create these lists, take a day or two to observe exactly how the day flows.

- Always review these lists with the sitter or your spouse to be certain there are no questions.

HOUSEHOLD MANAGEMENT LIST

Monday

7 A.M.: Feed dog 3 biscuits.

Tidy kitchen after breakfast.

Sweep floor.

Change beds.

Check grocery list; pick up any necessary items.

5 P.M.: Feed dog one bowl dry food, 2 biscuits.

Prepare school lunches after dinner.

Run dishwasher.

Empty dishwasher; lay out breakfast dishes.

Tuesday

7 A.M.: Feed dog 3 biscuits.

Tidy kitchen after breakfast.

Start laundry; fold and put away.

5 P.M.: Feed dog one bowl of dry food, 2 biscuits.

Prepare school lunches after dinner.

Run dishwasher.

Empty dishwasher; lay out breakfast dishes.

CHILDREN'S SCHEDULE

Monday, September 28

6:45 A.M.   Wake Heather (dresses self).

7:10   Wake Charlie—help him get dressed.

7:30   Breakfast (Heather: orange juice, cereal, and toast; Charlie: milk, muffin, and apple slices).

8:05   Bus comes for Heather. (She should have her backpack and lunch; sweater if it's chilly.)

8:45   Drive Charlie to nursery school.

12:00 P.M.   Nursery school pickup. Jamie comes for play date. Mother: Susan Miller, 833–2211. She'll pick up Jamie about 2:30.

3:40   Meet Heather's bus.

4:15-4:30   Heather should start homework. May need you to sit with her. Generally spends about thirty minutes on it.

5:30   Bath time. Make sure Heather washes her hair and dries it well.

6:00   Dinner. Lasagna in the refrigerator.

8:00   Charlie goes to bed. (Brush teeth.) He gets two stories and must have his stuffed monkey. If you can't find it, check the kitchen cupboard where I keep pots—he often hides it there.

8:15   Heather gets in bed. We read for fifteen minutes, then lights out.

■ If you were leaving a baby, you would note all feedings and the amounts given. A complete schedule for the morning might look like this:

BABY'S MORNING SCHEDULE	
7:00 A.M.	Baby wakes; change diaper.
7:30	Breakfast
	3 T mashed bananas
	3 T rice cereal
	7 oz. formula
8:00	One dropper baby vitamins; clean up and put into clothes.
9:00	Morning walk (don't forget sunblock and hat)
10:00–11:30	Nap
12:00 P.M.	Lunch
	3 T strained vegetables (peas or sweet potatoes)
	3 T fruit (applesauce or pear)
	7 oz. formula

Step #3: Helpful Tips

■ The more routine the children's lives are while you're gone, the better. Try not to change sitters right before a trip, and while it's nice to let the sitter offer a few special privileges, the children are better off sticking with the schedule and knowing what the limits are.

■ If the person with whom you are leaving the kids is a spouse, an unpaid relative, or a sitter covering for more than a week, set up a support system to help *them*. Consider budgeting for a teenager to help out a couple of afternoons while you're away. Also ask the children to pitch in: help with their lunches and meals, do dishes, feed pets, et cetera.

- Ask that a neighbor or a relative drop in both announced *and* unannounced. The feedback you receive will likely give you peace of mind.

If Your Child Stays Elsewhere While You Are Away

Perhaps Grandma has offered to help with the kids, but they'll be at her house for the first time, not yours. Here are some ideas:

- Talk with your children about other "firsts" at which they have succeeded.
- Visit first and talk about some of the things that will happen when the children stay there.
- If a visit isn't possible, arrange for photographs to be taken to show (or remind) children of what it's like.
- Leave your relative with emergency information (including the emergency consent form), the page-a-day calendar you created, and a copy of your Children's Schedule list, including exactly when you'll pick them up. While you certainly don't want to dictate their day, Grandma should know meal times (and surefire meal hits) as well as nap and bedtimes so that the basic daily routine can remain the same.
- In-town grandparents should be given a list of telephone numbers of friends as well as any carpooling schedules that will be in operation while you're away.
- Talk of the experience as a double adventure: your business trip and their stay at Grandma's, for example.

While You Are Away

- In advance, agree upon a time when you'll phone each day. If possible, call at the same time so that a new ritual comes into play.
- Phone at the appointed hours. Don't be alarmed if your child cries while on the phone (or refuses to speak to you). It's his or her chance to unbottle some feelings, and as long as the sitter reports that things are going well, you needn't be overly concerned.

- If you do speak with your children, don't get involved in any heated discussions. Expressing anger or disappointment about something that happened when you're not there leaves a child with a difficult set of emotions to handle on his or her own.

- Don't let the conversation be one-sided. Let them know how you're doing and what's going on.

Preparing for Your Return

- If your trip was for business, try to get related memos, letters, and thank-you notes written before you return. Do it at night in the hotel room or on the plane coming home.

- Should you bring a gift? Of course. It needn't be costly. It's another ritual for the children to anticipate, and it eases the pain of separation.

- Don't come home feeling compelled to "set everything right." Ask family members to pitch in with any family task that must be attended to, and otherwise, catch up with home chores gradually so that you can spend the time with the children.

- If you feel you must go right back to the office the first morning home, try to come home from work an hour earlier that day.

- Upon your return, do something special as a family. That first weekend you're home, set aside some time for family as well as for catching up on work and/or home chores.

An Occasional Alternative: Taking the Kids Along

- If you or your spouse travel frequently, consider taking your children along sometimes and leaving them with a hotel sitter while you're busy during the day. One lawyer takes just one of his children with him when schedules permit, providing a special time for both child and parent.

- Make yourself available periodically during the day, even if it's meeting for half an hour at lunch time before you return to your meeting. Take your child on a different trip if you're going to be in back-to-back meetings or under extreme pressure.

- Call the hotel to see what family services are offered. Some hotels now have playgrounds; many have pools; most will recommend sitters or a bonded service. Some even offer on-site "day camps" over weekends, during major conferences, and during the summer.

- If you're booking a sitter long-distance, do so through a bonded service recommended by the hotel, and speak to the sitter in advance of the trip. You'll feel better having heard his or her voice. (Or if you didn't like the sound of the sitter, ask the service to recommend someone more to your liking.)

- If you're renting a car, request a car seat, if needed.

- Book a room with a refrigerator. It's much easier (and less expensive) to feed children if you can keep milk and cheese and other favorites in the room with you.

- Maintain your child's normal sleeping and eating patterns as much as possible while away.

- Sightseeing can make your trip one that both of you will remember for a long time to come. Those special business trips will make up for all the ones where you have to leave the children behind!

ABOUT THE AUTHORS

Ronni Eisenberg is a nationally recognized time management and organizational expert. She has run organizing workshops and has lectured on time management for major corporations and national business associations. In addition, she frequently does one-on-one consulting regarding organization in the workplace.

Ronni Eisenberg has also served as spokesperson for several major consumer product campaigns and created her own line of organizing products.

Kate Kelly, a professional writer, is the author of *The Complete Idiot's Guide to Parenting a Teenager* and *Election Day: An American Holiday, An American History*. She has also co-authored a book on home remodeling, *Renovating with a Contractor*, and has ghostwritten several other titles.

In addition to *Organize Yourself!*, Ronni Eisenberg and Kate Kelly together have written four other books: *The Overwhelmed Person's Guide to Time Management, Organize Your Office!, Organize Your Home!*, and *Organize Your Family!*

If you would like to write to comment on the book or send in your organizing suggestions, please write to Ronni Eisenberg & Associates, P.O. Box 3272, Westport, CT 06880.

INDEX

A

Address book, on computer, 45–46
Answering machine. *See* Telephone
  answering machine
Appointments, 20, 23, 71, 206
"At the door" planning, 22
Automatic teller machines (ATMs), 85, 86

B

Babysitters, 11, 25, 125, 267, 271,
  274–75, 289, 299
Banking, 83–88
Beauty routine, 221–23
Beepers, 17
Better Business Bureau, 180
Bill-paying, 70, 89–95
  electronic, 93–95
  household affairs folder for, 70,
    89–90, 92
  system for, 90–93
Birthday book, 51, 224–25
Birthday cards, 3, 224
Birthday gifts, 236–38
Books, 33–35, 269
  baby care, 269
  catalog system for, 35
  donating to charities, 34
  establishing home library, 33–35
Briefcase, 242–44
Budgeting, 96–102
  charting monthly expenses,
    100–101
  establishing a system for, 97–98
  expenses, 97
  goal setting, 96–97
  identifying trouble spots in, 98–100
  personal allowance, 97–98
  sample charts for, 99, 101
  savings, 98
Bulletin board, 52, 53
Business cards, filing of, 64

C

Calendars, 36–41, 240
  computer, 38–40
  recording on, 37
  useful features of, 37
  wall, 38
Canceled checks folder, 51, 84–85, 95
Card catalog system, for resource file,
  76–80
Career goals, 191–92
Carry-on luggage, 215–16, 289
Cash receipts file, 59, 92
Catalogs, 64, 71
  shopping by, 238
Categorization, 33–35, 58–60, 79–80,
  121, 134, 245–46
  of books, 33–35
  of clothes in closets, 134
  of deductions for income taxes,
    121
  of files, 58–60
  of frequently used items, 245–46
  of home resources, 79–80
Change of address, 72, 182, 187, 190
Charity, donating to, 93, 173, 181, 185,
  280
Charts, 16, 65, 77, 79, 101, 107, 108, 109,
  112, 114, 144, 148, 212–13, 283, 284,
  296, 297, 298, 299

Charts *(cont.)*
  babysitter, 299
  budgeting, 101
  contact resource cards, 77, 79
  gift shopping, 237
  grocery list, 148
  household chores, 283, 284
  household help, 297, 298, 299
  investment, 107, 108, 109
  medical records, 65, 112
  message center, 144
  personal property, 114
  phone logs, 16
  travel checklist, 212–13
  travel itinerary, 296
Checkbook, 83–85, 119–20
  canceled check folder, 84–85
  keeping detailed entries for income
    taxes, 119–20
Checklists, *See* Charts
Child care provider, 161, 162, 163. *See
  also* Babysitters
Children, 11, 26, 30, 38, 47, 65–66,
  127–28, 156, 157, 163, 178–79,
  181–82, 207, 261–302
  child care provider, 161–63
  coping with absent parents,
    293–301
  emergency training, 127–28
  health records of, 65–66
  medicine chest, 156
  moving, 178–79, 181–82, 185,
    187, 190
  pre-birth checklist, 263–69
  rooms of, 276–80, 282–83
  schoolwork, 285
  self-reliance, 283–85
  teaching organization to, 281–86
  traveling with, 287–92, 301–2
  waiting time, 30
  weeding out children's items,
    279–80
Chores, family, 283–84, 285
Cleaning, household, 130–31, 188
Clocks, 24, 51

  desk, 51, 54
  set a few minutes ahead, 24
  traveling, 211, 213
Closets, 133–37, 251, 258–59
  front hall, 136
  linen, 136
  redesigning, 136–37
  reorganizing, 134
  tips for men, 258–59
Clothes shopping. *See* Wardrobe shopping
Clothing, 22, 196, 250–59, 265, 266, 267,
  268, 273–74, 287. *See also* Wardrobe
  shopping
  baby, 265, 267, 268, 273–74, 287
  choice of, the night before, 22
  job interviews, 196
  maternity, 266
  seasonality of, 253, 256
  shopping for men, 255–59
  shopping for women, 250–54
  travel, 207–8, 210–17
Clothing care for men, 259
Clutter, reducing, 27, 53, 132, 279–80
  See also Tag sales
  weeding out children's rooms,
    279–80
Color-coded filing system, 57–58, 276–77
Computer, 42–48
  address books on, 45–46
  backing up, 43–44
  becoming literate, 43
  gift shopping, 237
  income taxes, 119
  investment-tracking, 109–10
  laptop, 47–48
  modem for, 46
  online sevices on, 46–47, 109–10
  organizational tasks accomplished
    on, 44–45
  purchase of, 42–43
  réumés, 192–93
Cooking, 202–3, 268, 271
  party preparation, 202–3
  preparing for post-pregnancy,
    268, 271

Correspondence, handling, 72
Cover letters, 193–94
Credit cards, 103, 213, 233, 239–40

D

Daily routine, 22–24, 223
Dates, remembering, 224–26
Day planner, 36–37, 240
Deadlines, setting personal, 6
Delegation of work, 27
Desk, 49–55
    additional storage around, 52–53
    building new space for, 50–51
    establishing better work habits at,
      53–55
    organization of area, 51–52
    purchase of, 50
    tools at, 51–52
Desk workbook, 35, 53–54
Doctor search, 227–30

E

Electronic organizers, 40–41
E-mail, 67, 73–74
Emergencies, preparing for, 125–28
Employment file, 59
Entertaining. *See* Party planning
Errands, 231–35
Events, major, 165–217
    house painting, 174–77
    job search, 191–98
    moving, 178–90
    parties, 198–203
    tag sales, 167–73
    travel, 204–17

F

Family, 11, 26, 38, 65–66, 132, 144,
    149, 151, 153, 161–63, 177, 178–
    79, 231–32, 235, 247–49. *See also*
    Children
    errands, 231–32, 235
    health records of, 65–66
    household help, 161–63

    laundry organization for the larger
      family, 153
    message center, 144
    moving, 178–79
    preservation of personal time, 11,
      26
    spouse, organizing with, 247–49
Family computer. *See* Computer
Faxes, 21, 67, 74–75
Filing systems, 53, 54, 56–64, 70,
    76–80, 115, 225–26, 236–37
    common mistakes in, 56
    developing good habits, 61–62
    establishing, 57–63
    for gift shopping, 236–37
    maintaining, 62–63
    materials not to incorporate in, 64
    resource, 76–80
    tickler files, 53, 54, 63–64, 70,
      115, 225–26, 237
Financial master list, 103–5
Financial records, 81–122
    banking, 83–88
    bill-paying, 89–95
    budgeting, 97–102
    financial master list, 103–5
    income taxes, 119–22
    investments, 106–10
    medical payments and insurance
      reimbursements, 111–12
    personal property inventory,
      113–15
First-aid supplies, 156–57
Folders, 63–64, 89–90, 92, 95, 112,
    119–21
    canceled checks, 95, 120, 121
    household affairs, 70, 89–90, 92,
      95, 112, 119, 121, 237
    tickler files, 63–64, 115
Food shopping, 147–51

G

General household, 129–32
    cleaning, 130–31
    clutter reduction, 132

Gift shopping, 236–38
Grocery lists, 148–49

H

Handbag, 233, 239–41
Health records, 65–66
Hiring household help, 158–63
Home service resource cards, 78–80
Hospital stay, for childbirth, 266, 268
Hotels, 208, 289, 291
Household affairs folder, 70, 89–90, 92,
    95, 112, 119, 121, 237
Household help, 130, 158–63, 206. *See
    also* Babysitters
    checking references, 161–62
    defining the job, 158
    interviewing, 160–61
    prescreening applicants, 159–60
    tips for child care provider, 163
Household matters, 123–63
    emergency preparation, 125–28
    general upkeep, 129–32
    grocery shopping, 147–51
    hiring help, 158–63
    kitchen, 138–46
    laundry, 152–53
    medicine chest, 154–57
Household notebook, 129–30, 131, 176,
    203, 231, 251

I

Income, 97–100
    tracking for investment, 108–9
Income taxes, 119–22
Index cards, for resource file, 76–79
Infant care, 270–76. *See also* Children
Insurance, 60, 91, 92, 97, 103, 111–12,
    113–15, 163, 180, 186, 264, 266–67
    childbirth, 264, 266–67
    file, 60
    household help, 163
    moving, 180, 186
    payments, 91, 92, 97
    personal property inventory for,
        113–15

policy numbers, 103
reimbursements, 111–12, 115
Interruptions, managing, 10–12,
    19–20
Interview strategies, 160–61, 195–97
    during job search, 195–97
    for hiring household help,
        160–61
Inventory control, 113–15, 151
    for groceries, 151
    for personal property, 113–15
Investments, 104, 106–10

J

Job search, 191–97
    cover letter, 193–94
    identifying goal, 192
    interview strategies, 195–97
    organization of, 191–92
    résumé, 192–93
    techniques, 194–95
Junk mail, 71, 74

K

Keys, placement of, 22, 207, 240, 246
Kitchen, 138–44. *See also* Refrigerator
    cabinet storage, 140–41
    counter space, 142
    drawers, 141
    on-the-wall storage, 142–43
Kitchen timer, use of, 29–30

L

Labeling, 135, 176, 185, 246
Laptop computers, 47–48
Lateness, avoidance of, 22–24
Laundry, 152–53, 273
Legal documents, 70, 117, 118
Leisure time, setting aside, 8
Letter writing, 72
Library, home, organization of, 33–35
Linen closet, 136
Losing things, how to stop, 245–46
Luggage, 215–16, 289. *See also* Travel

M

Magazines, 67, 68, 182, 238
  as gifts, 238
Mail, 67–74
  filing, 70
  junk, 71, 74
  methods for dealing with, 68–71
  reading, 70–71
  "rip and read" method, 73
  sorting, 68
Mail Preference Service, 71
Makeup, 212, 221, 222–23
Medical care, 227–30, 263–64, 267
  choice of, 227–30, 263–64, 267
  pregnancy, 263–64, 267
Medical history records, 60, 65–66, 183
Medical payments, 111–12
Medicine, 154–57, 213, 288, 289
  chest, 154–57
  for children, 288, 289
  for traveling, 213, 288
Misplacing items, 245–46
Motivation, 7–8
Moving, 178–90

N

Neighbors, phone numbers of, 125
Newspaper ads, for household help, 159
Numbers, emergency, 125–28

O

Online services, use of, 46–47, 86, 110

P

Packing tips, 183–85, 210–17, 244
  for briefcase, 244
  for moving, 183–85
  for travel, 210–17
Painting the home, 174–77
Palmtop computer, 40–41
Pantry area, 150
Paperwork, controlling, 31–80
  calendars, 36–41
  correspondence, 67–75

  family computer, 42–48
  filing systems, 56–64
  health records, 65–66
  organizing desk area, 49–55
  resource file, 76–80
Party planning, 198–203
Personal digital assistants, 40–41
Personal property inventory, 113–15
Personal time, preserving, 25–26
Pets, 183, 206
  care during absence, 206
  moving, 183
Post-pregnancy, 269–75
Pregnancy checklist, 263–68. *See also*
  Post-pregnancy
Procrastination, 3–9

R

Reading, 25, 240, 243
Receipts, shopping, 90, 233
Recipes, 151, 199
Records, packing, 185
Referrals, 159, 179–80, 227–28
  for doctors, 227–28
  for household help, 159
  for movers, 179–80
Refrigerator, 145–46
Resource file, 64, 76–80, 126
  contact cards for, 77–78
  establishing, 76–77
  home service, 78–80, 126
Résumé preparation, 192–93
Rewards, as incentive, 7, 9, 11

S

Safe-deposit box, 116–18
Shopping, 42–43, 50, 75, 147–51,
  199–201, 236–40, 250–59, 264,
  266, 267, 268, 273
  baby, 264, 266, 267, 268, 273
  computer, 42–43
  desk, 50
  fax machine, 75
  gift, 236–40

Shopping *(cont.)*
grocery, 147–51
mail or phone, 238
party, 199–201
wardrobe, 250–59
Spouse, organizing with, 38, 247–49
Storage, 52–53, 116–19, 140–41,
142–43, 146, 246, 278–79
children's rooms, 278–79
desk area, 52–53
kitchens, 140–41, 142–43
refrigerator, 146
safe-deposit boxes, 116–19
Strongbox, need for, 118
Supermarket shopping, 147–51

T

Tag sales, 167–73
Tax deductions, opportunties for, 34, 92,
119–20, 237
Taxes, 3, 89–90, 97, 119–22, 182
Telephone, 11, 13–21, 29, 70, 71,
125–27, 209, 275
answering machine, 11, 19–20
ending annoying calls, 71
ending conversations, 15
extension in baby's room, 275
habits, 14–15
important numbers for emergencies, 125–26, 127
leaving messages, 20
logging calls, 16
organizing area around, 13
screening calls, 19–20
timing conversations, 15, 29
tips, 20–21, 209
types of, 16–17, 18
useful added features, 17–18
Telephone Preference Service, 71
Tickler files, 53, 54, 63–64, 70, 115,
225–26, 237

Time management, 36–41
calendar maintenance, 36–41
controlling your time, 1–30
kitchen timer, 29
managing interruptions, 10–12
preserving personal time, 25–26
Time wasters, avoiding, 27–28
Toiletry kit, for traveling, 214–15, 223
Toys, 276–80, 288, 290, 292
children's room, 276–80
traveling, 288, 290, 292
Travel, 204–9
advance planning, 205–7,
211–14
carry-on bag, 215–16
checklist before, 207, 212–13
children, 287–93, 301
equipment and accessories for,
210–11, 214–16
hotel stay, 208
leaving children behind, 293–302
packing tips, 210–17
toiletry kit preparation, 214–15

V

Voice-mail, 11, 19–20

W

Wallet organization, 233, 239
Wardrobe shopping, 250–59
men, 255–59
personal shopper, 254
planning clothing needs, 250–51,
255–56
simplifying, 251–53, 256–57
what to wear while, 252–53, 257
women, 250–54
Wasting time, tips for avoiding, 27–28
Workspace, importance of, 6, 275. *See also*
Desk